That Time I Got Reincarnated as a SLIME
The Ways of the Monster Nation

2

Sho Okagiri Original Story: **FUSE** Character Design: **Mitz Vah**

The Story So Far

Framea, a girl of the rabbitfolk race, pays a visit to the land of Tempest inside the Forest of Jura. After a few chance encounters, Tempest's ruler, the Demon Lord Rimuru, asks her to write a guidebook for his fledgling nation.

Given full freedom to explore the realm, Framea happily gathers material for the book, but one day, Rimuru summons her again, asking her to tackle the dungeon he's about to open to the world!

Teaming up with Elen and her band of adventurers, Framea dives in so she can write a strategy guide for would-be challengers. What awaits them in the depths...?

Contents

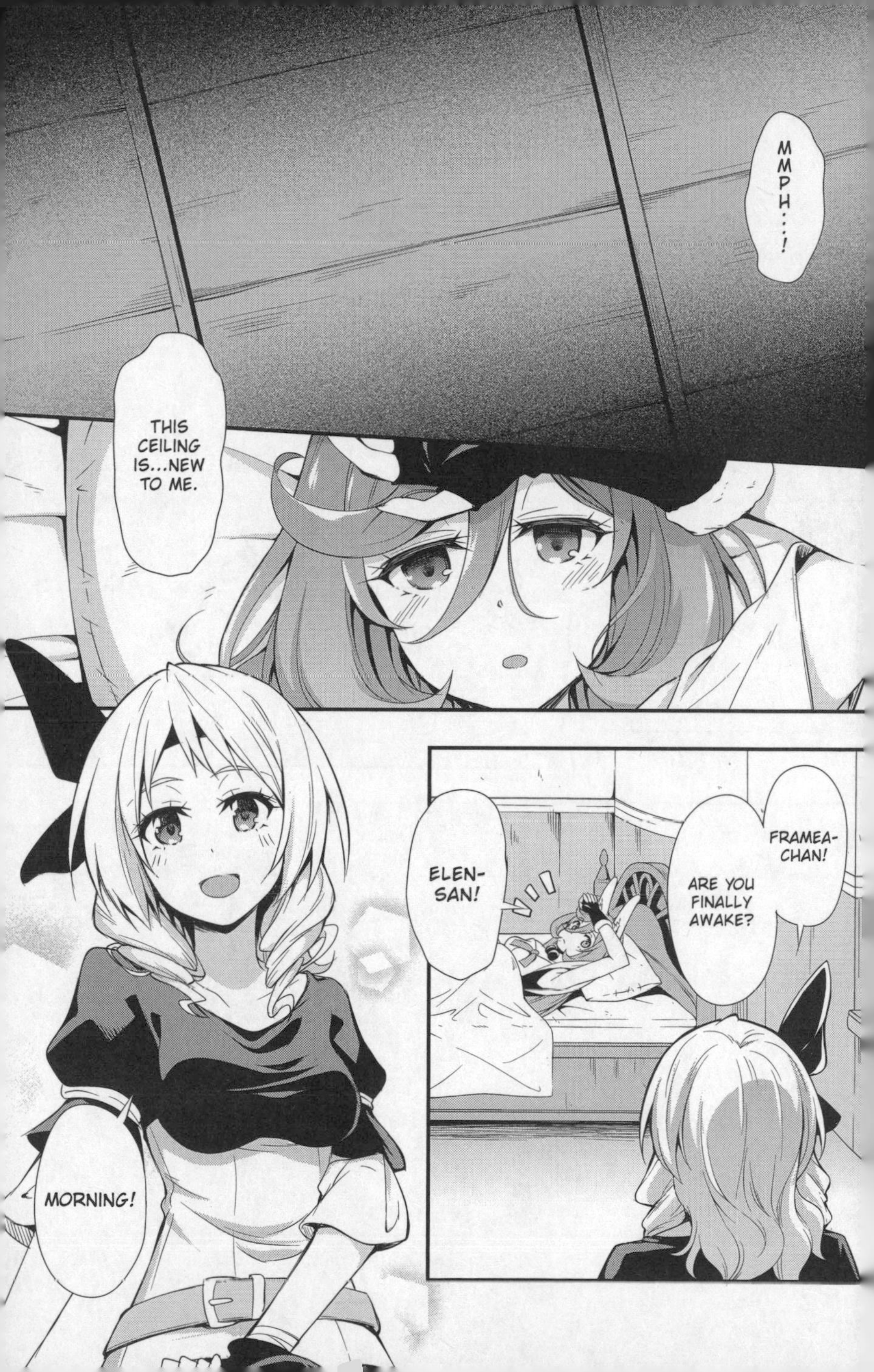
MMPH...!
THIS CEILING IS...NEW TO ME.
FRAMEA-CHAN! ARE YOU FINALLY AWAKE?
ELEN-SAN!
MORNING!

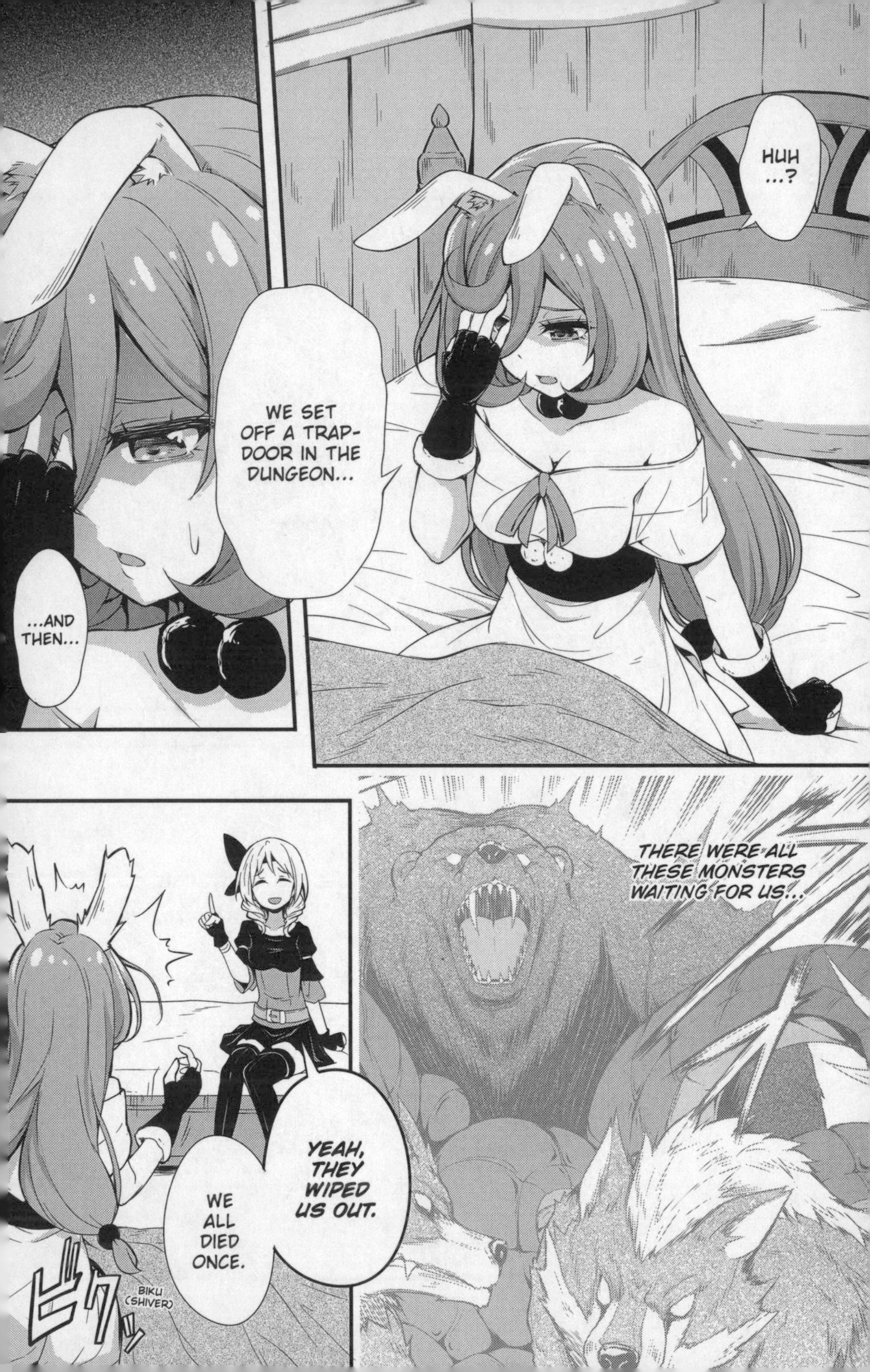
HUH ...?
WE SET OFF A TRAP-DOOR IN THE DUNGEON...
...AND THEN...
THERE WERE ALL THESE MONSTERS WAITING FOR US...
YEAH, THEY WIPED US OUT.
WE ALL DIED ONCE.
BIKU (SHIVER)

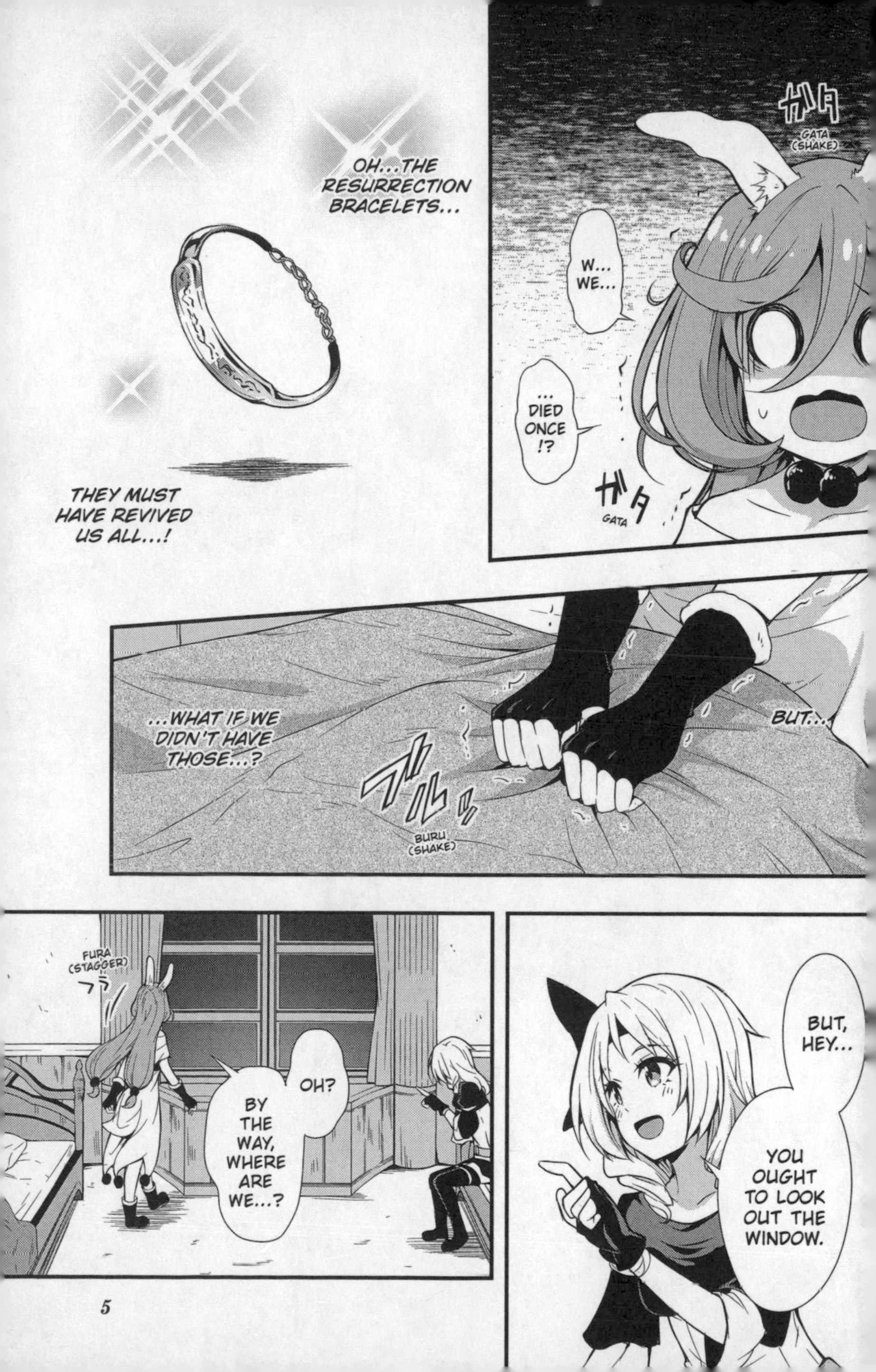
GATA (SHAKE)
W... WE...
...DIED ONCE!?
GATA
OH...THE RESURRECTION BRACELETS...
THEY MUST HAVE REVIVED US ALL...!
BUT...
...WHAT IF WE DIDN'T HAVE THOSE...?
BURU (SHAKE)
BUT, HEY...
YOU OUGHT TO LOOK OUT THE WINDOW.
OH?
BY THE WAY, WHERE ARE WE...?
FURA (STAGGER)

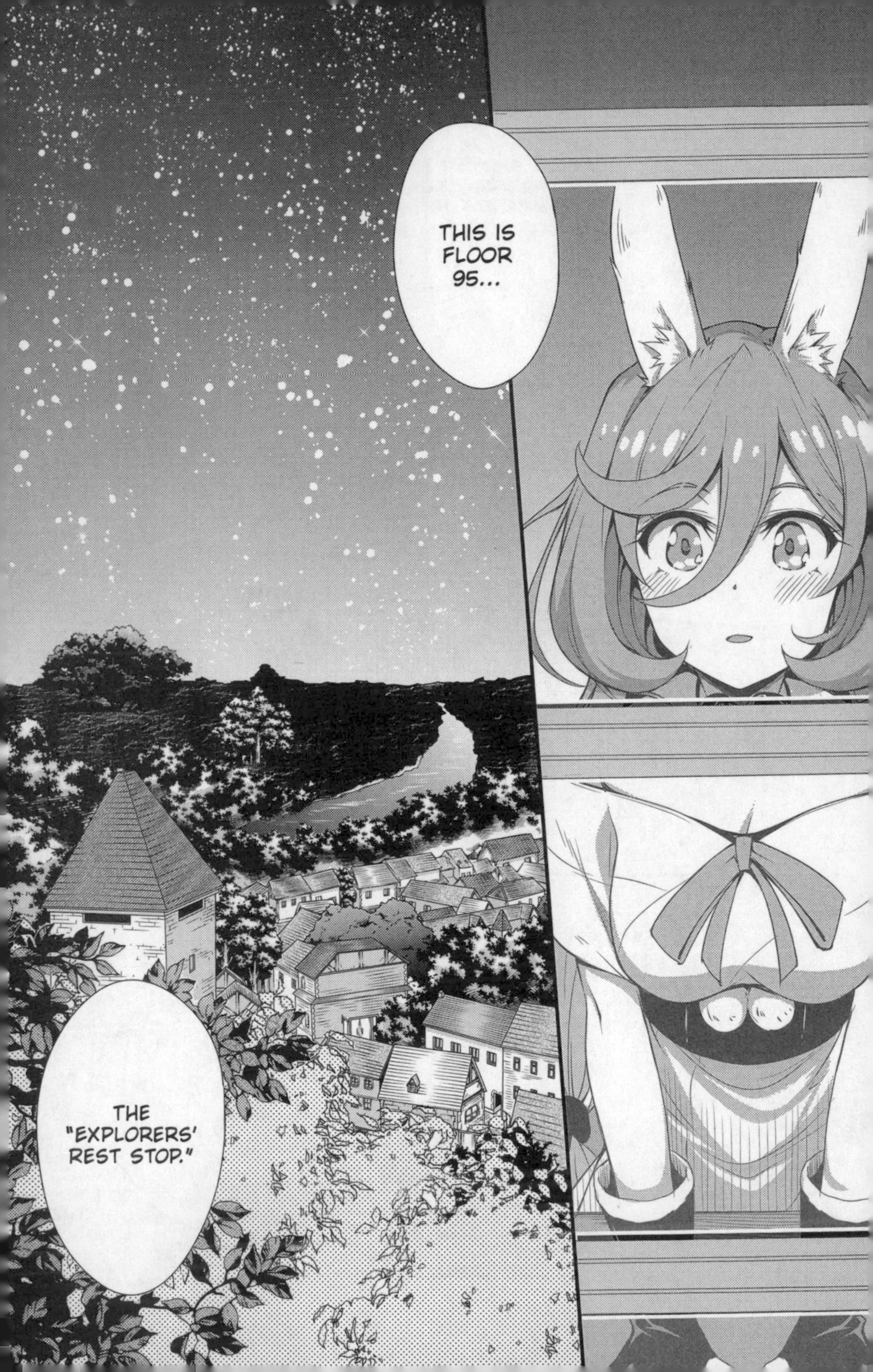
THIS IS FLOOR 95...
THE "EXPLORERS' REST STOP."

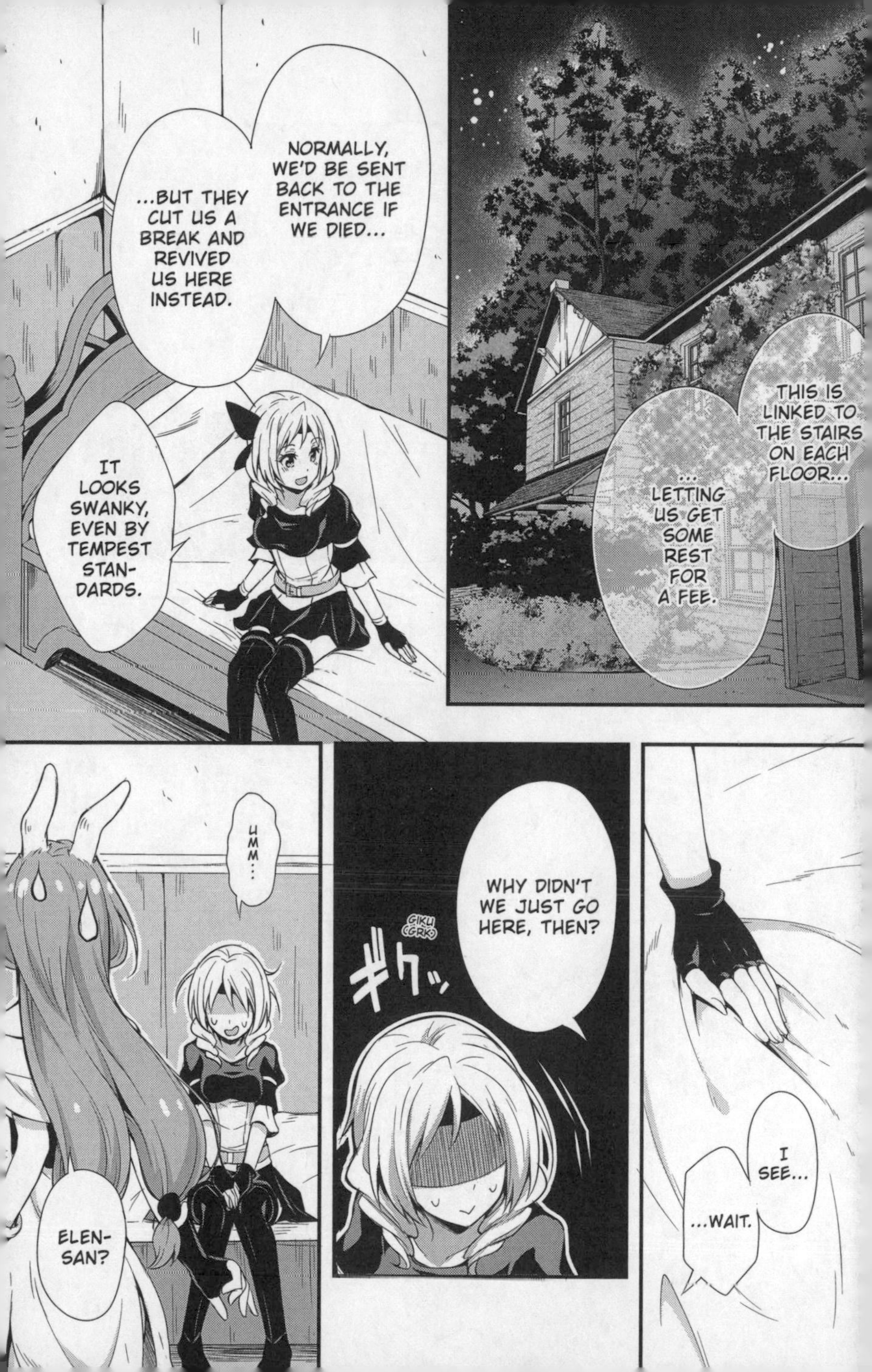
THIS IS LINKED TO THE STAIRS ON EACH FLOOR...
...LETTING US GET SOME REST FOR A FEE.
NORMALLY, WE'D BE SENT BACK TO THE ENTRANCE IF WE DIED...
...BUT THEY CUT US A BREAK AND REVIVED US HERE INSTEAD.
IT LOOKS SWANKY, EVEN BY TEMPEST STAN-DARDS.
I SEE...
...WAIT.
WHY DIDN'T WE JUST GO HERE, THEN?
ギクッ
GIKU (GRK)
UMM...
ELEN-SAN?

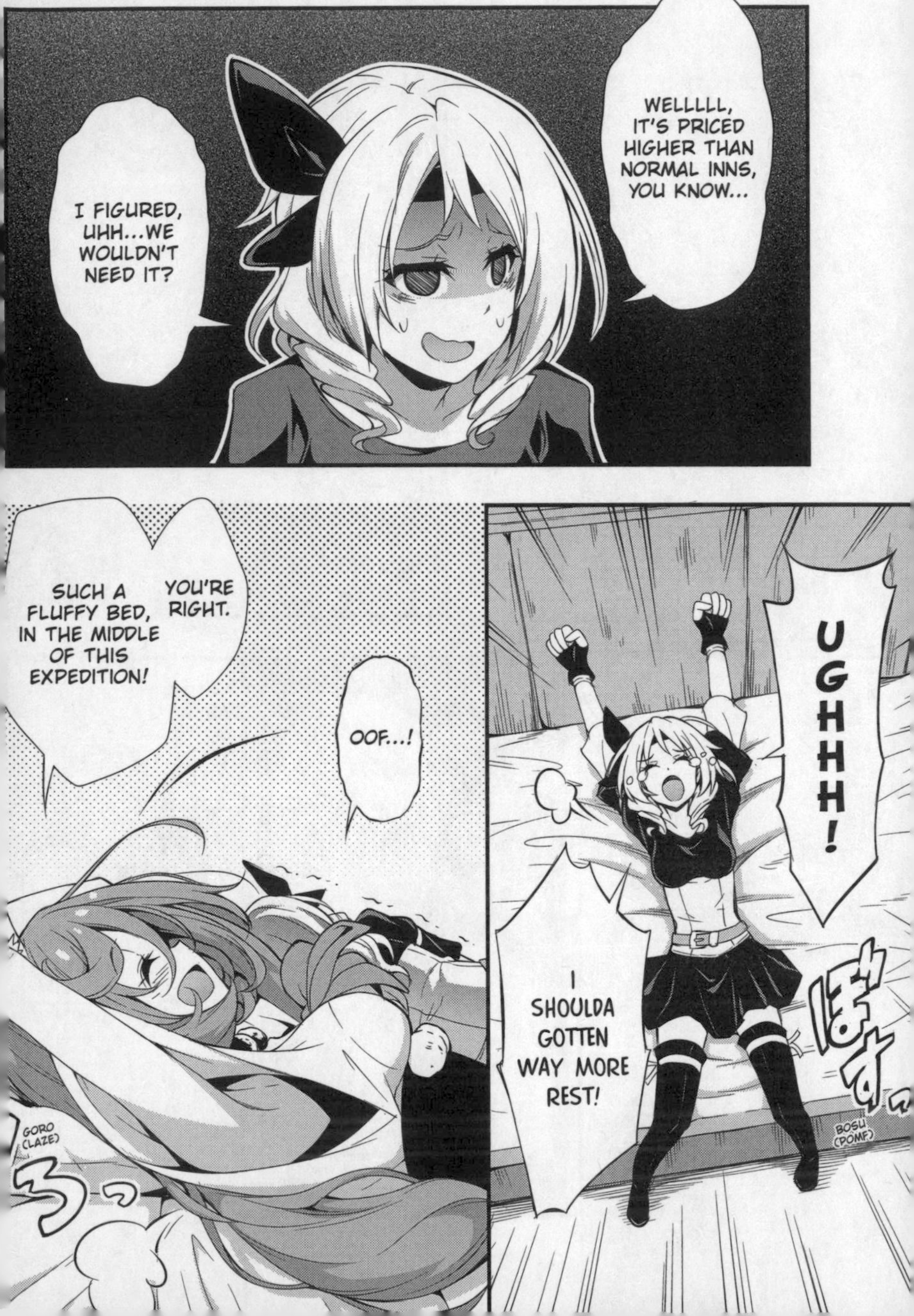
WELLLLL, IT'S PRICED HIGHER THAN NORMAL INNS, YOU KNOW...
I FIGURED, UHH...WE WOULDN'T NEED IT?
UGHHH!
I SHOULDA GOTTEN WAY MORE REST!
ぼすっ
BOSU (POMF)
YOU'RE RIGHT.
SUCH A FLUFFY BED, IN THE MIDDLE OF THIS EXPEDITION!
OOF...!
GORO (LAZE)
ごろっ

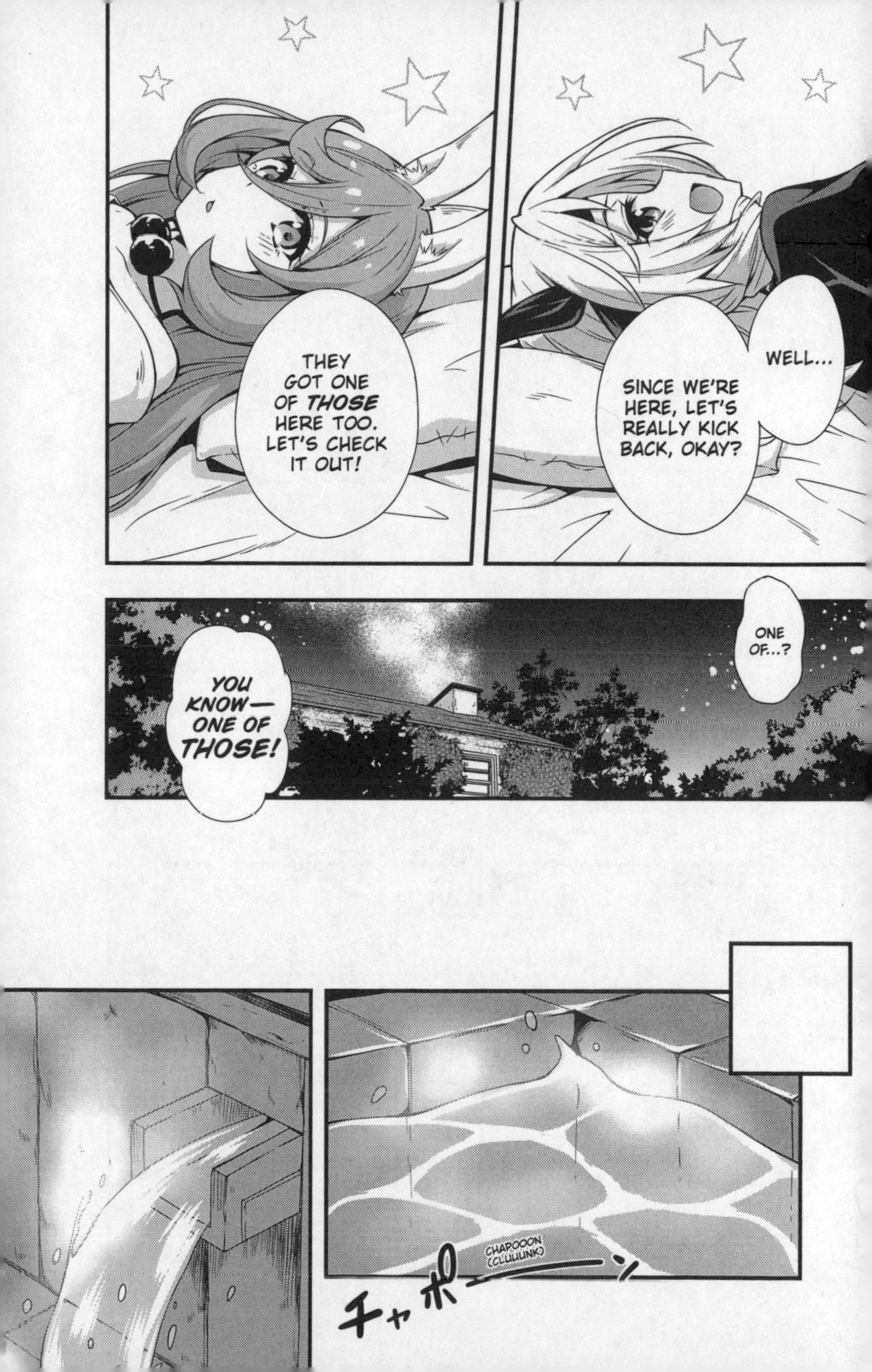
WELL...
SINCE WE'RE HERE, LET'S REALLY KICK BACK, OKAY?
THEY GOT ONE OF *THOSE* HERE TOO. LET'S CHECK IT OUT!
ONE OF...?
YOU KNOW—ONE OF THOSE!
CHAPOOON (CLUUUUNK)
チャポーン

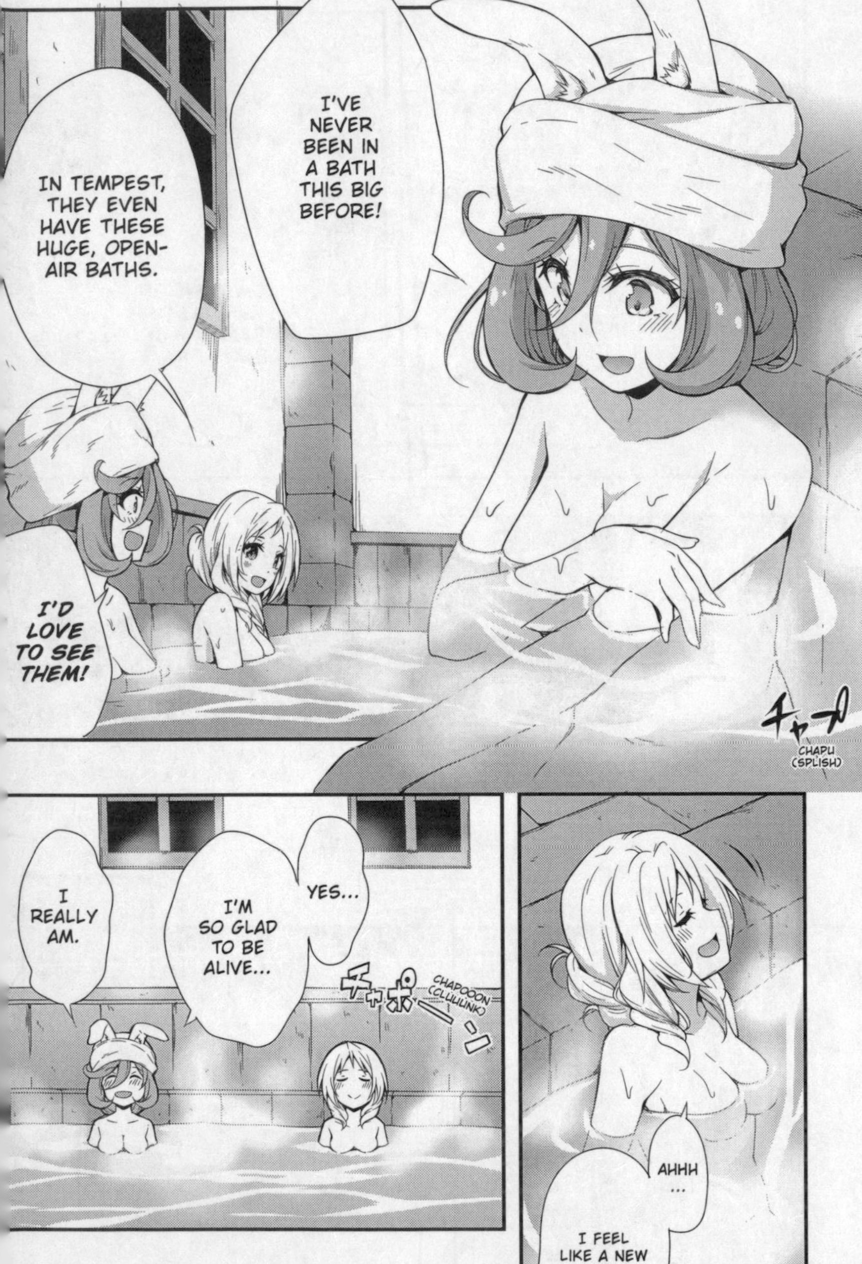
I'VE NEVER BEEN IN A BATH THIS BIG BEFORE!
IN TEMPEST, THEY EVEN HAVE THESE HUGE, OPEN-AIR BATHS.
チャプ
CHAPU (SPLISH)
I'D LOVE TO SEE THEM!
AHHH...
I FEEL LIKE A NEW WOMAN!
YES...
I'M SO GLAD TO BE ALIVE...
I REALLY AM.
チャポーン
CHAPOOON (CLUUUNK)

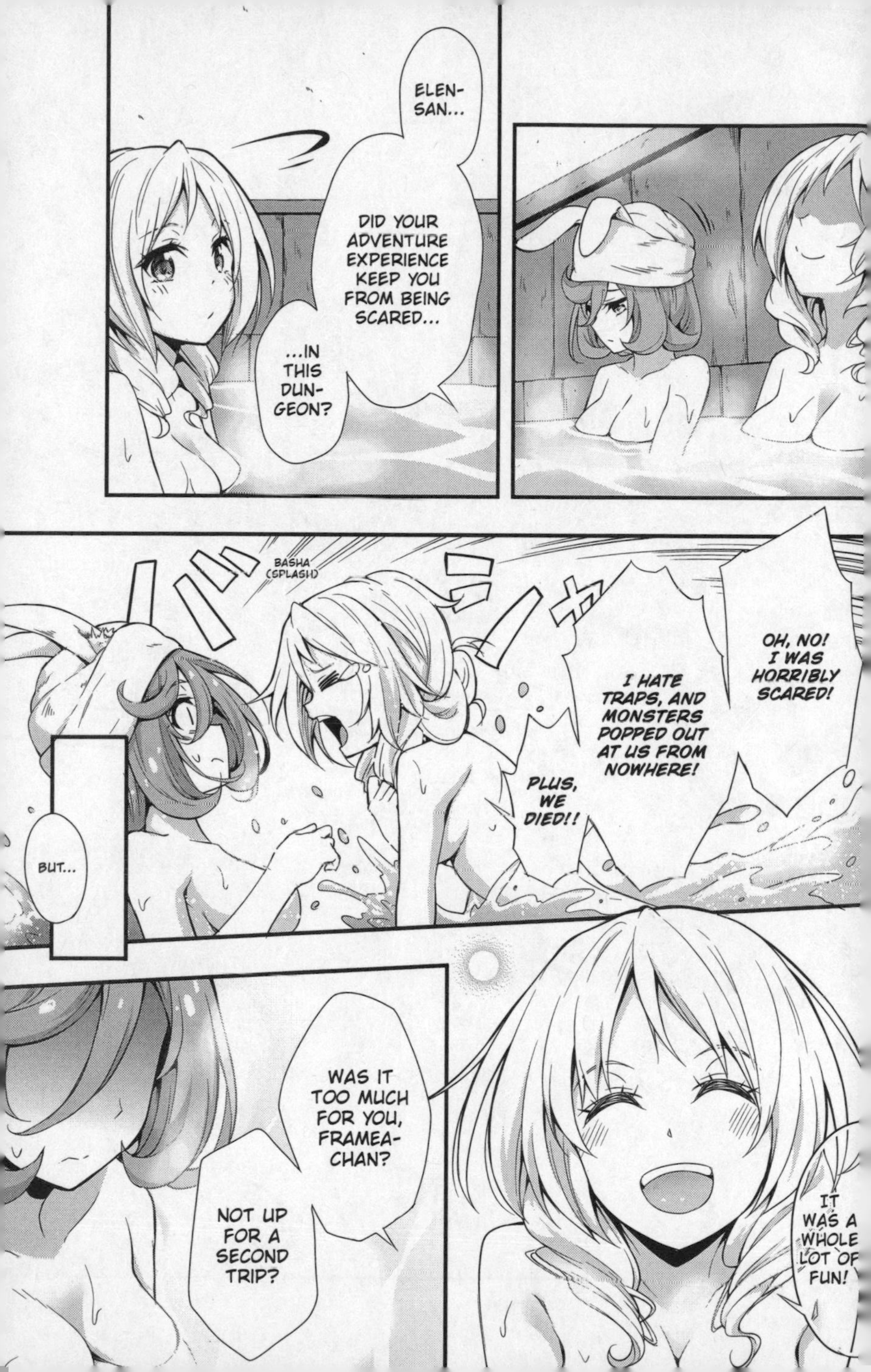
ELEN-SAN...
DID YOUR ADVENTURE EXPERIENCE KEEP YOU FROM BEING SCARED...
...IN THIS DUN-GEON?
OH, NO! I WAS HORRIBLY SCARED!
I HATE TRAPS, AND MONSTERS POPPED OUT AT US FROM NOWHERE!
PLUS, WE DIED!!
BASHA (SPLASH)
BUT...
IT WAS A WHOLE LOT OF FUN!
WAS IT TOO MUCH FOR YOU, FRAMEA-CHAN?
NOT UP FOR A SECOND TRIP?

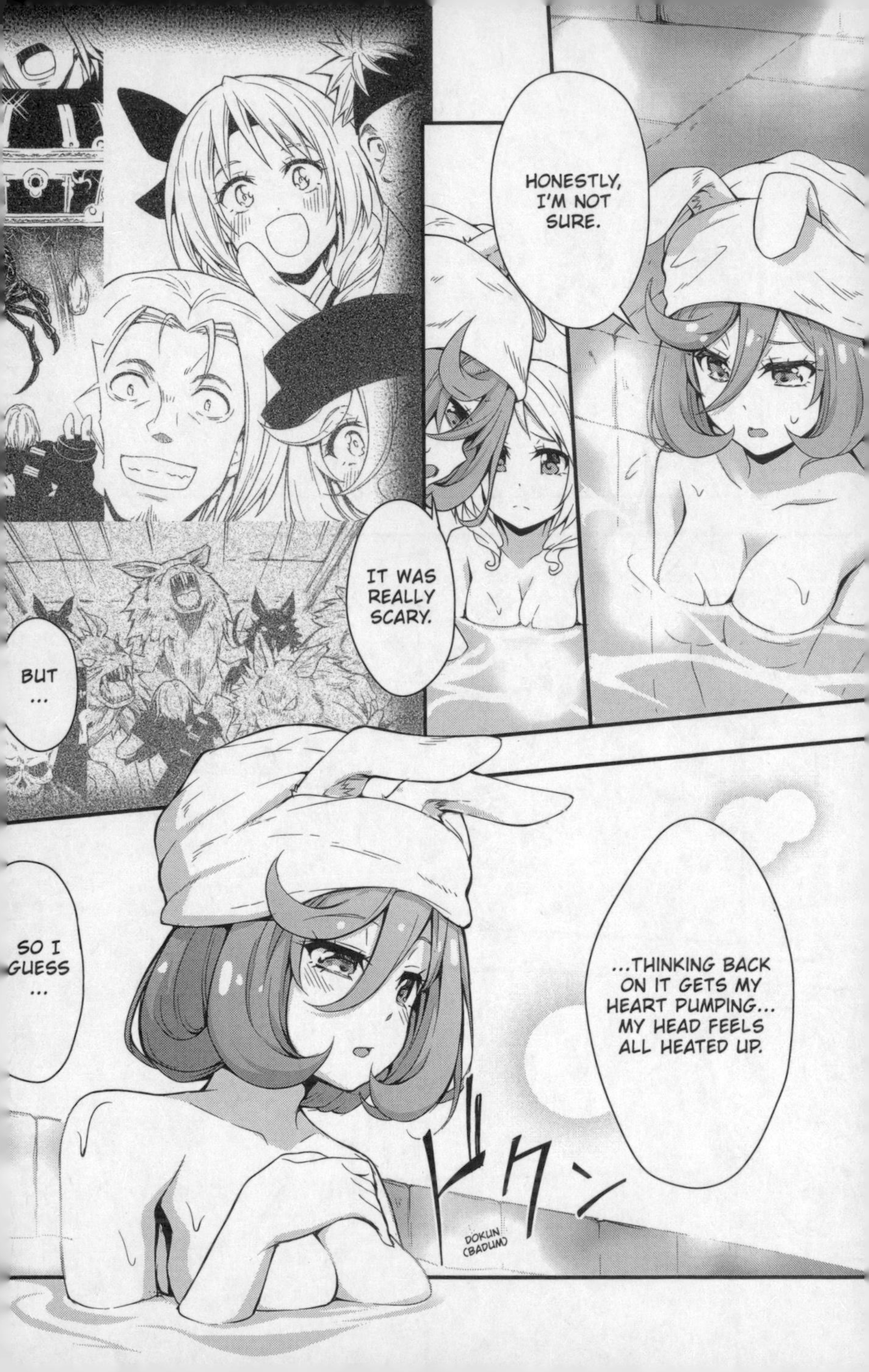
HONESTLY, I'M NOT SURE.
IT WAS REALLY SCARY.
BUT ...
SO I GUESS ...
...THINKING BACK ON IT GETS MY HEART PUMPING... MY HEAD FEELS ALL HEATED UP.
DOKUN (BADUM)

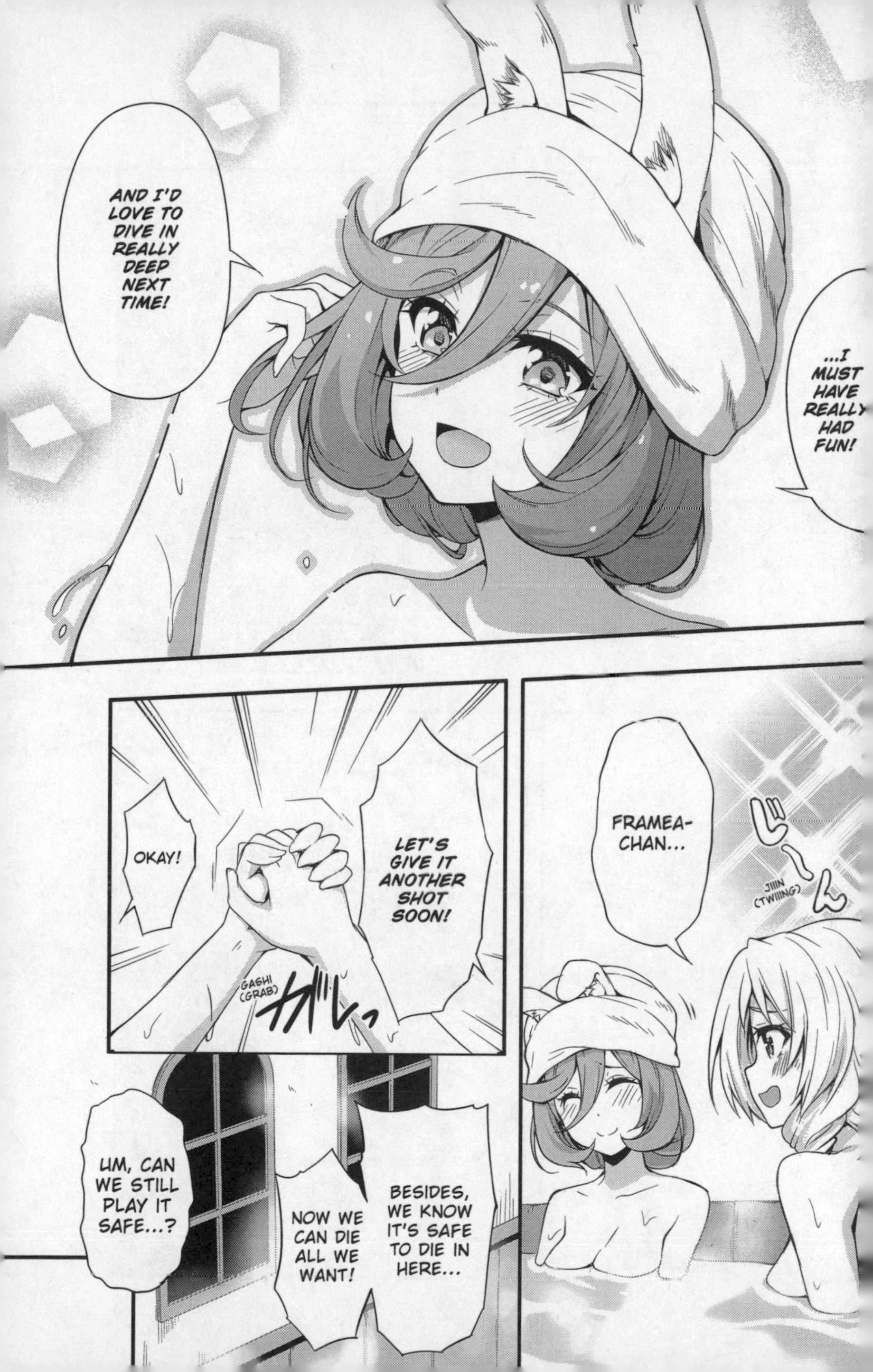
...I MUST HAVE REALLY HAD FUN!
AND I'D LOVE TO DIVE IN REALLY DEEP NEXT TIME!
FRAMEA-CHAN...
JIIN (TWIIING)
LET'S GIVE IT ANOTHER SHOT SOON!
OKAY!
GASHI (GRAB)
BESIDES, WE KNOW IT'S SAFE TO DIE IN HERE...
NOW WE CAN DIE ALL WE WANT!
UM, CAN WE STILL PLAY IT SAFE...?

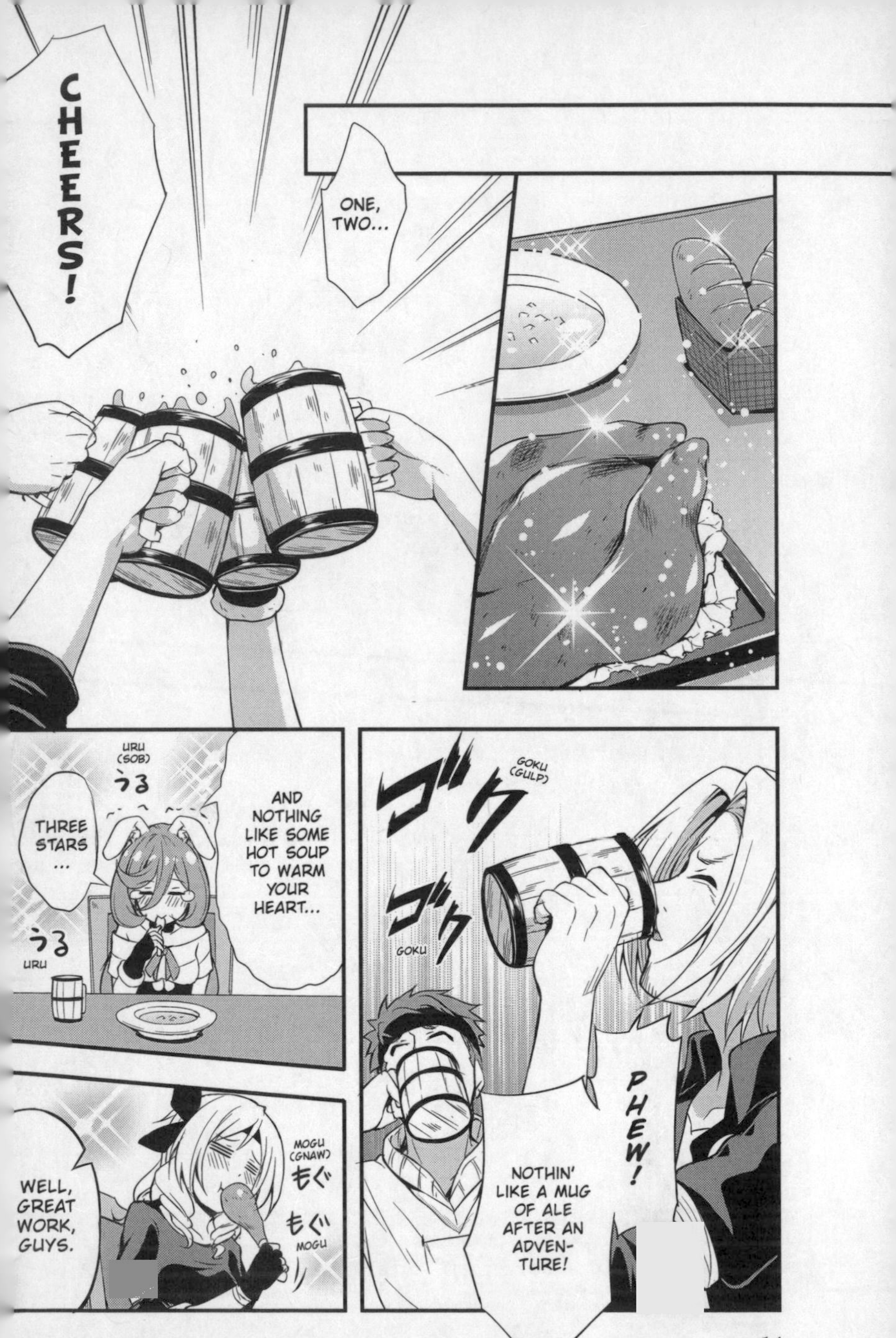
ONE, TWO...
CHEERS!
GOKU (GULP)
ゴク
ゴク
GOKU
NOTHIN' LIKE A MUG OF ALE AFTER AN ADVEN-TURE!
PHEW!
AND NOTHING LIKE SOME HOT SOUP TO WARM YOUR HEART...
URU (SOB)
うる
THREE STARS ...
うる
URU
MOGU (GNAW)
もぐ
もぐ
MOGU
WELL, GREAT WORK, GUYS.

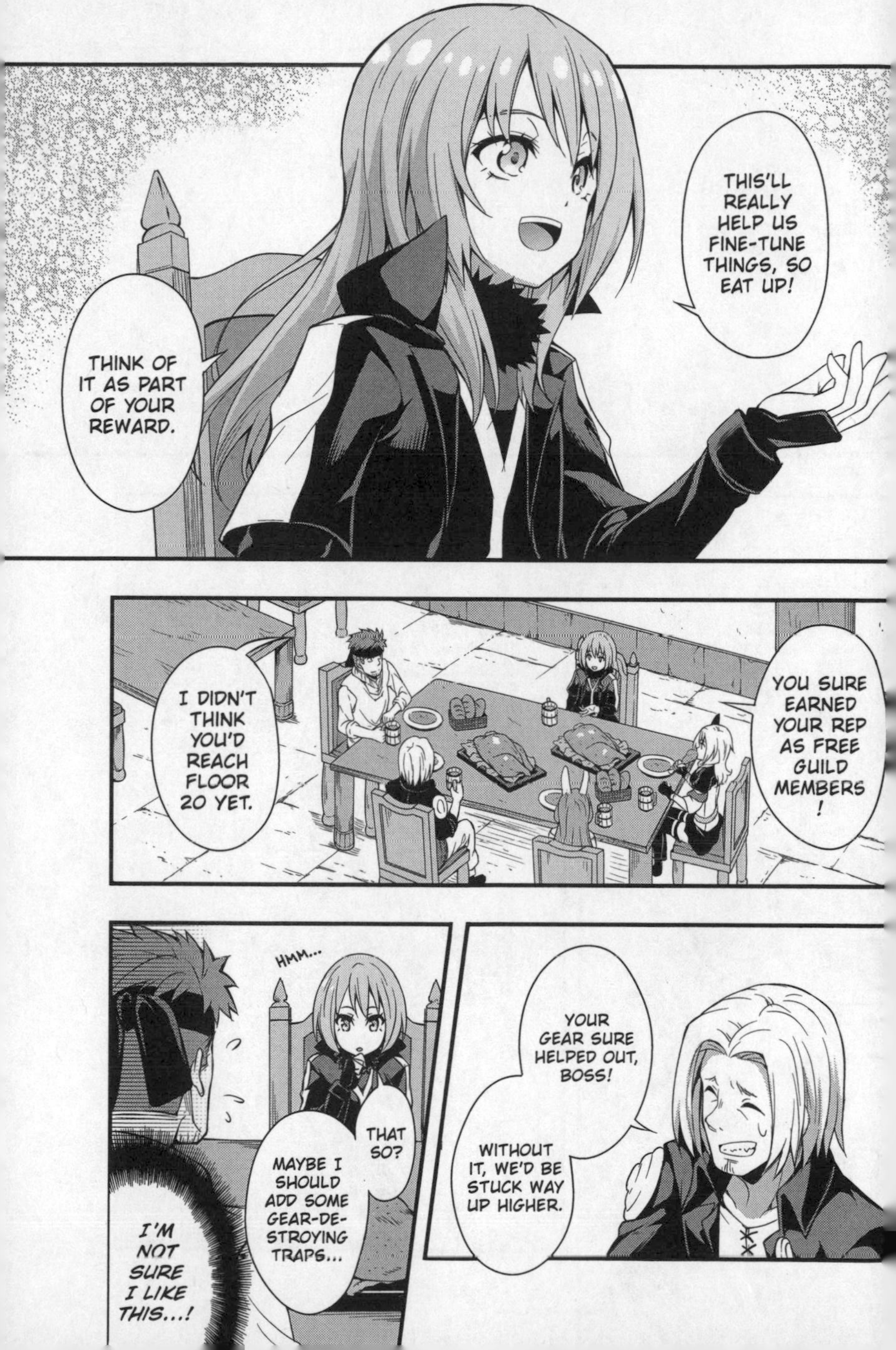
THIS'LL REALLY HELP US FINE-TUNE THINGS, SO EAT UP!
THINK OF IT AS PART OF YOUR REWARD.
YOU SURE EARNED YOUR REP AS FREE GUILD MEMBERS!
I DIDN'T THINK YOU'D REACH FLOOR 20 YET.
YOUR GEAR SURE HELPED OUT, BOSS!
WITHOUT IT, WE'D BE STUCK WAY UP HIGHER.
HMM...
THAT SO?
MAYBE I SHOULD ADD SOME GEAR-DE-STROYING TRAPS...
I'M NOT SURE I LIKE THIS...!

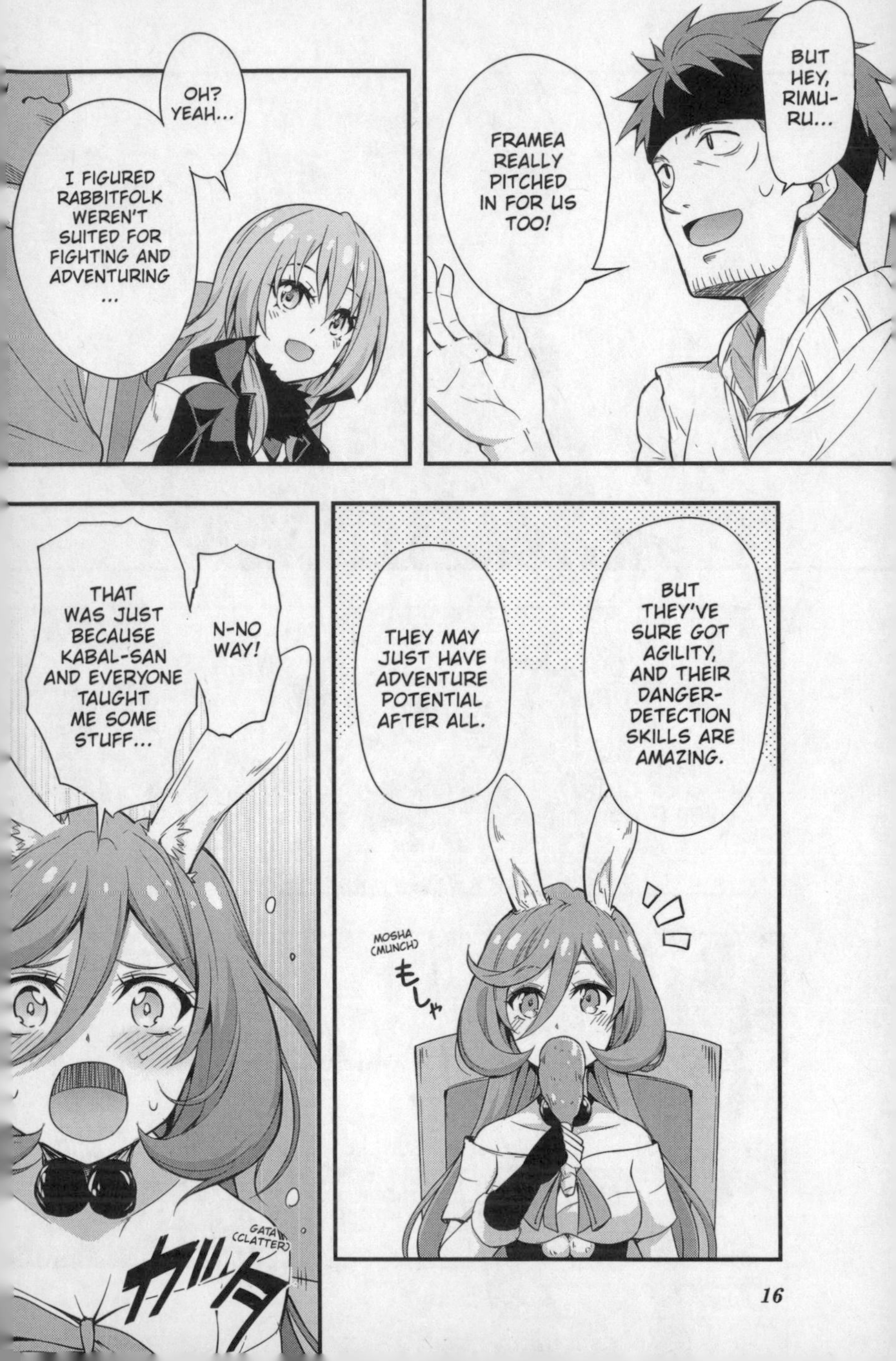
BUT HEY, RIMU-RU...
FRAMEA REALLY PITCHED IN FOR US TOO!
OH? YEAH...
I FIGURED RABBITFOLK WEREN'T SUITED FOR FIGHTING AND ADVENTURING ...
BUT THEY'VE SURE GOT AGILITY, AND THEIR DANGER-DETECTION SKILLS ARE AMAZING.
THEY MAY JUST HAVE ADVENTURE POTENTIAL AFTER ALL.
MOSHA (MUNCH)
もしゃ
N-NO WAY!
THAT WAS JUST BECAUSE KABAL-SAN AND EVERYONE TAUGHT ME SOME STUFF...
GATA (CLATTER)
ガタッ

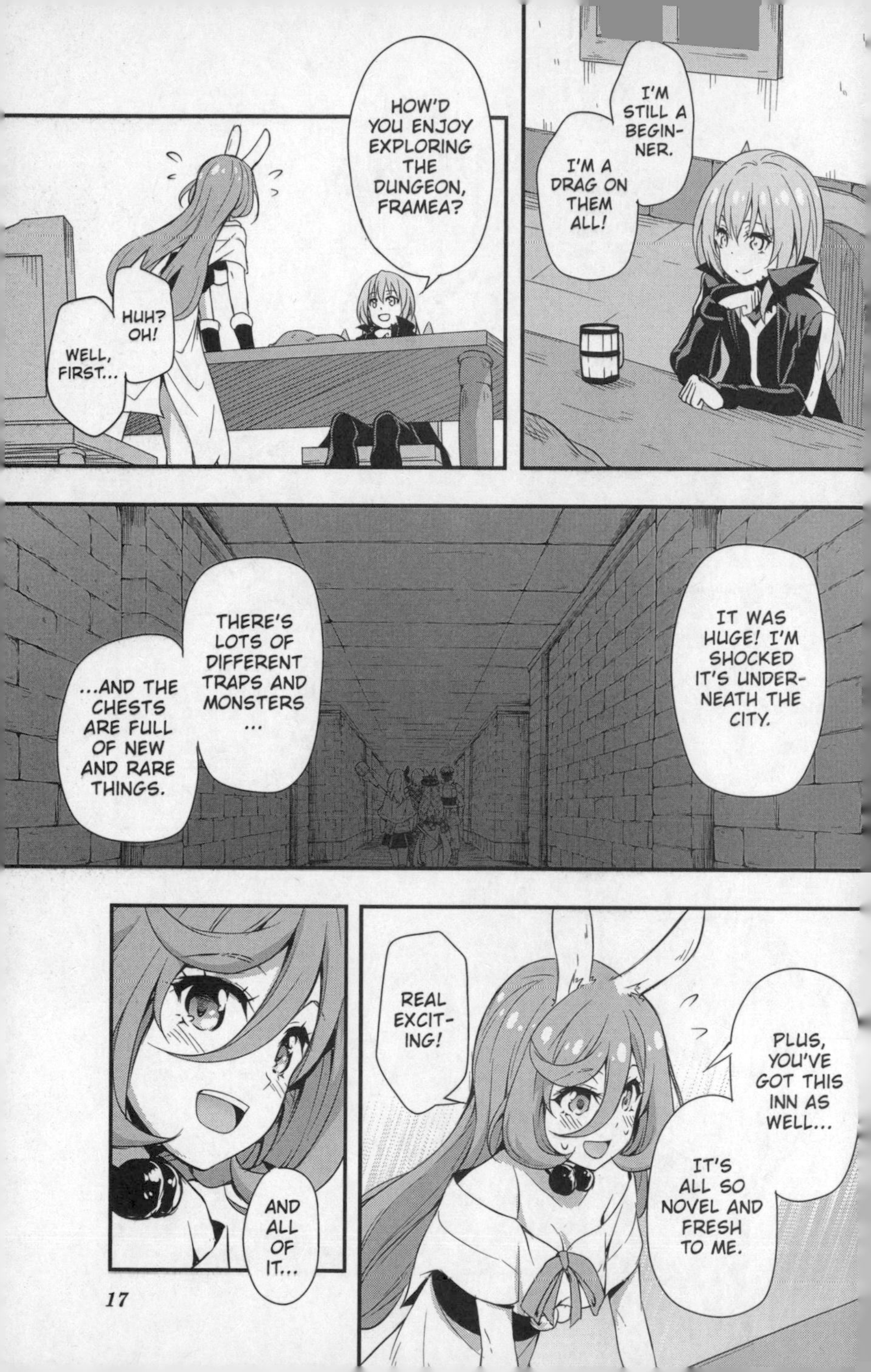
I'M STILL A BEGIN-NER.
I'M A DRAG ON THEM ALL!
HOW'D YOU ENJOY EXPLORING THE DUNGEON, FRAMEA?
HUH? OH!
WELL, FIRST...
IT WAS HUGE! I'M SHOCKED IT'S UNDER-NEATH THE CITY.
THERE'S LOTS OF DIFFERENT TRAPS AND MONSTERS ...
...AND THE CHESTS ARE FULL OF NEW AND RARE THINGS.
REAL EXCIT-ING!
PLUS, YOU'VE GOT THIS INN AS WELL...
IT'S ALL SO NOVEL AND FRESH TO ME.
AND ALL OF IT...

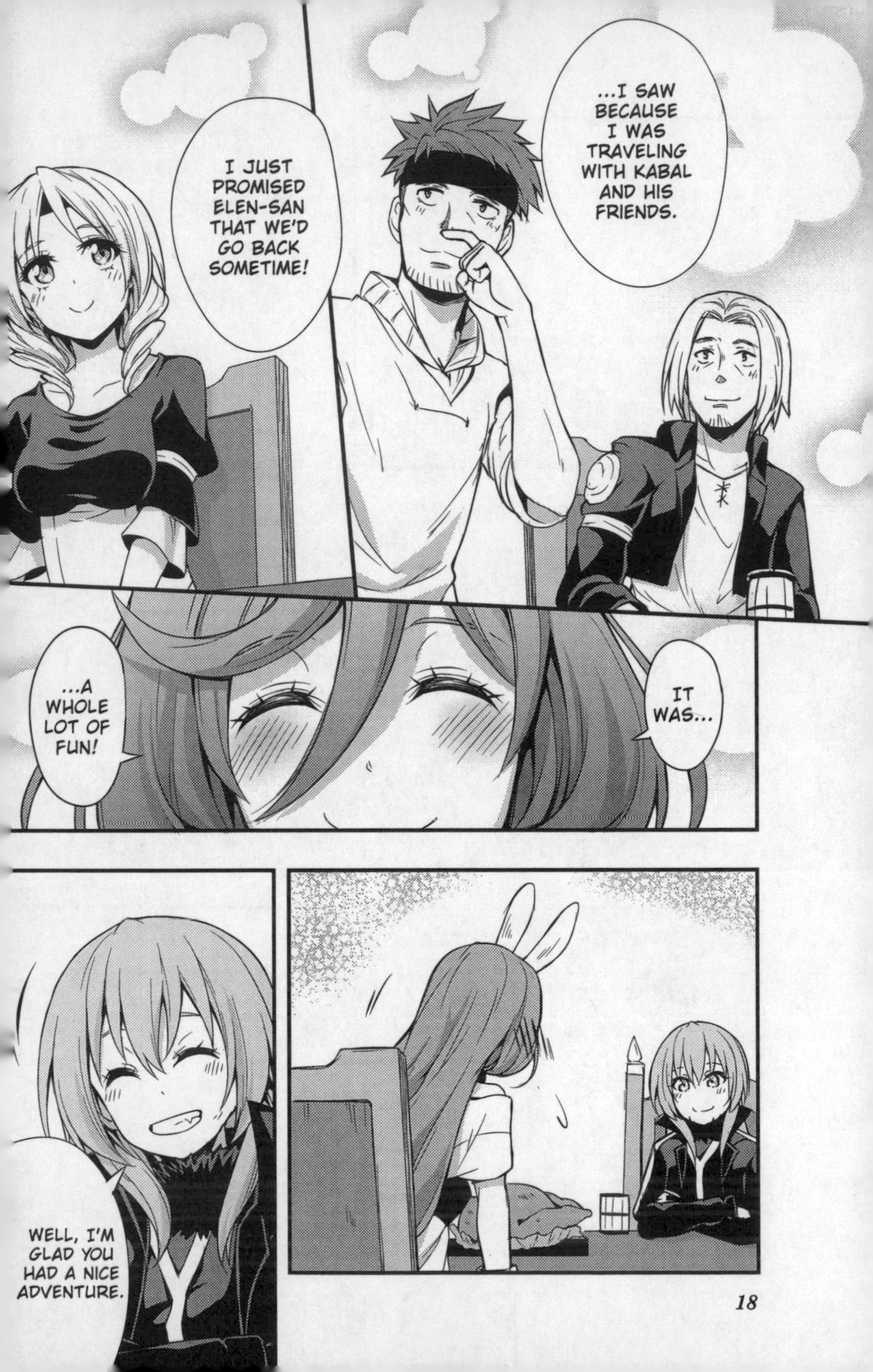
...I SAW BECAUSE I WAS TRAVELING WITH KABAL AND HIS FRIENDS.
I JUST PROMISED ELEN-SAN THAT WE'D GO BACK SOMETIME!
IT WAS...
...A WHOLE LOT OF FUN!
WELL, I'M GLAD YOU HAD A NICE ADVENTURE.

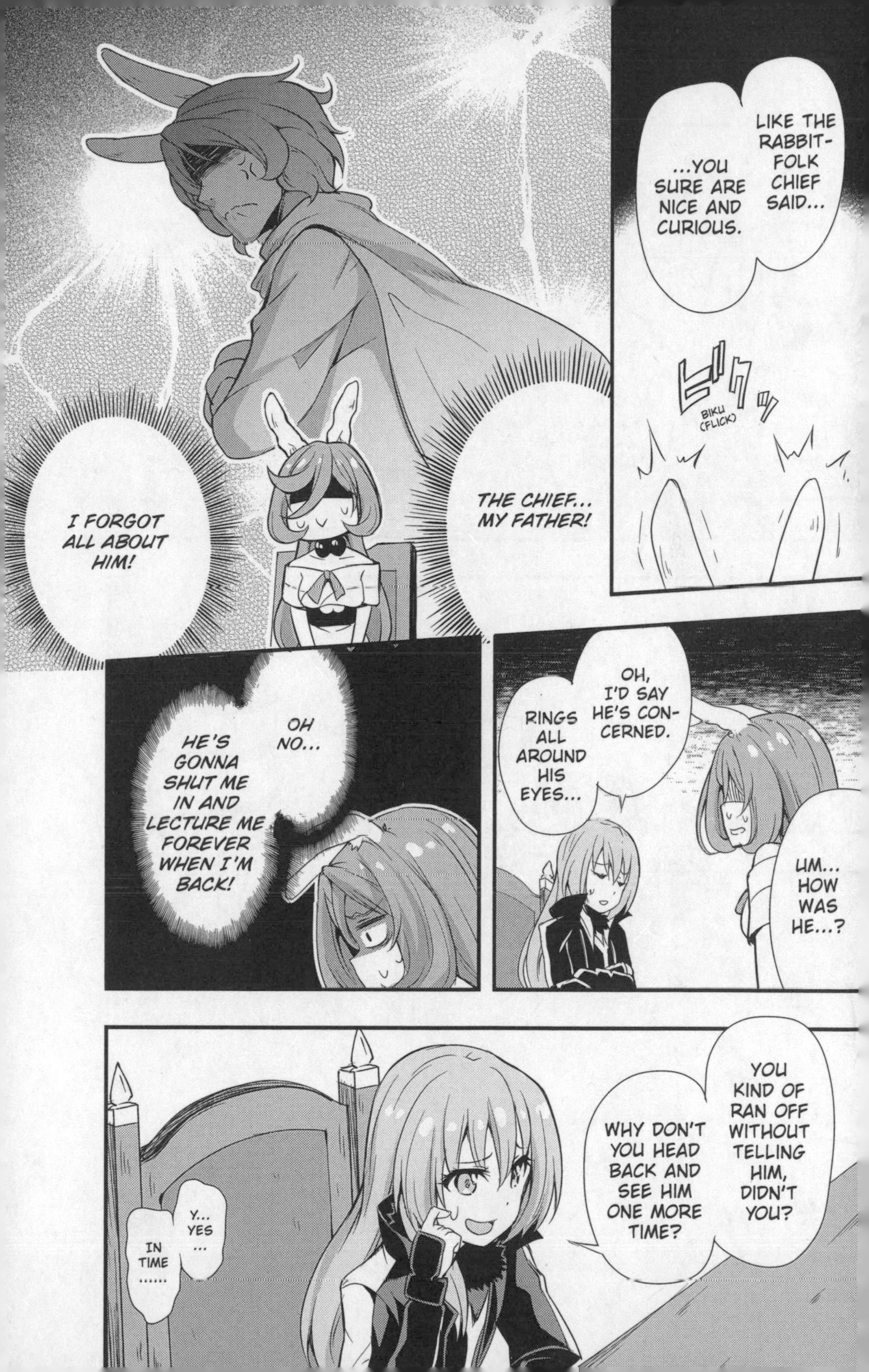
LIKE THE RABBIT-FOLK CHIEF SAID...
...YOU SURE ARE NICE AND CURIOUS.
BIKU (FLICK)
THE CHIEF... MY FATHER!
I FORGOT ALL ABOUT HIM!
UM... HOW WAS HE...?
OH, I'D SAY HE'S CONCERNED.
RINGS ALL AROUND HIS EYES...
OH NO...
HE'S GONNA SHUT ME IN AND LECTURE ME FOREVER WHEN I'M BACK!
YOU KIND OF RAN OFF WITHOUT TELLING HIM, DIDN'T YOU?
WHY DON'T YOU HEAD BACK AND SEE HIM ONE MORE TIME?
Y... YES...
IN TIME ......

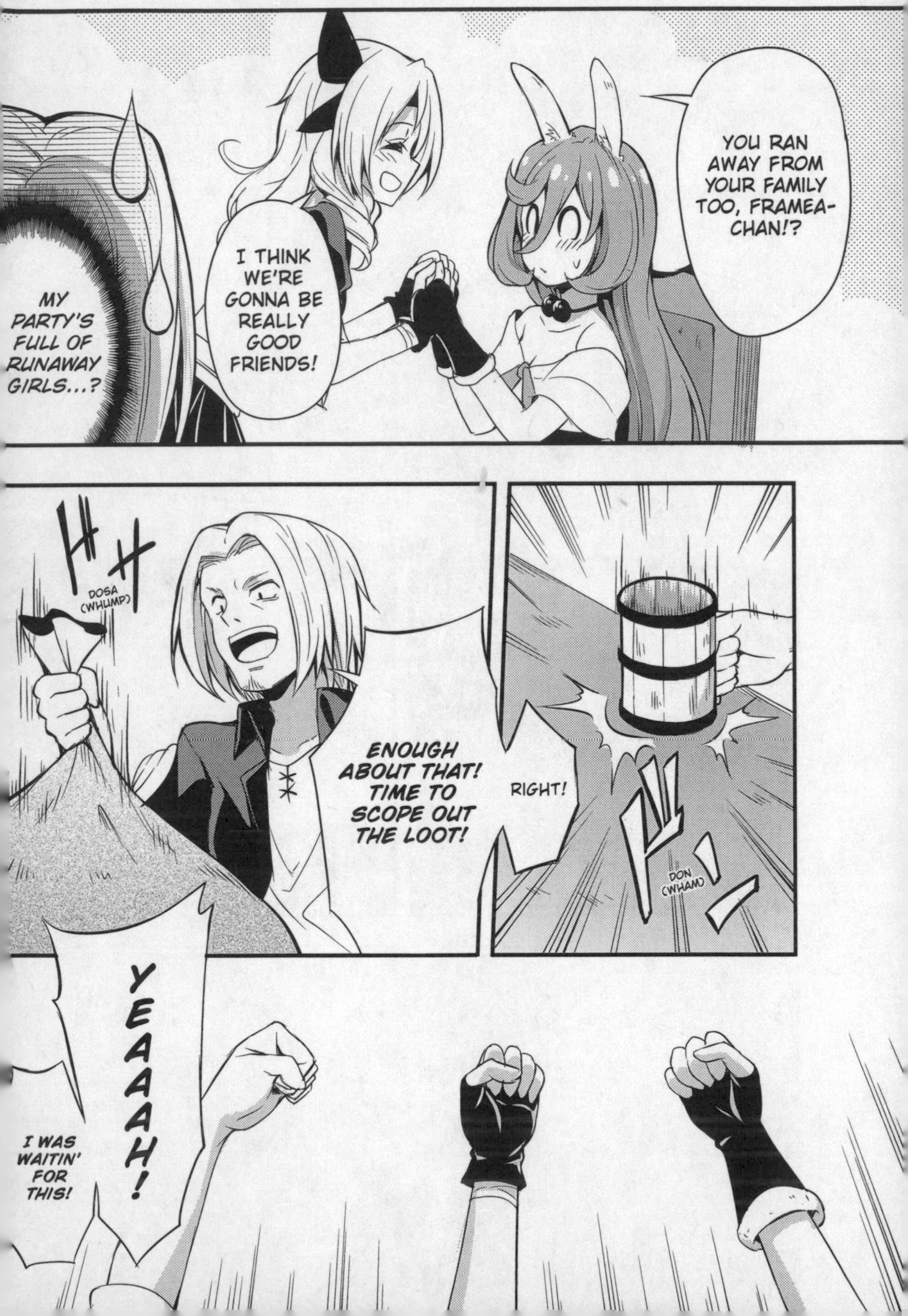
YOU RAN AWAY FROM YOUR FAMILY TOO, FRAMEA-CHAN!?
I THINK WE'RE GONNA BE REALLY GOOD FRIENDS!
MY PARTY'S FULL OF RUNAWAY GIRLS...?
RIGHT!
DON (WHAM)
DOSA (WHUMP)
ENOUGH ABOUT THAT! TIME TO SCOPE OUT THE LOOT!
YEAAAAH!
I WAS WAITIN' FOR THIS!

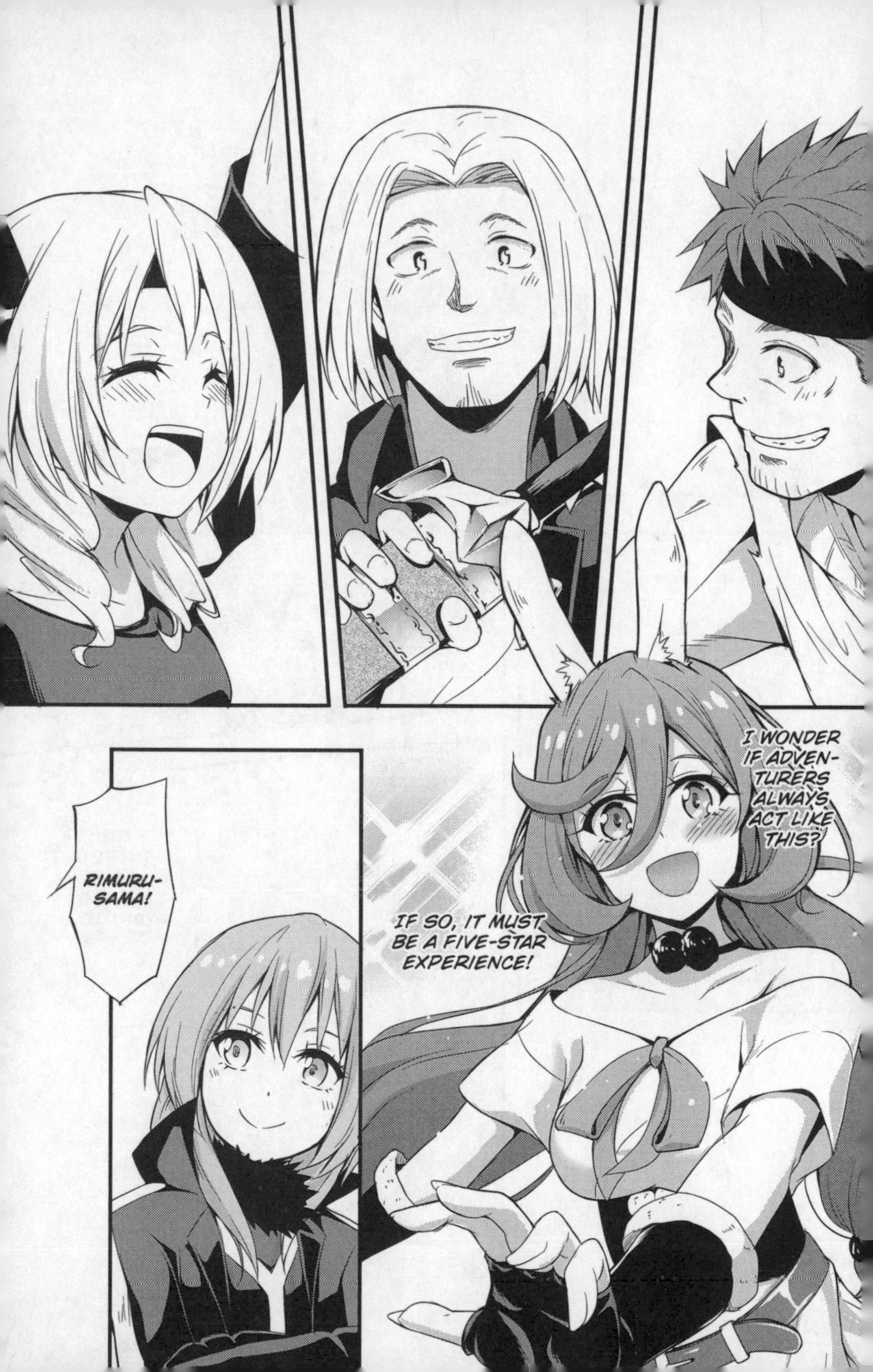
I WONDER IF ADVENTURERS ALWAYS ACT LIKE THIS?
IF SO, IT MUST BE A FIVE-STAR EXPERIENCE!
RIMURU-SAMA!

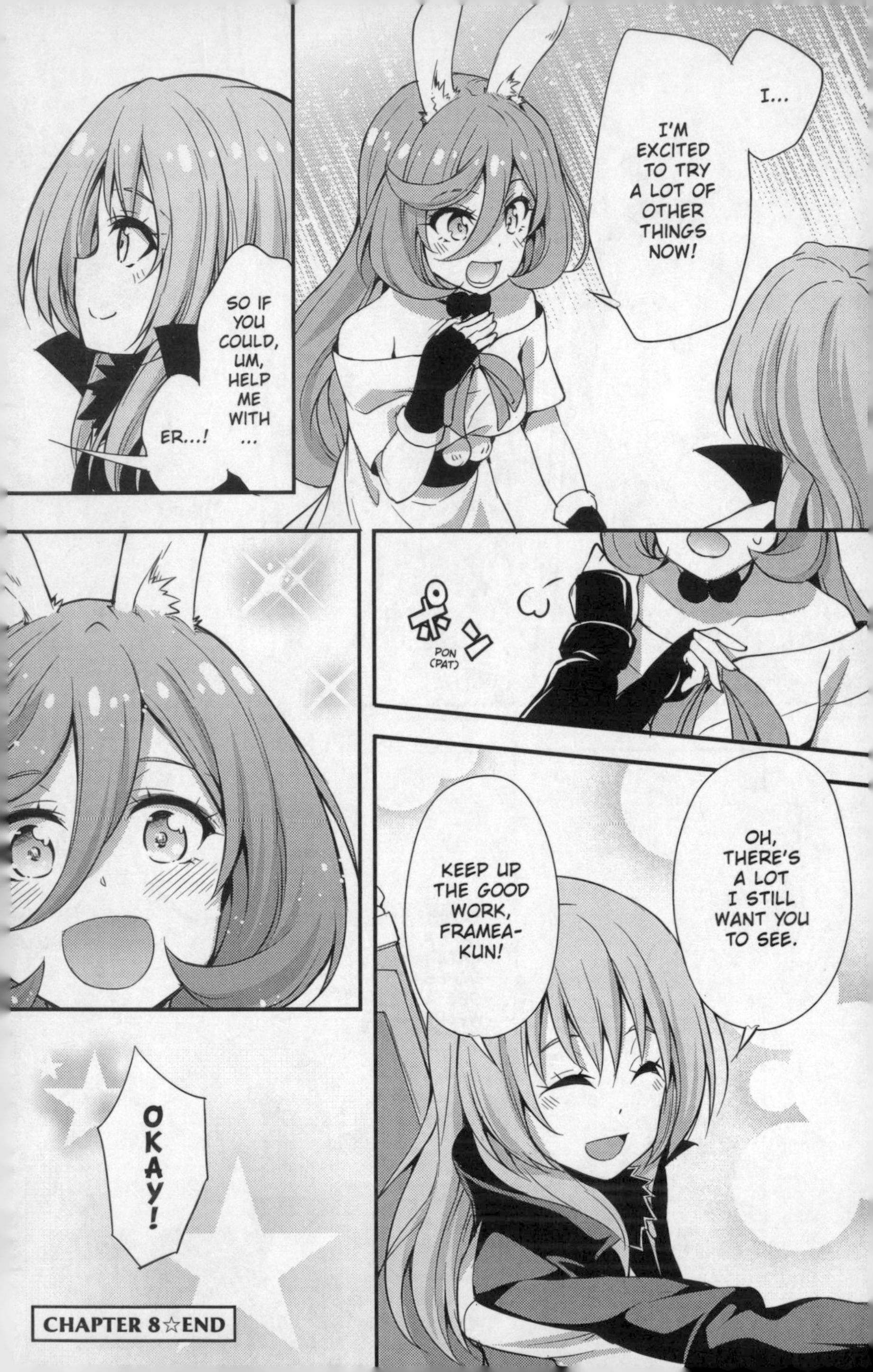
I...
I'M EXCITED TO TRY A LOT OF OTHER THINGS NOW!
SO IF YOU COULD, UM, HELP ME WITH ...
ER...!
PON (PAT)
OH, THERE'S A LOT I STILL WANT YOU TO SEE.
KEEP UP THE GOOD WORK, FRAMEA-KUN!
OKAY!
CHAPTER 8☆END

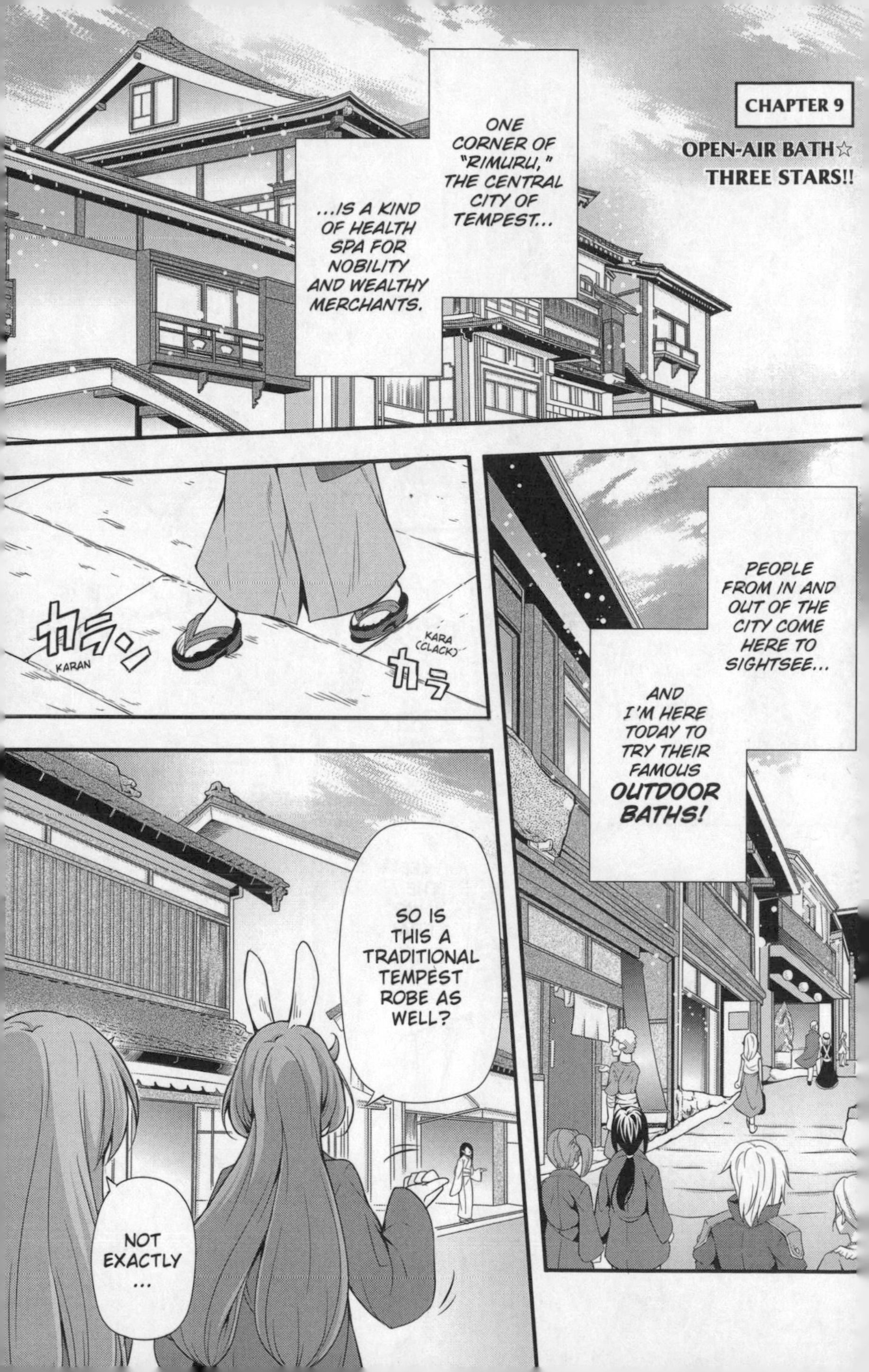
CHAPTER 9
OPEN-AIR BATH☆ THREE STARS!!
ONE CORNER OF "RIMURU," THE CENTRAL CITY OF TEMPEST...
...IS A KIND OF HEALTH SPA FOR NOBILITY AND WEALTHY MERCHANTS.
PEOPLE FROM IN AND OUT OF THE CITY COME HERE TO SIGHTSEE...
AND I'M HERE TODAY TO TRY THEIR FAMOUS OUTDOOR BATHS!
カラ
KARA (CLACK)
カラン
KARAN
SO IS THIS A TRADITIONAL TEMPEST ROBE AS WELL?
NOT EXACTLY ...

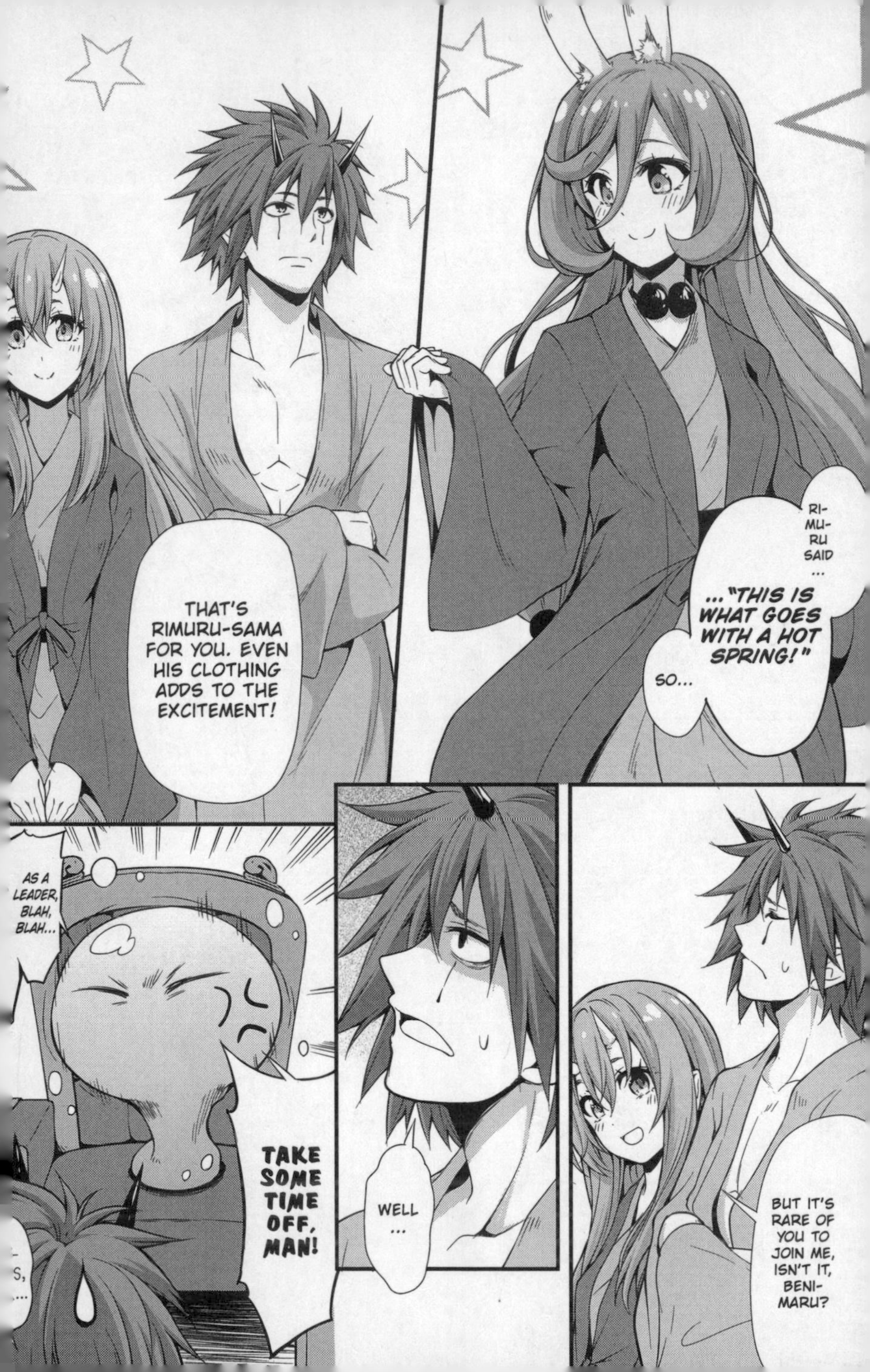
RI-MU-RU SAID...
..."THIS IS WHAT GOES WITH A HOT SPRING!"
SO...
THAT'S RIMURU-SAMA FOR YOU. EVEN HIS CLOTHING ADDS TO THE EXCITEMENT!
BUT IT'S RARE OF YOU TO JOIN ME, ISN'T IT, BENI-MARU?
WELL...
TAKE SOME TIME OFF, MAN!
AS A LEADER, BLAH, BLAH...

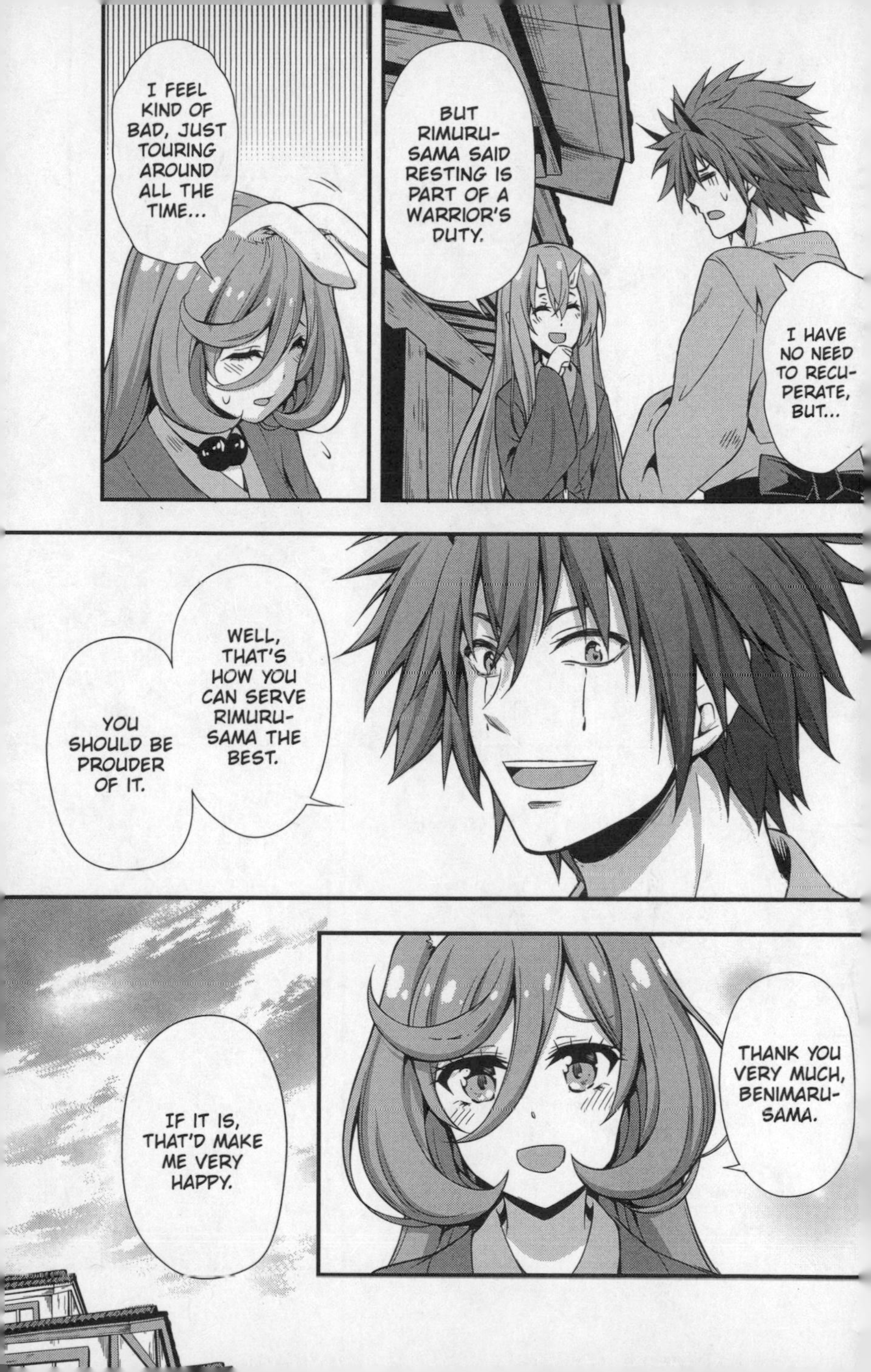
I HAVE NO NEED TO RECUPERATE, BUT...
BUT RIMURU-SAMA SAID RESTING IS PART OF A WARRIOR'S DUTY.
I FEEL KIND OF BAD, JUST TOURING AROUND ALL THE TIME...
WELL, THAT'S HOW YOU CAN SERVE RIMURU-SAMA THE BEST.
YOU SHOULD BE PROUDER OF IT.
THANK YOU VERY MUCH, BENIMARU-SAMA.
IF IT IS, THAT'D MAKE ME VERY HAPPY.

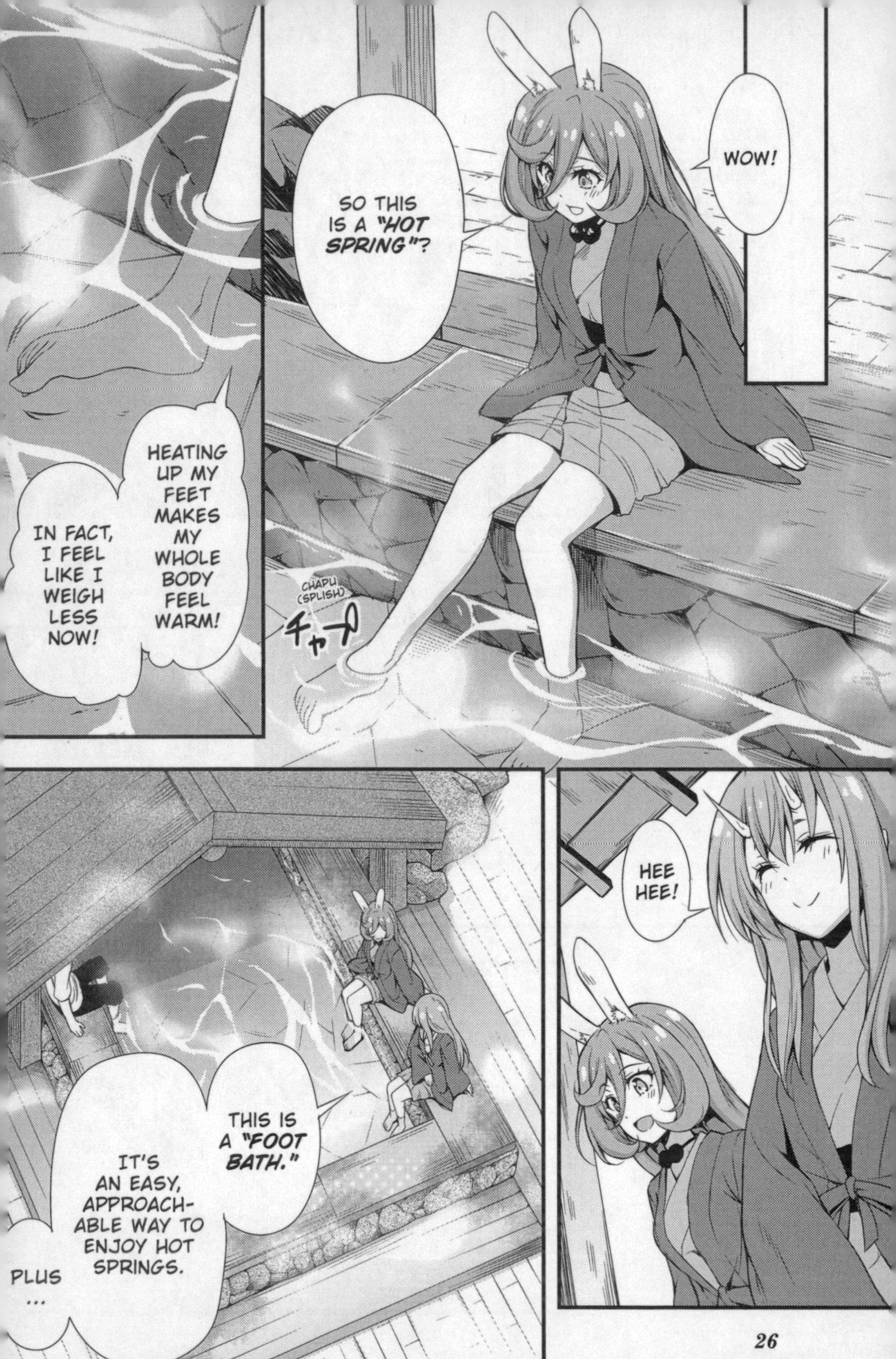
WOW!
SO THIS IS A "HOT SPRING"?
CHAPU (SPLISH)
チャプ
HEATING UP MY FEET MAKES MY WHOLE BODY FEEL WARM!
IN FACT, I FEEL LIKE I WEIGH LESS NOW!
HEE HEE!
THIS IS A "FOOT BATH."
IT'S AN EASY, APPROACHABLE WAY TO ENJOY HOT SPRINGS.
PLUS ...

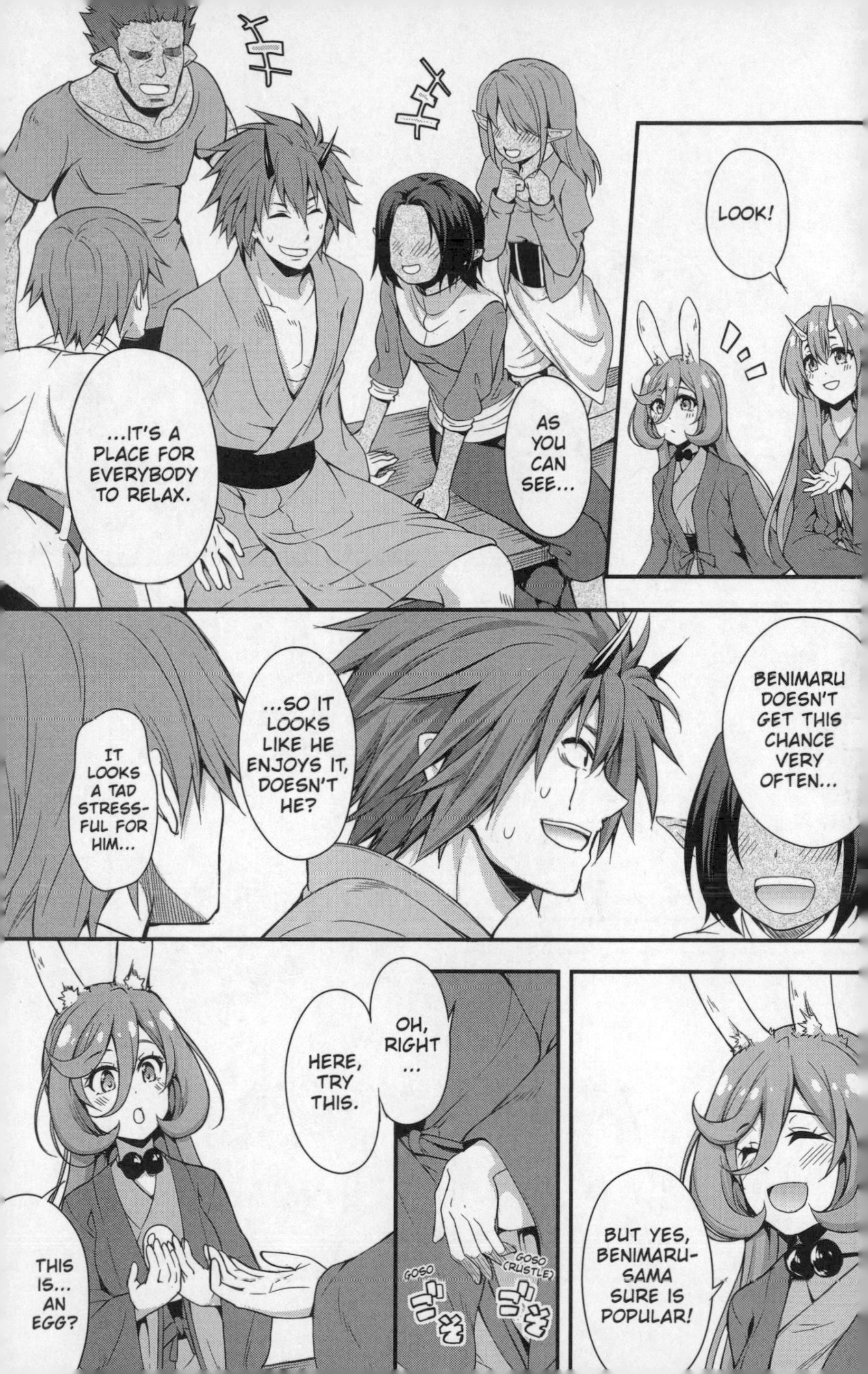
LOOK!
AS YOU CAN SEE...
...IT'S A PLACE FOR EVERYBODY TO RELAX.
BENIMARU DOESN'T GET THIS CHANCE VERY OFTEN...
...SO IT LOOKS LIKE HE ENJOYS IT, DOESN'T HE?
IT LOOKS A TAD STRESSFUL FOR HIM...
BUT YES, BENIMARU-SAMA SURE IS POPULAR!
OH, RIGHT...
HERE, TRY THIS.
GOSO (RUSTLE)
GOSO
THIS IS... AN EGG?

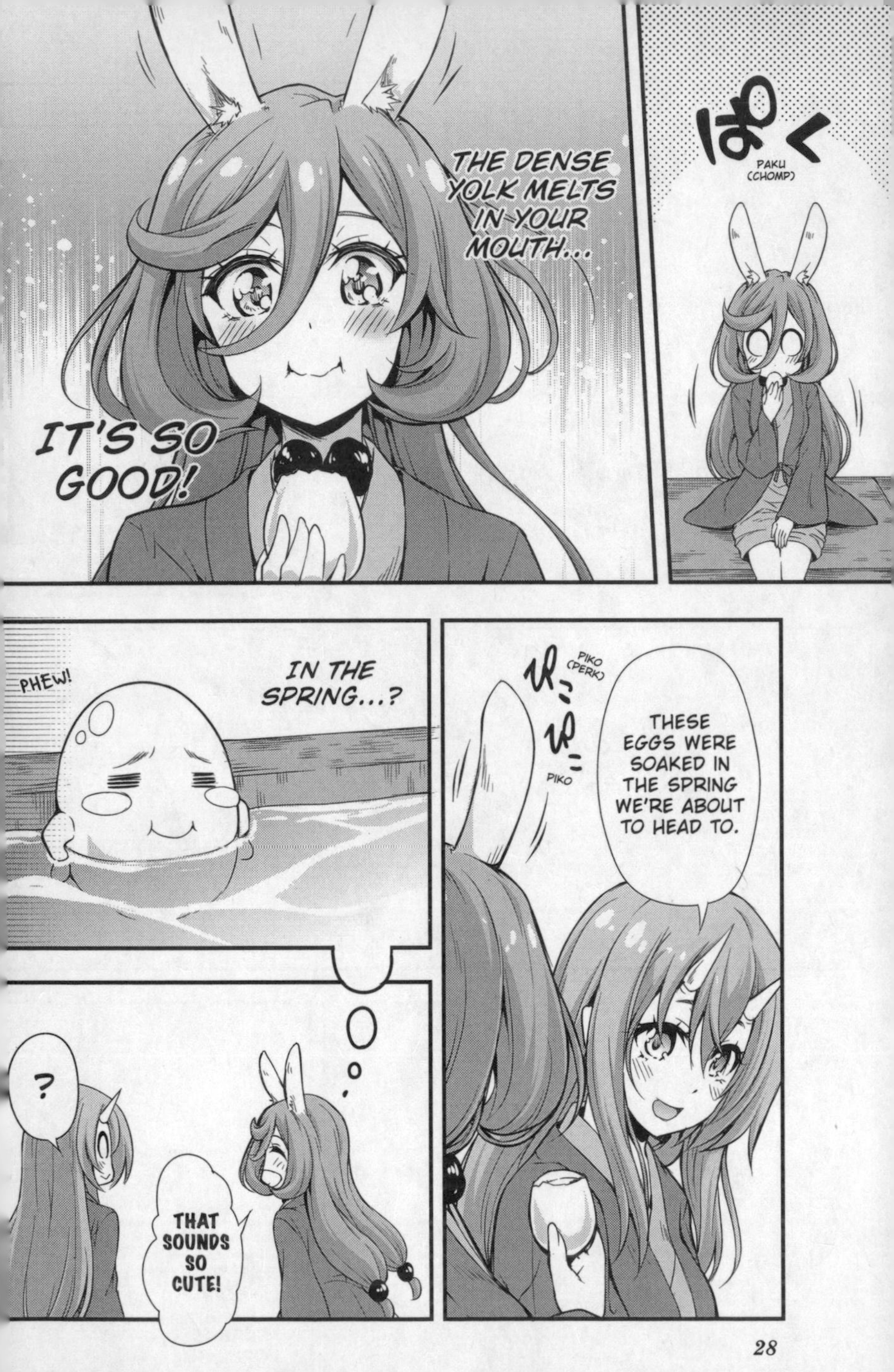
ぱく
PAKU (CHOMP)
THE DENSE YOLK MELTS IN YOUR MOUTH...
IT'S SO GOOD!
ぴこぴこ
PIKO (PERK) PIKO
THESE EGGS WERE SOAKED IN THE SPRING WE'RE ABOUT TO HEAD TO.
IN THE SPRING...?
PHEW!
THAT SOUNDS SO CUTE!
?

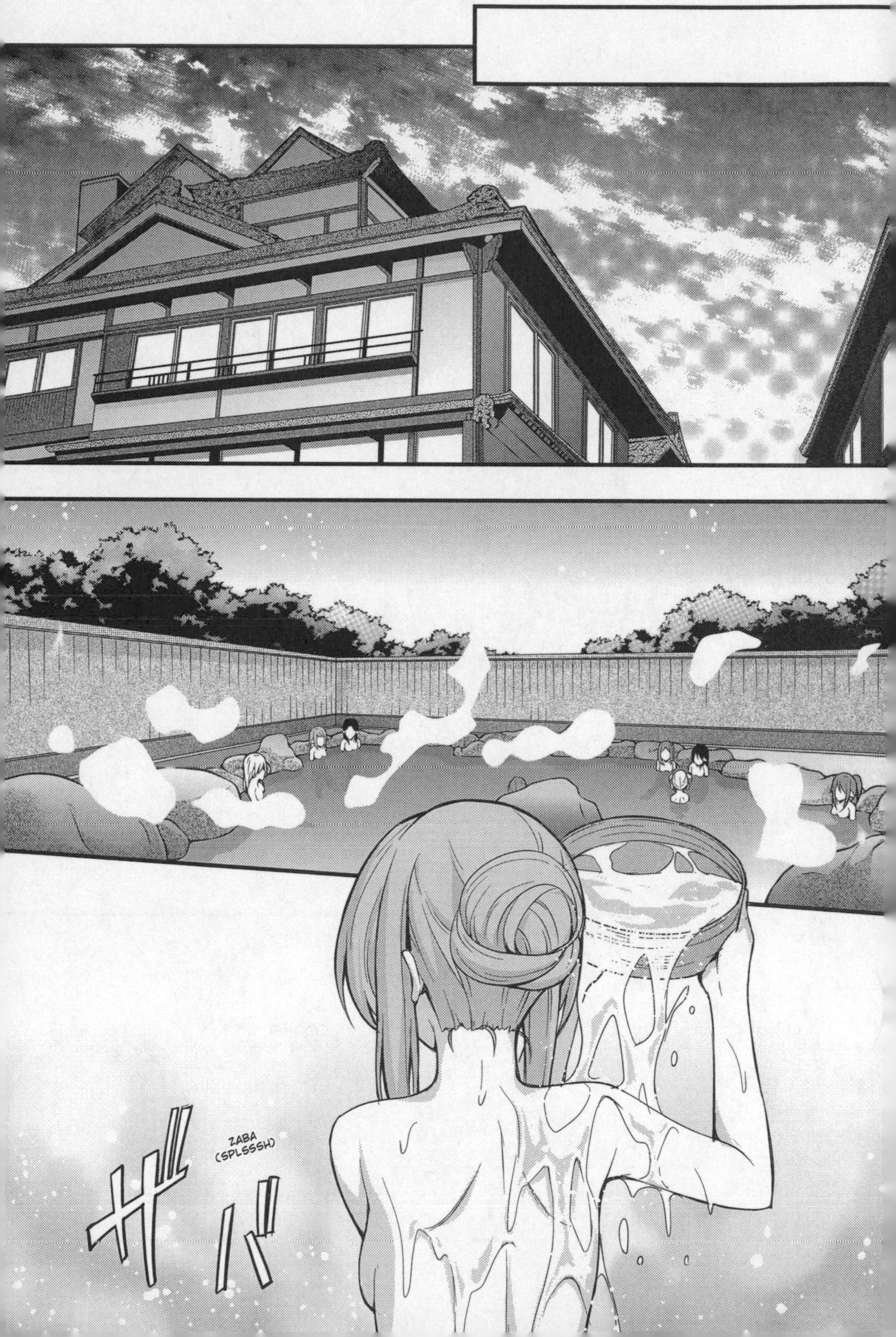
ZABA
(SPLSSSH)

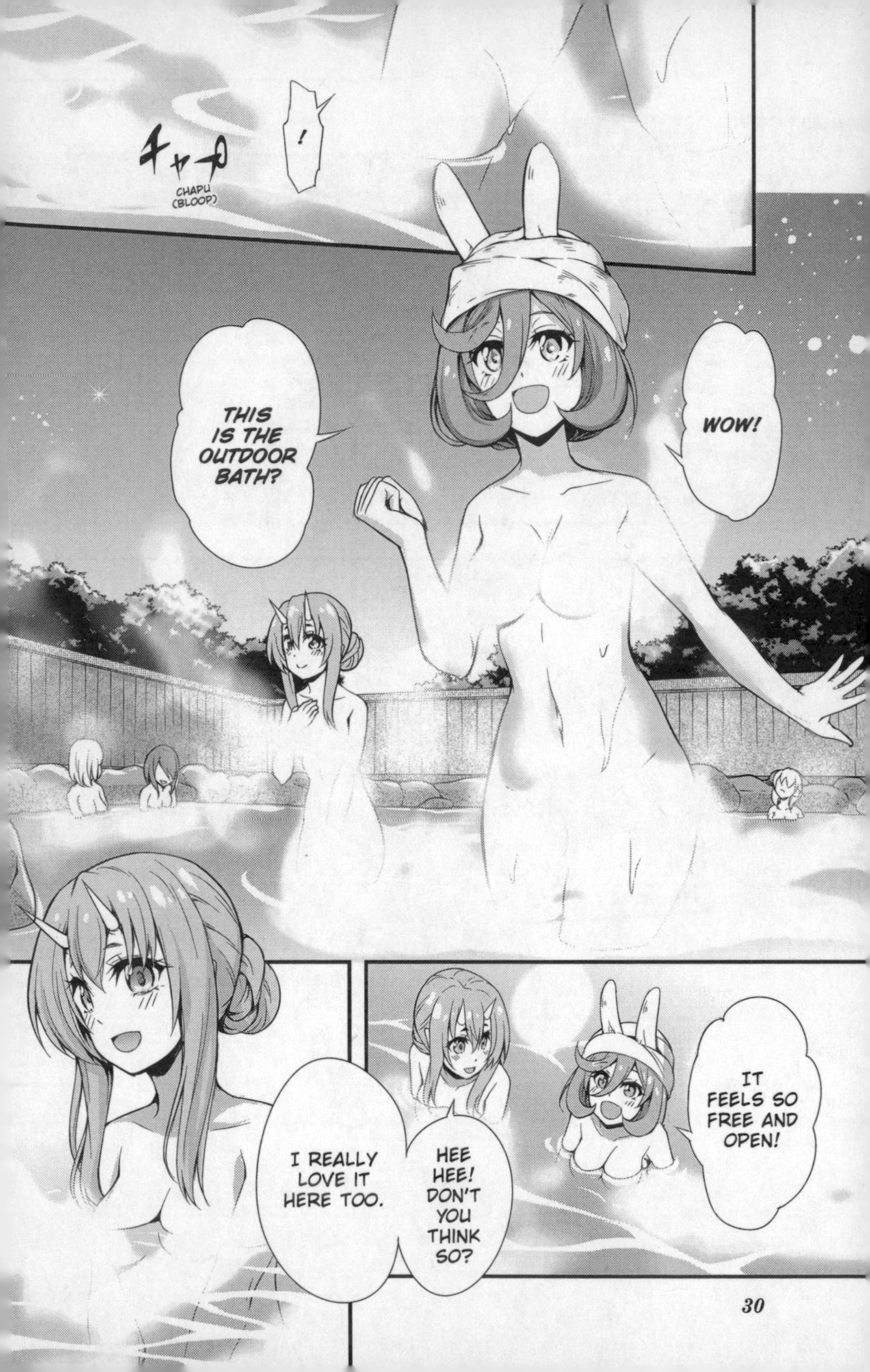
!
チャプ
CHAPU (BLOOP)
WOW!
THIS IS THE OUTDOOR BATH?
IT FEELS SO FREE AND OPEN!
HEE HEE! DON'T YOU THINK SO?
I REALLY LOVE IT HERE TOO.

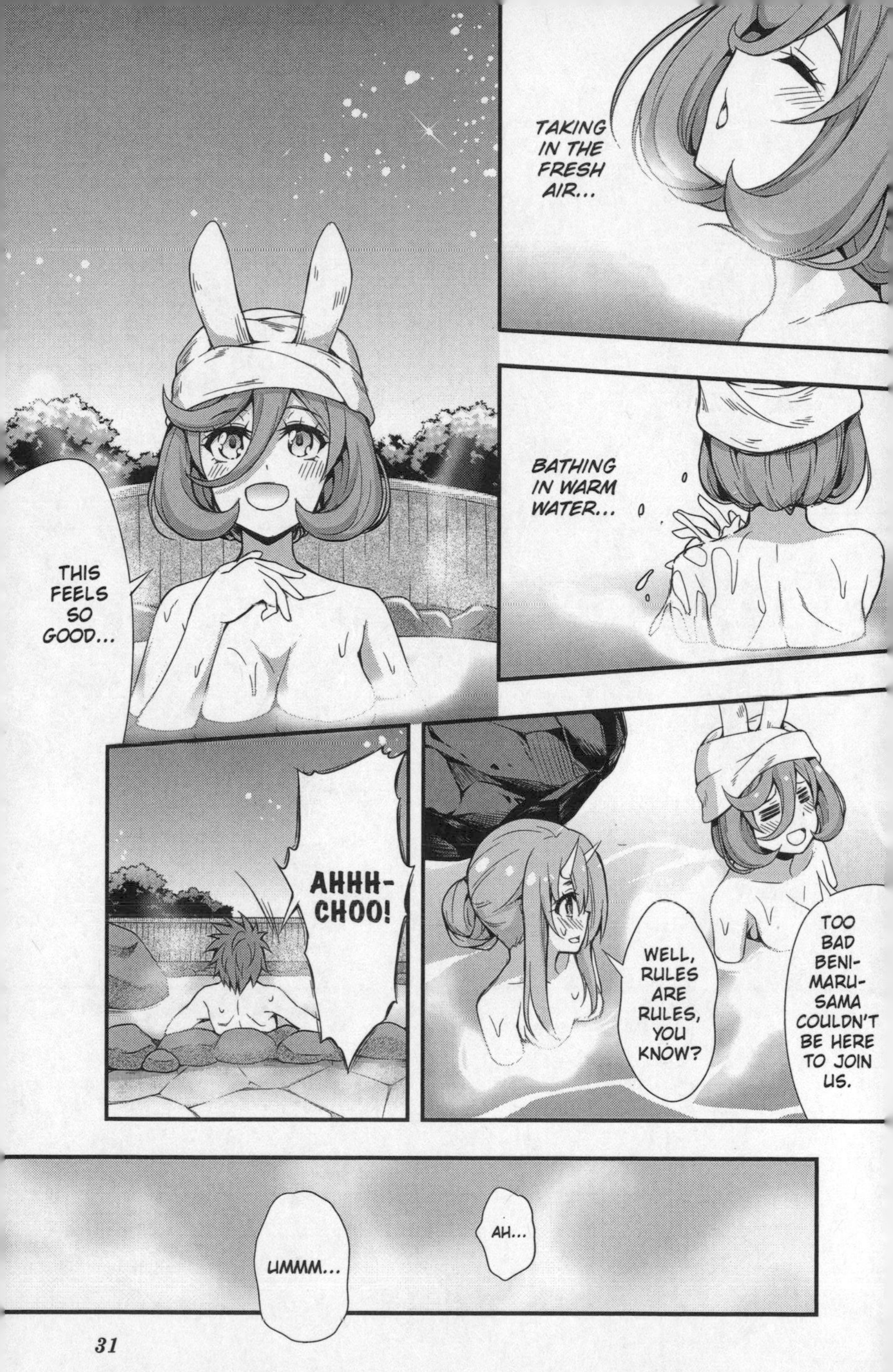
TAKING IN THE FRESH AIR...
BATHING IN WARM WATER...
THIS FEELS SO GOOD...
TOO BAD BENI-MARU-SAMA COULDN'T BE HERE TO JOIN US.
WELL, RULES ARE RULES, YOU KNOW?
AHHH-CHOO!
AH...
UMMM...

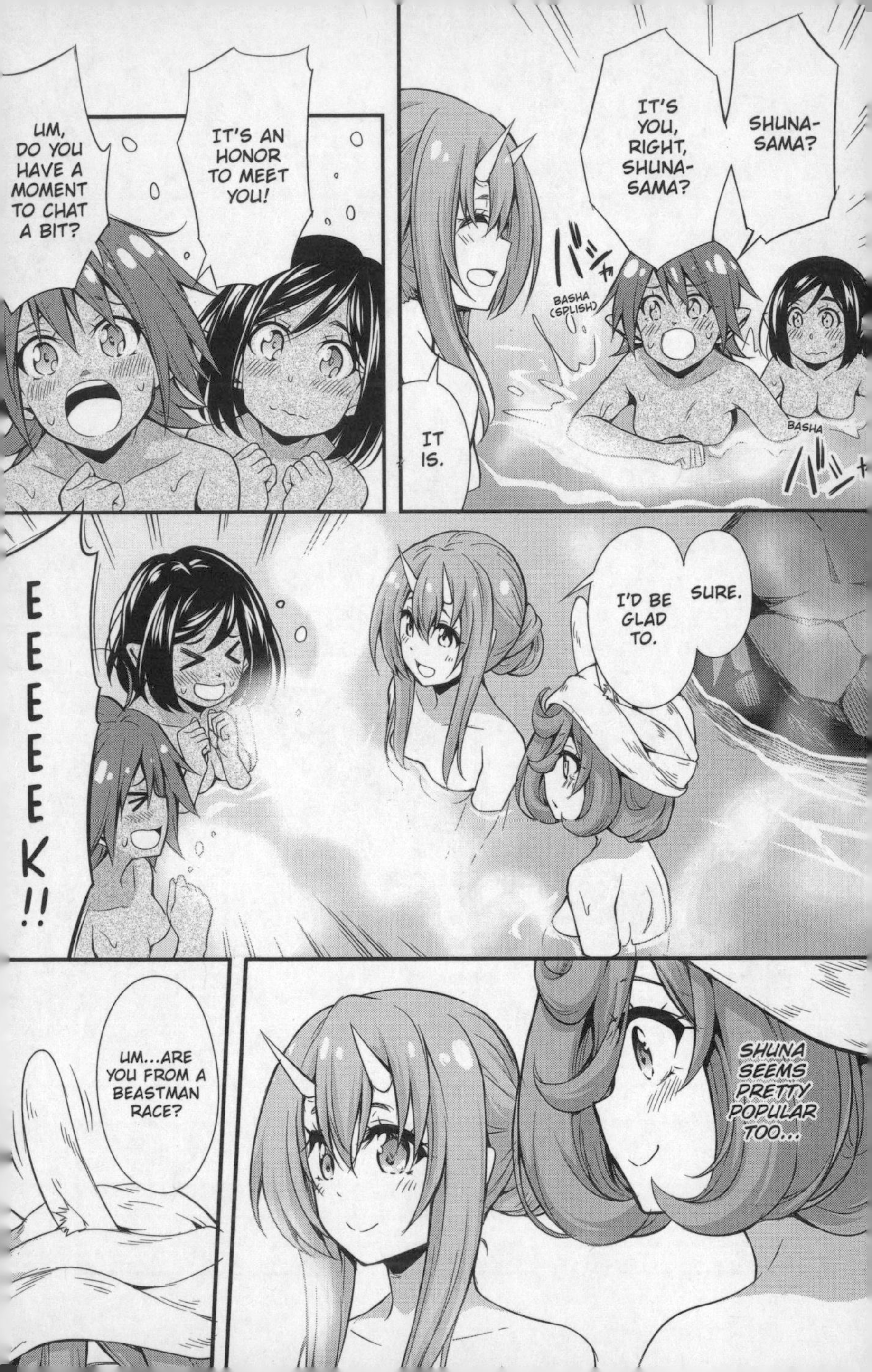
SHUNA-SAMA?
IT'S YOU, RIGHT, SHUNA-SAMA?
BASHA (SPLISH)
BASHA
IT IS.
IT'S AN HONOR TO MEET YOU!
UM, DO YOU HAVE A MOMENT TO CHAT A BIT?
SURE.
I'D BE GLAD TO.
EEEEEK!!
SHUNA SEEMS PRETTY POPULAR TOO...
UM...ARE YOU FROM A BEASTMAN RACE?

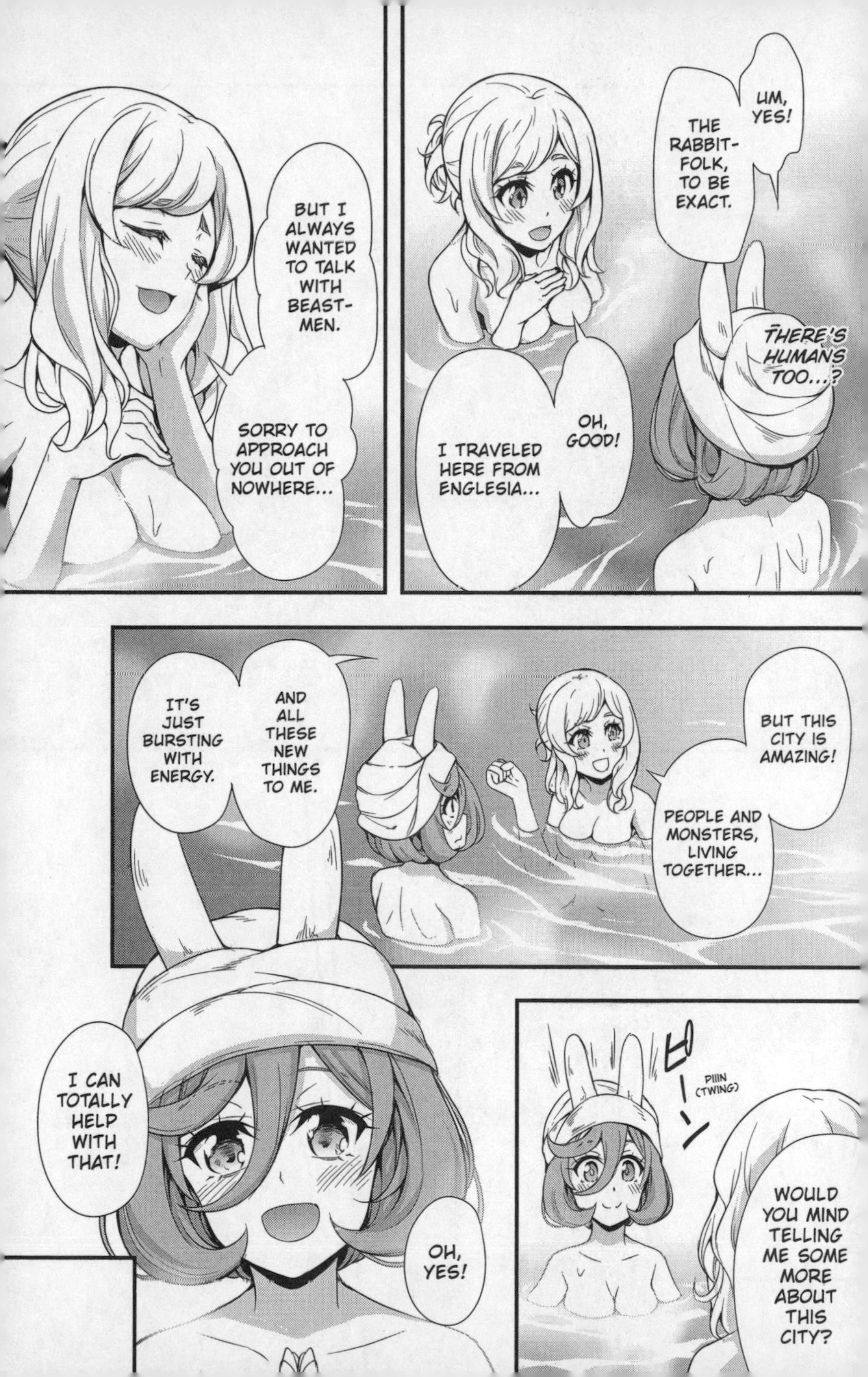
UM, YES!
THE RABBIT-FOLK, TO BE EXACT.
THERE'S HUMANS TOO...?
OH, GOOD!
I TRAVELED HERE FROM ENGLESIA...
BUT I ALWAYS WANTED TO TALK WITH BEAST-MEN.
SORRY TO APPROACH YOU OUT OF NOWHERE...
BUT THIS CITY IS AMAZING!
PEOPLE AND MONSTERS, LIVING TOGETHER...
AND ALL THESE NEW THINGS TO ME.
IT'S JUST BURSTING WITH ENERGY.
PIIIN (TWING)
WOULD YOU MIND TELLING ME SOME MORE ABOUT THIS CITY?
OH, YES!
I CAN TOTALLY HELP WITH THAT!

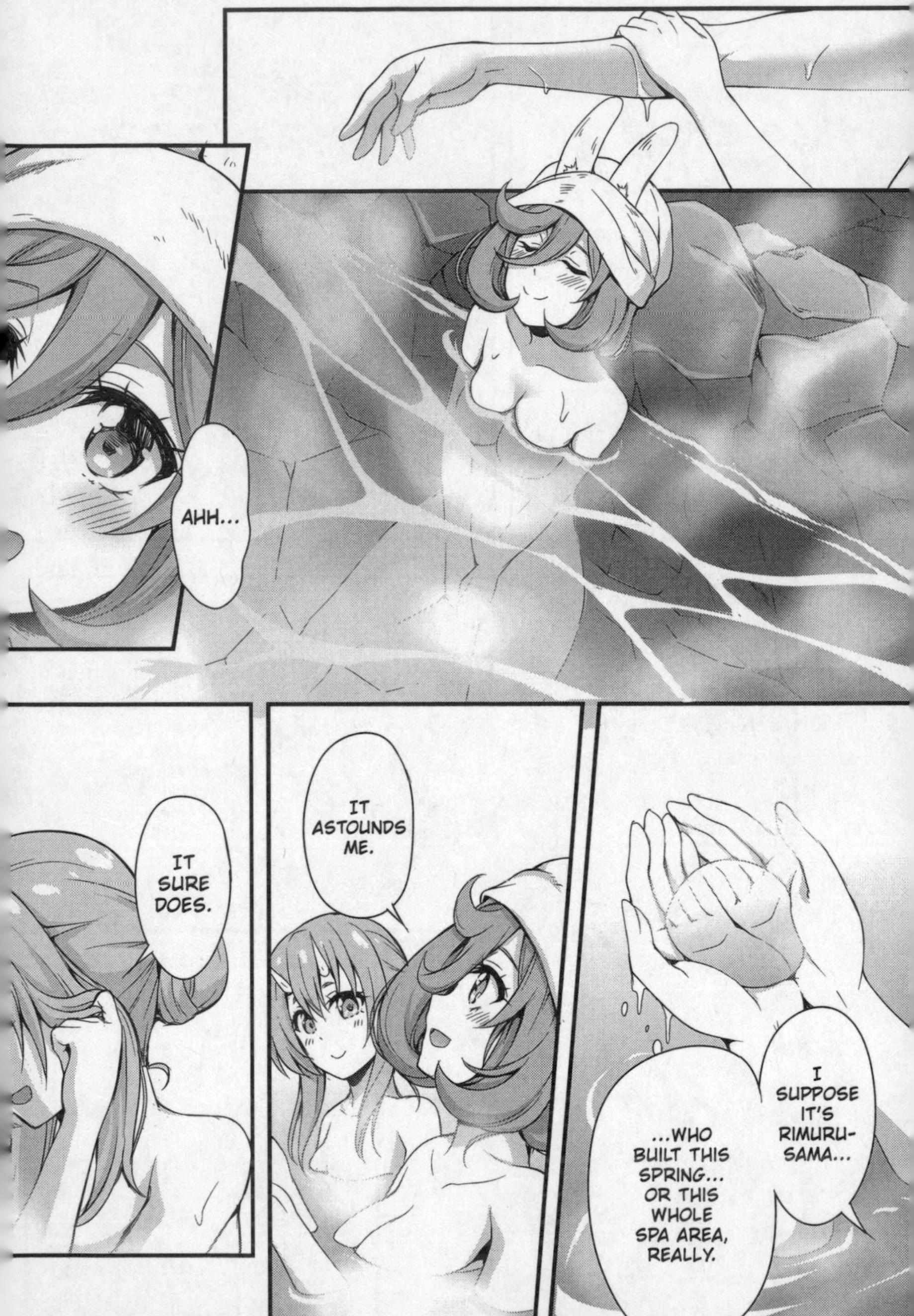
AHH...
I SUPPOSE IT'S RIMURU-SAMA...
...WHO BUILT THIS SPRING... OR THIS WHOLE SPA AREA, REALLY.
IT ASTOUNDS ME.
IT SURE DOES.

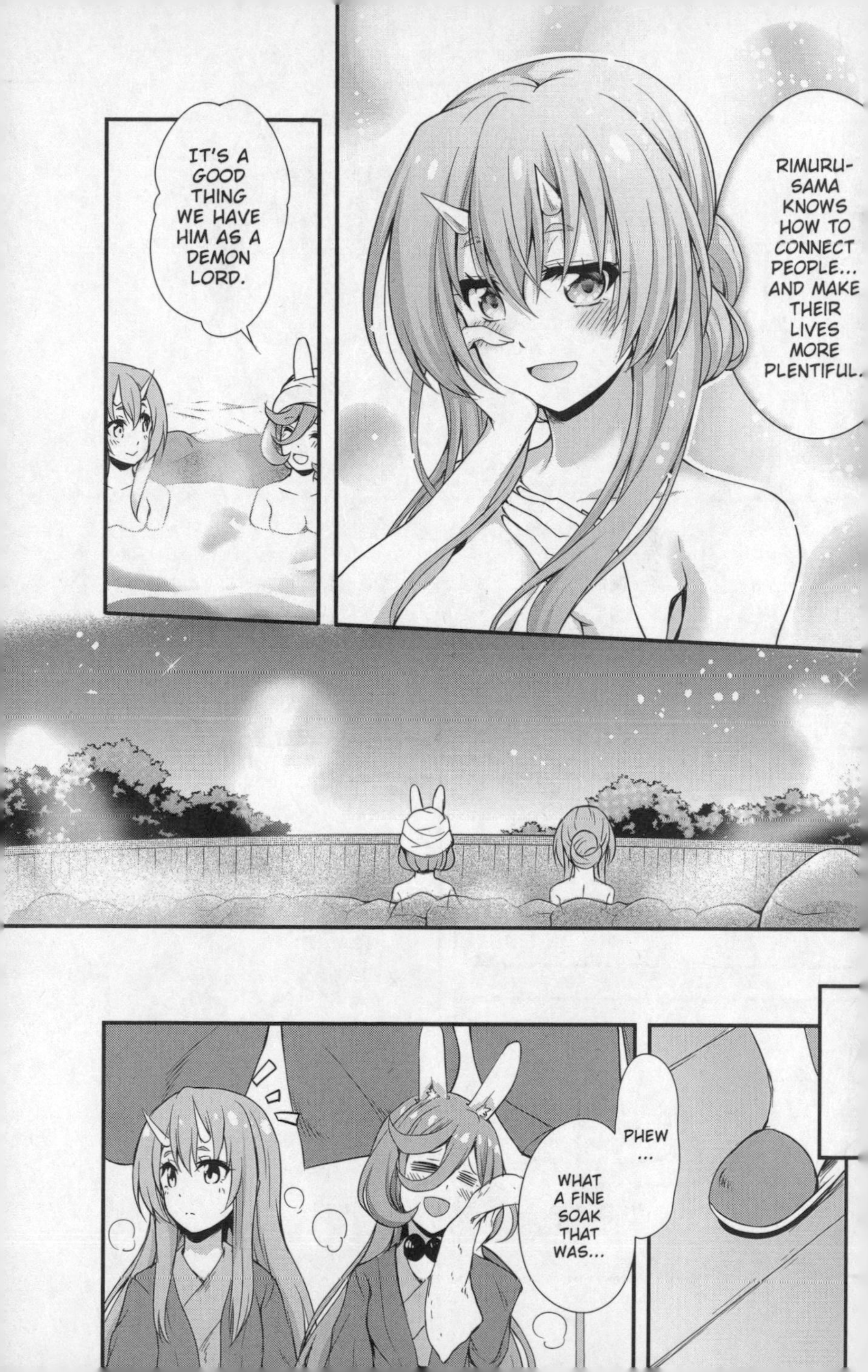
RIMURU-SAMA KNOWS HOW TO CONNECT PEOPLE... AND MAKE THEIR LIVES MORE PLENTIFUL.
IT'S A GOOD THING WE HAVE HIM AS A DEMON LORD.
PHEW ... WHAT A FINE SOAK THAT WAS...

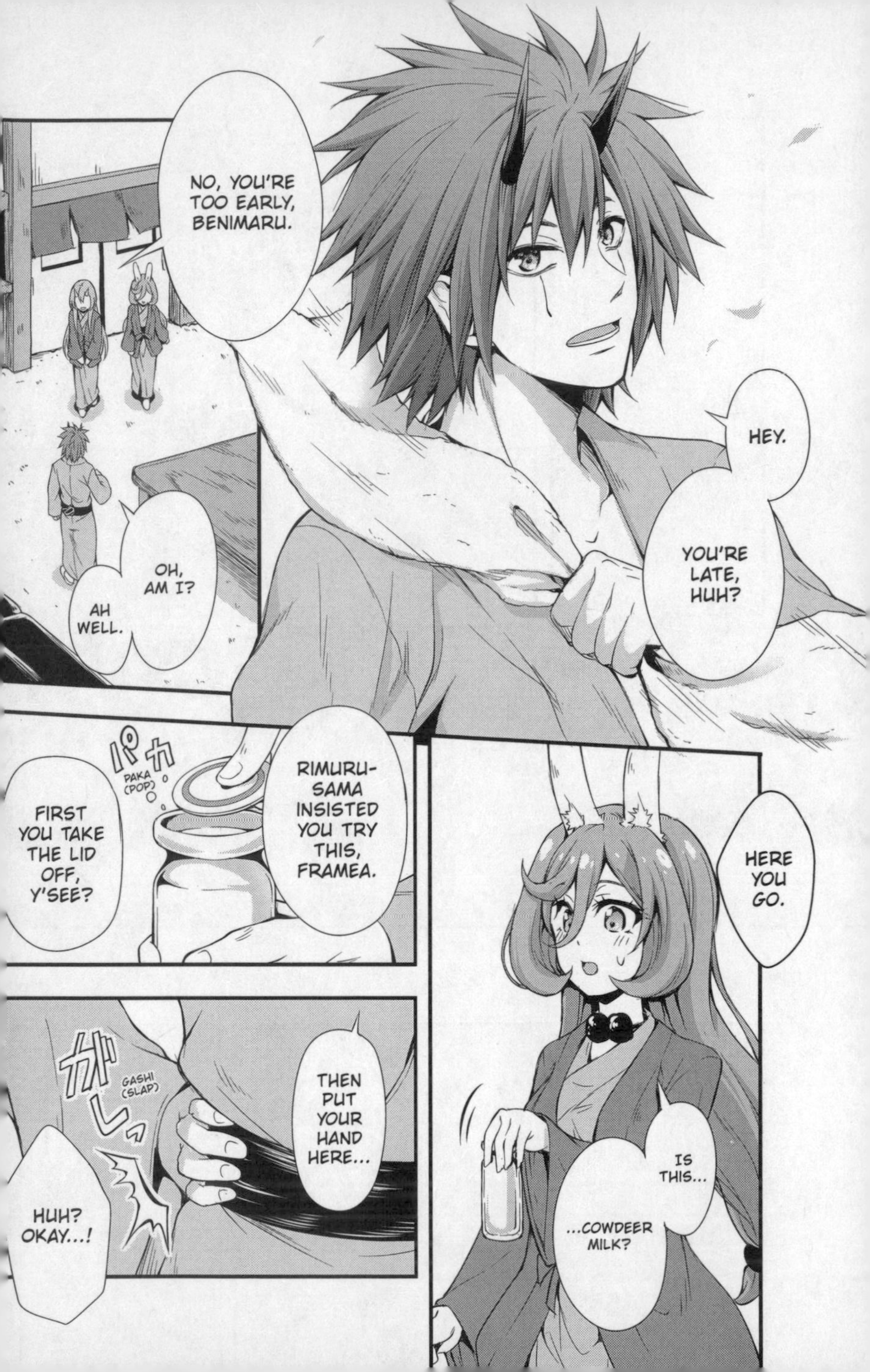
HEY.
YOU'RE LATE, HUH?
NO, YOU'RE TOO EARLY, BENIMARU.
OH, AM I?
AH WELL.
HERE YOU GO.
IS THIS...
...COWDEER MILK?
RIMURU-SAMA INSISTED YOU TRY THIS, FRAMEA.
PAKA (POP)
FIRST YOU TAKE THE LID OFF, Y'SEE?
THEN PUT YOUR HAND HERE...
GASHI (SLAP)
HUH? OKAY...!

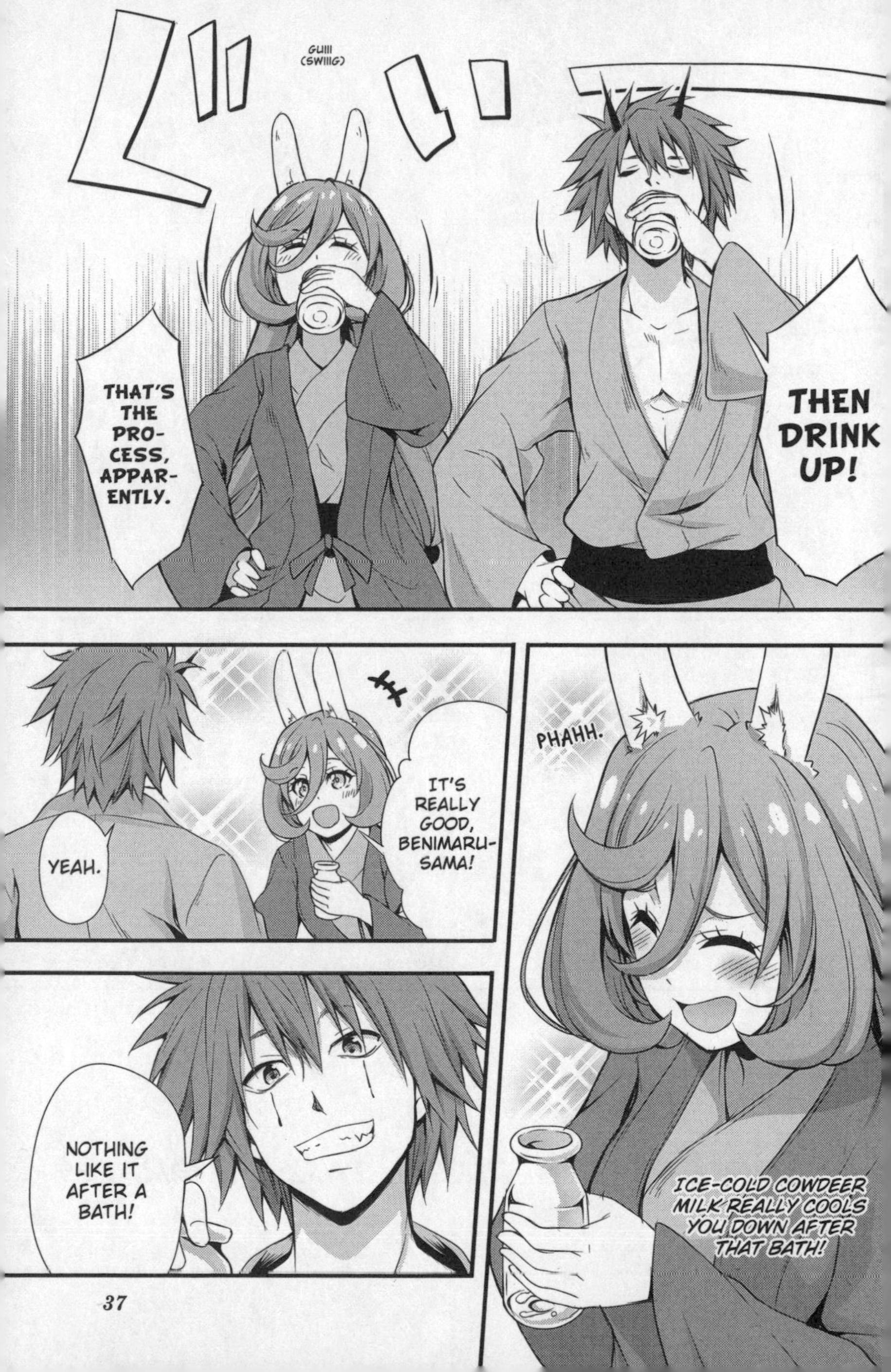
GUIII (SWIIIG)
THEN DRINK UP!
THAT'S THE PRO-CESS, APPAR-ENTLY.
PHAHH.
ICE-COLD COWDEER MILK REALLY COOLS YOU DOWN AFTER THAT BATH!
IT'S REALLY GOOD, BENIMARU-SAMA!
YEAH.
NOTHING LIKE IT AFTER A BATH!

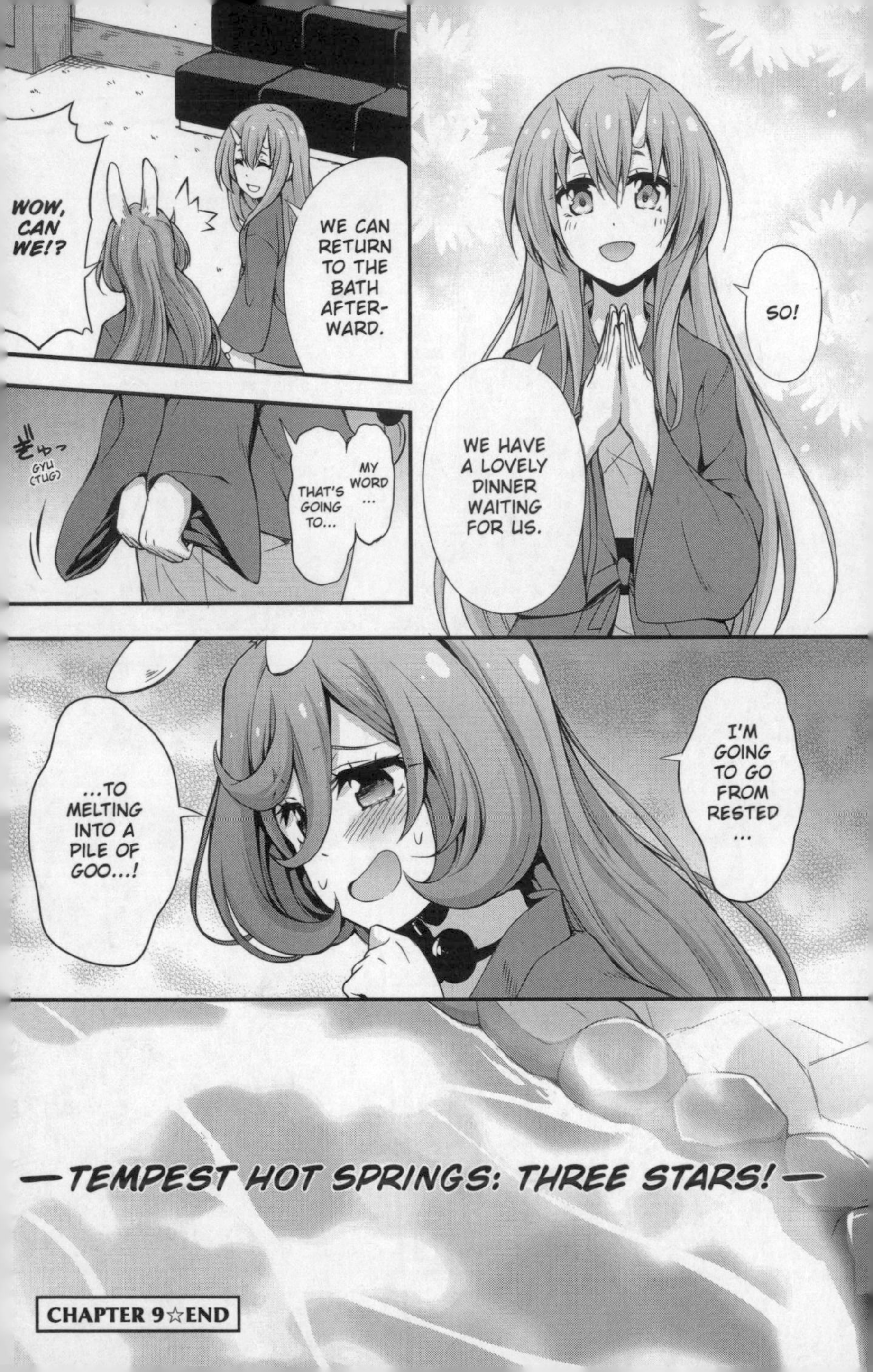
SO!
WE HAVE A LOVELY DINNER WAITING FOR US.
WE CAN RETURN TO THE BATH AFTER-WARD.
WOW, CAN WE!?
ぎゅっ
GYU (TUG)
MY WORD...
THAT'S GOING TO...
I'M GOING TO GO FROM RESTED...
...TO MELTING INTO A PILE OF GOO...!
—TEMPEST HOT SPRINGS: THREE STARS!—
CHAPTER 9☆END

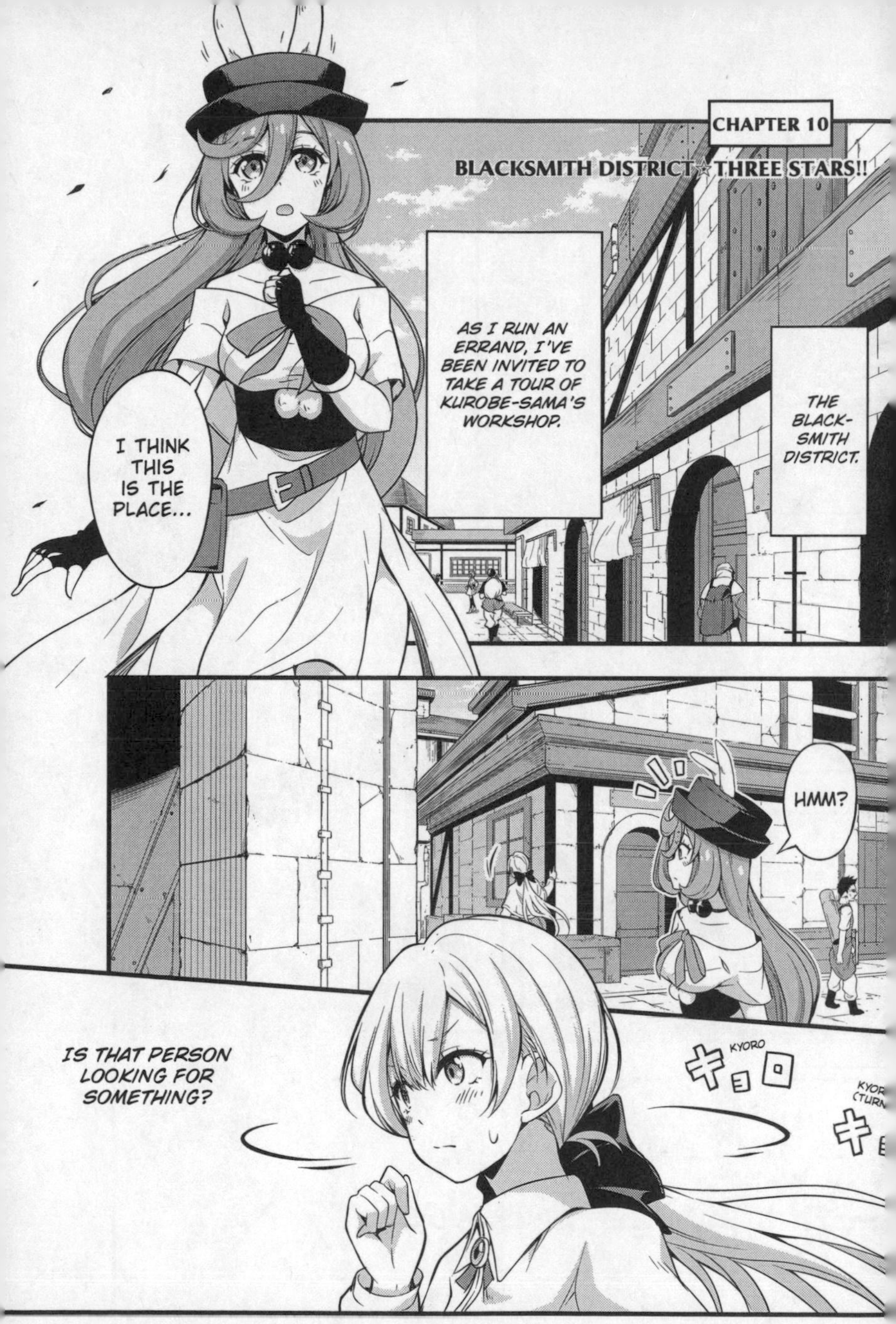
CHAPTER 10
BLACKSMITH DISTRICT☆THREE STARS!!
THE BLACK-SMITH DISTRICT.
AS I RUN AN ERRAND, I'VE BEEN INVITED TO TAKE A TOUR OF KUROBE-SAMA'S WORKSHOP.
I THINK THIS IS THE PLACE...
HMM?
キョロ
KYORO
IS THAT PERSON LOOKING FOR SOMETHING?

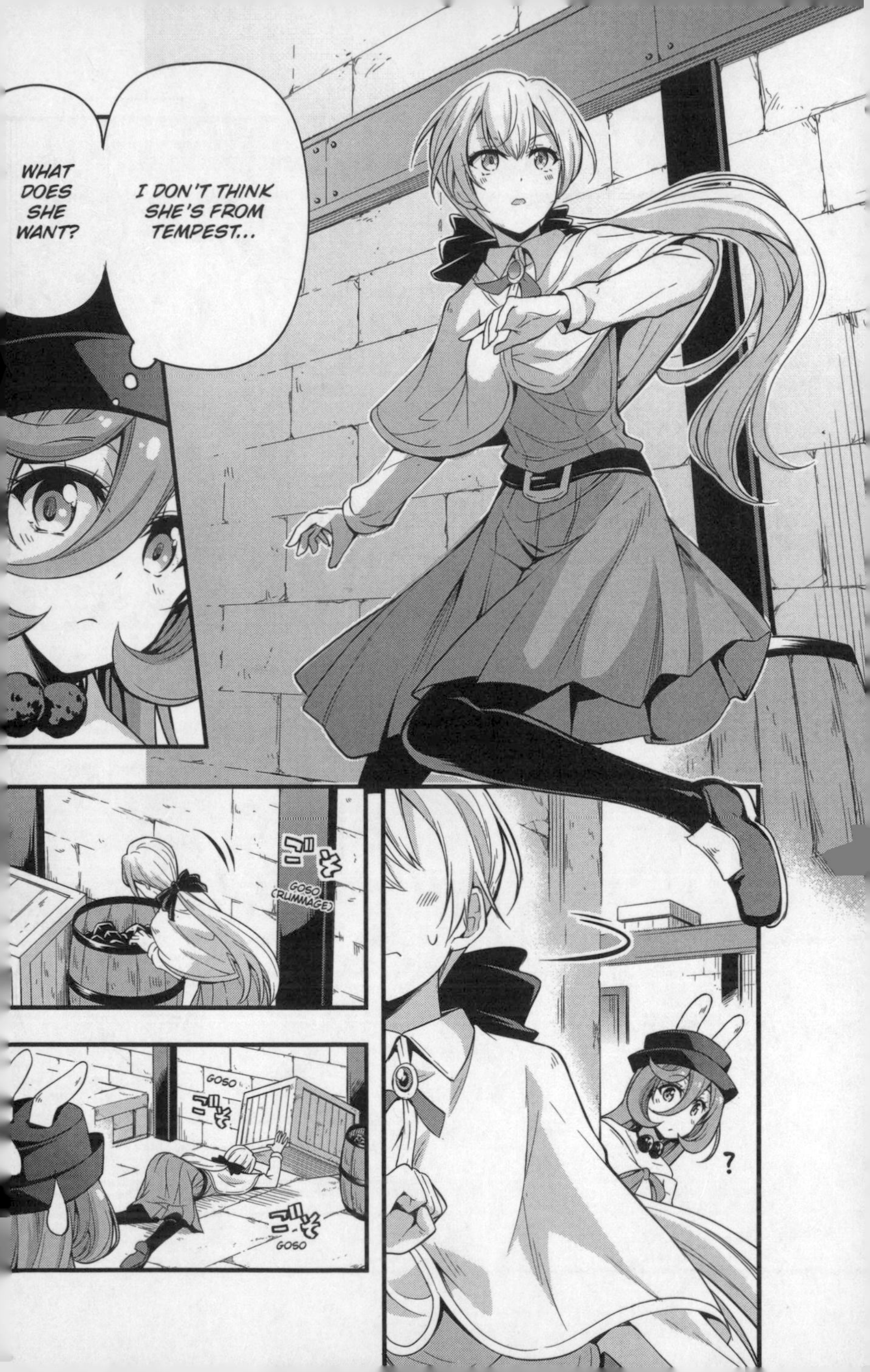
I DON'T THINK SHE'S FROM TEMPEST...
WHAT DOES SHE WANT?
?
ゴソ
GOSO (RUMMAGE)
GOSO
ゴソ
ゴソ
GOSO

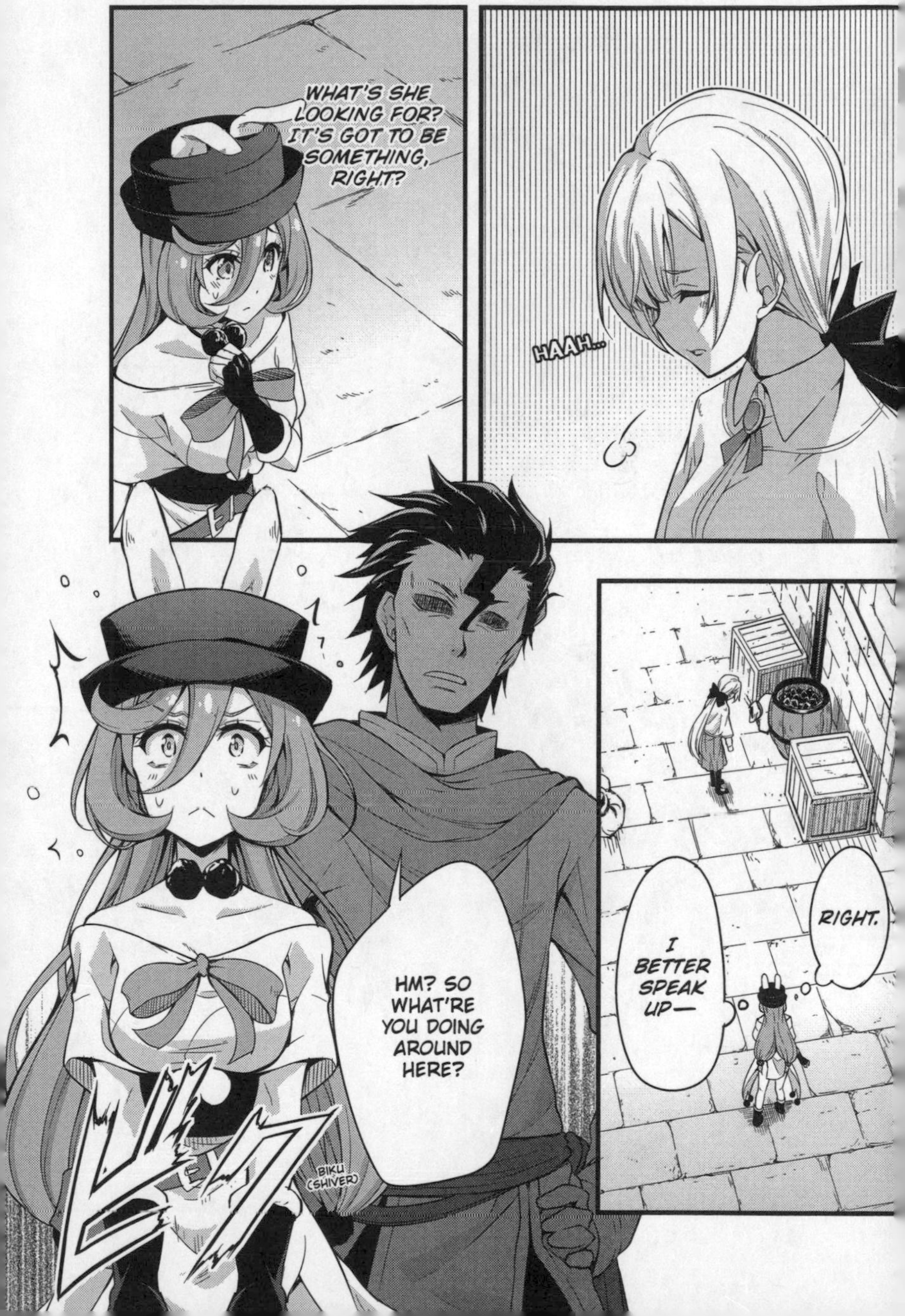
HAAAH...
WHAT'S SHE LOOKING FOR? IT'S GOT TO BE SOMETHING, RIGHT?
RIGHT.
I BETTER SPEAK UP—
HM? SO WHAT'RE YOU DOING AROUND HERE?
BIKU (SHIVER)

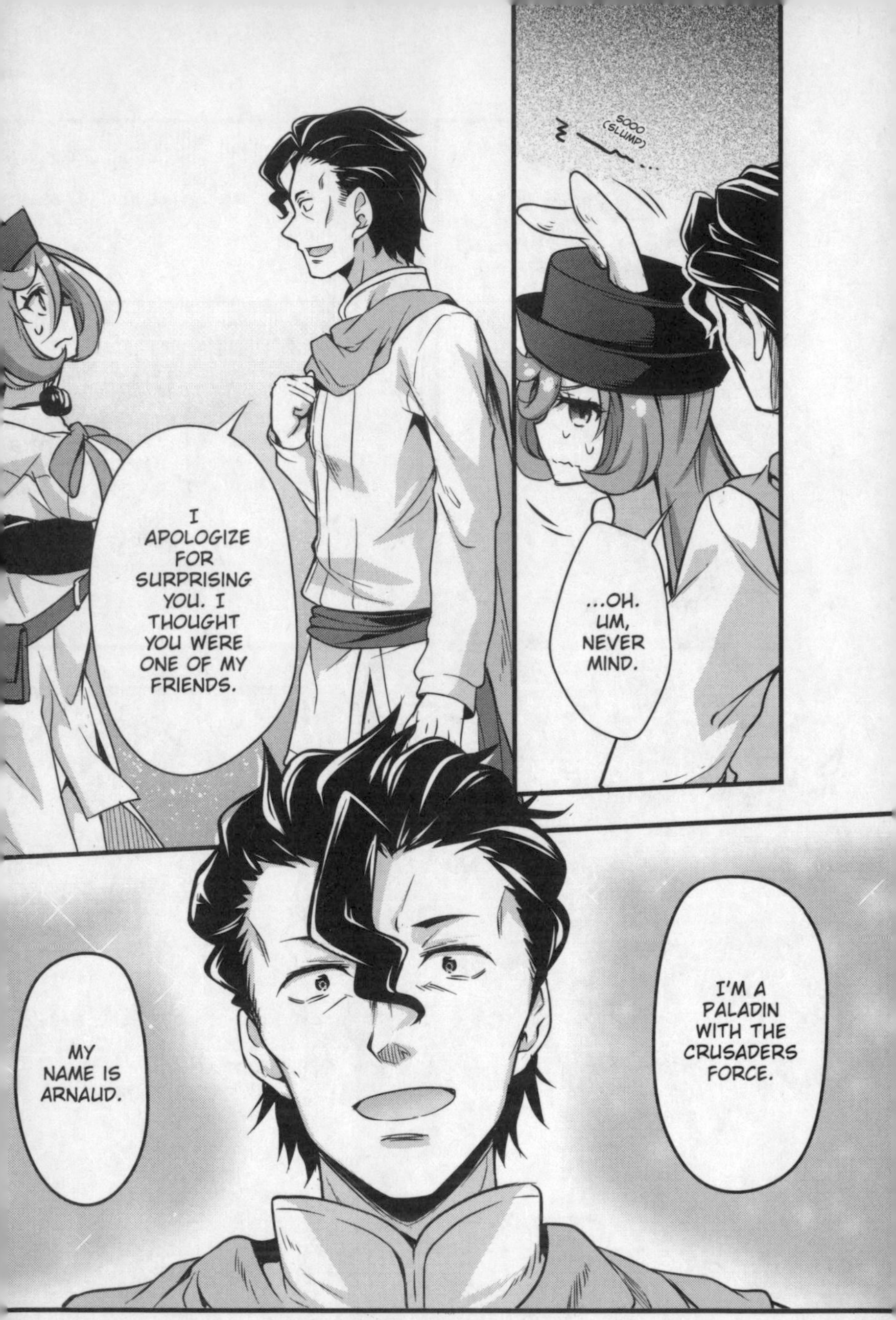
SOOO (SLUMP)
...OH. UM, NEVER MIND.
I APOLOGIZE FOR SURPRISING YOU. I THOUGHT YOU WERE ONE OF MY FRIENDS.
I'M A PALADIN WITH THE CRUSADERS FORCE.
MY NAME IS ARNAUD.

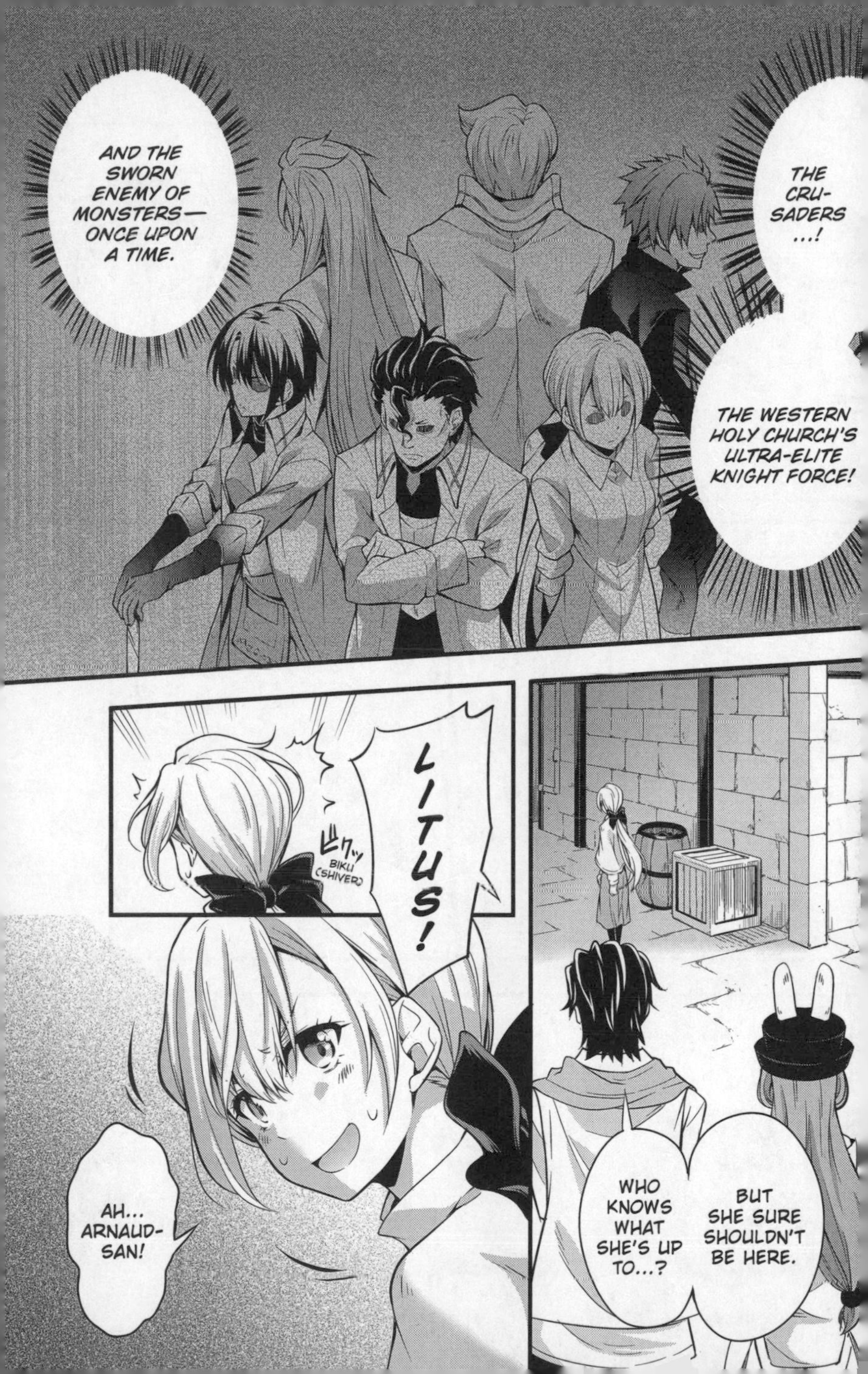
THE CRU-SADERS ...!
THE WESTERN HOLY CHURCH'S ULTRA-ELITE KNIGHT FORCE!
AND THE SWORN ENEMY OF MONSTERS—ONCE UPON A TIME.
WHO KNOWS WHAT SHE'S UP TO...?
BUT SHE SURE SHOULDN'T BE HERE.
LITUS!
ビクッ
BIKU (SHIVER)
AH... ARNAUD-SAN!

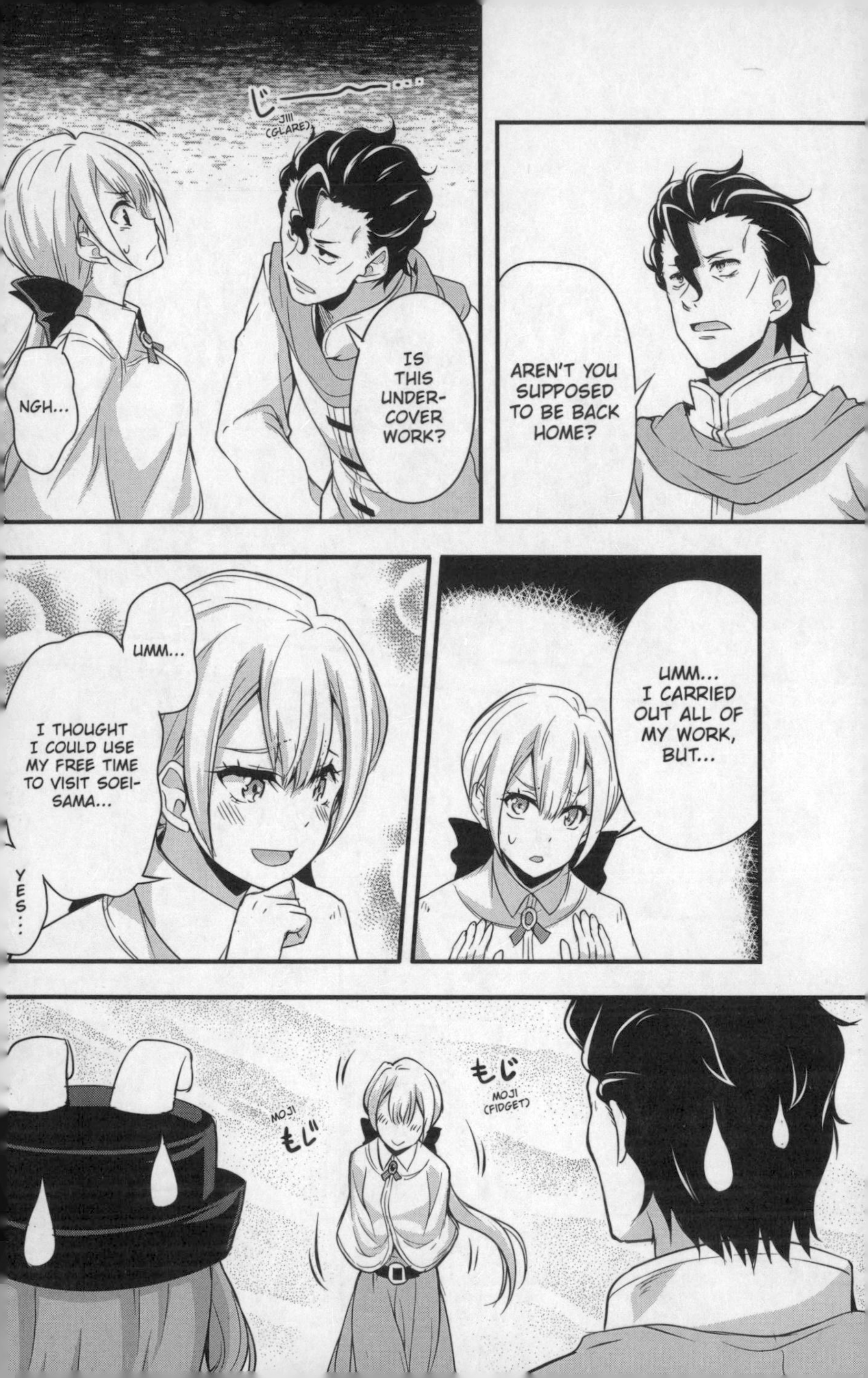
AREN'T YOU SUPPOSED TO BE BACK HOME?
じーー…
JIII (GLARE)
IS THIS UNDER-COVER WORK?
NGH...
UMM... I CARRIED OUT ALL OF MY WORK, BUT...
UMM...
I THOUGHT I COULD USE MY FREE TIME TO VISIT SOEI-SAMA...
YES...
もじ
MOJI (FIDGET)
MOJI
もじ

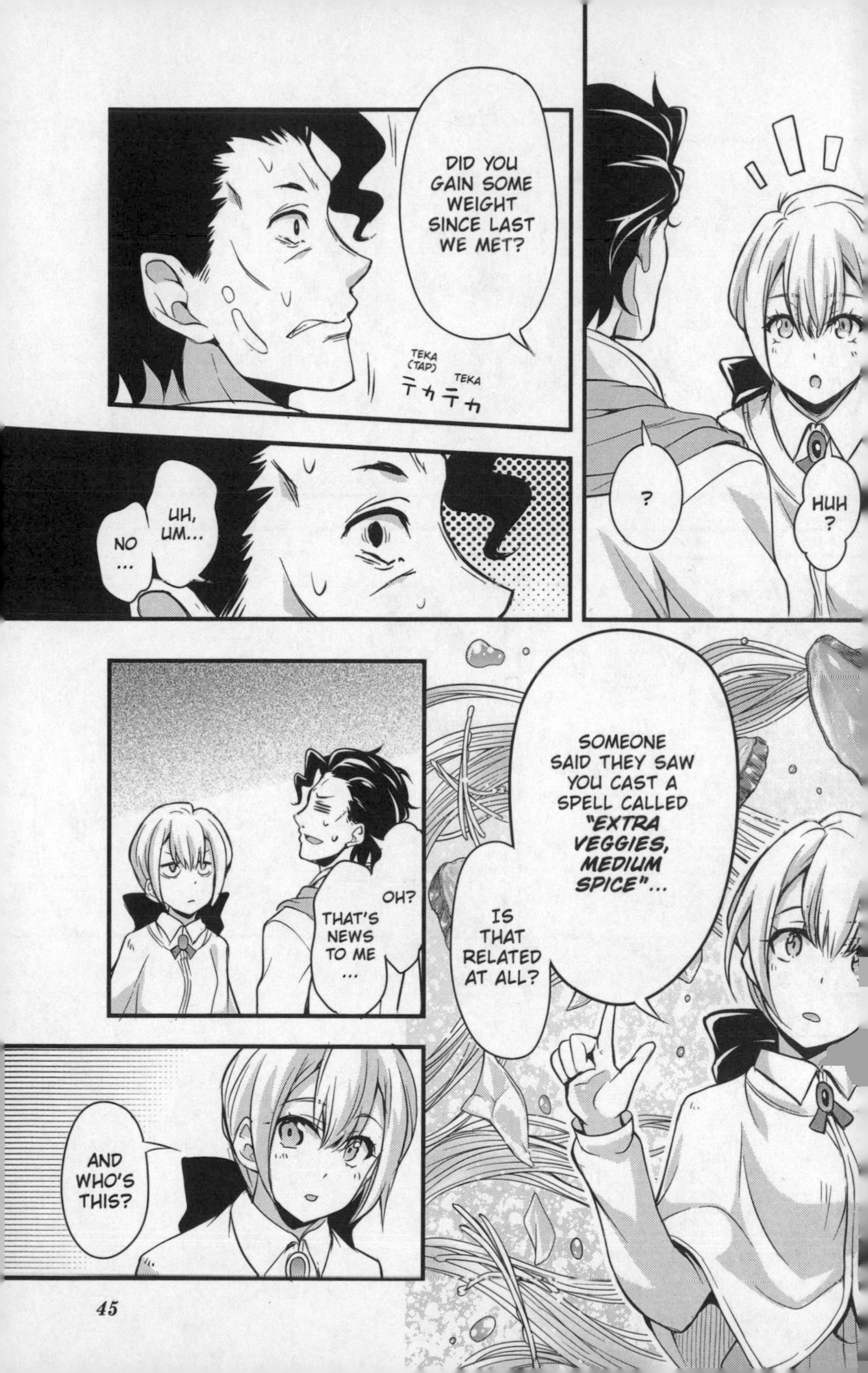
HUH?
?
DID YOU GAIN SOME WEIGHT SINCE LAST WE MET?
TEKA (TAP) TEKA
テカテカ
UH, UM...
NO...
SOMEONE SAID THEY SAW YOU CAST A SPELL CALLED "EXTRA VEGGIES, MEDIUM SPICE"...
IS THAT RELATED AT ALL?
OH?
THAT'S NEWS TO ME...
AND WHO'S THIS?

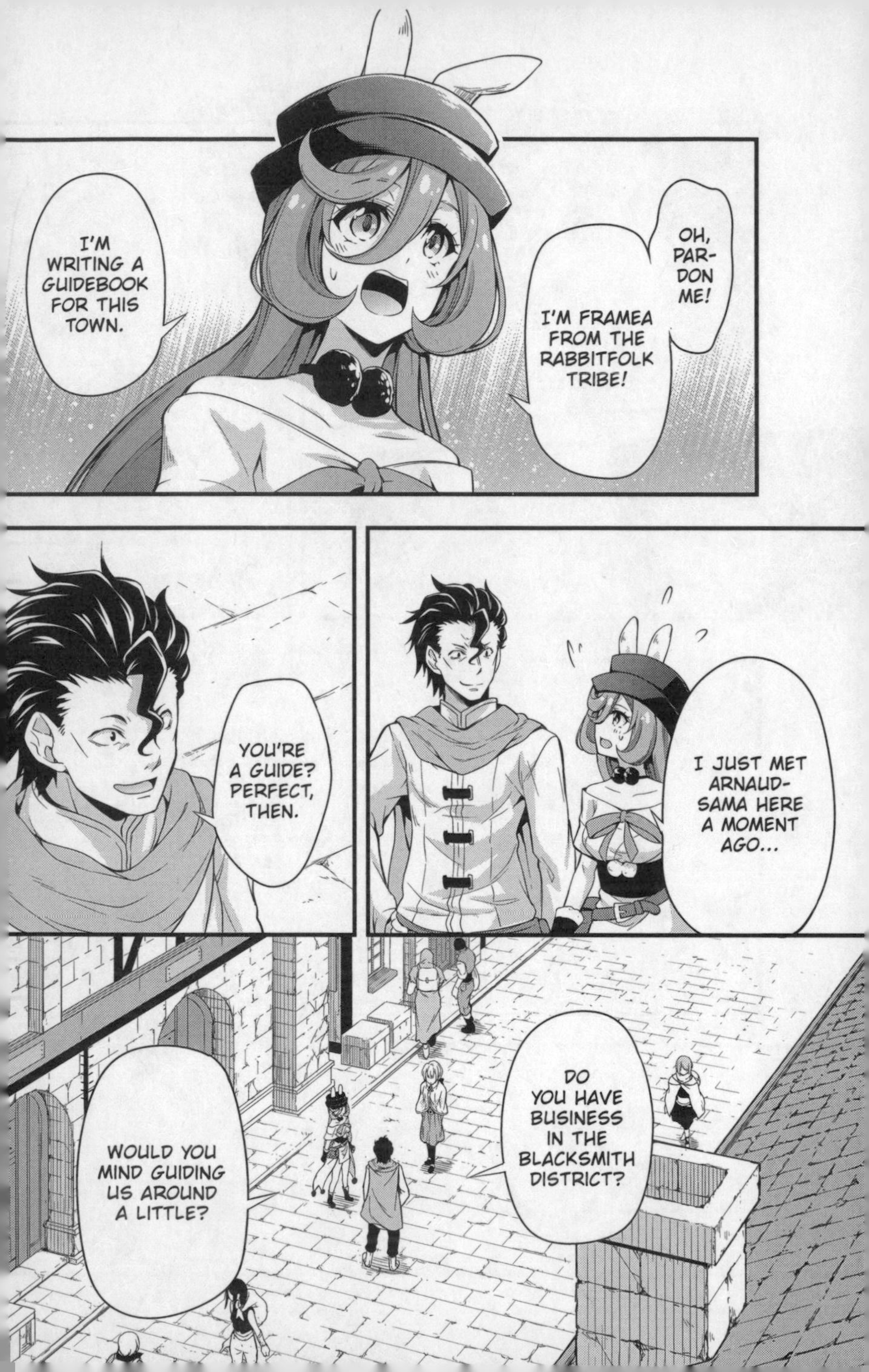
OH, PARDON ME!
I'M FRAMEA FROM THE RABBITFOLK TRIBE!
I'M WRITING A GUIDEBOOK FOR THIS TOWN.
I JUST MET ARNAUD-SAMA HERE A MOMENT AGO...
YOU'RE A GUIDE? PERFECT, THEN.
DO YOU HAVE BUSINESS IN THE BLACKSMITH DISTRICT?
WOULD YOU MIND GUIDING US AROUND A LITTLE?

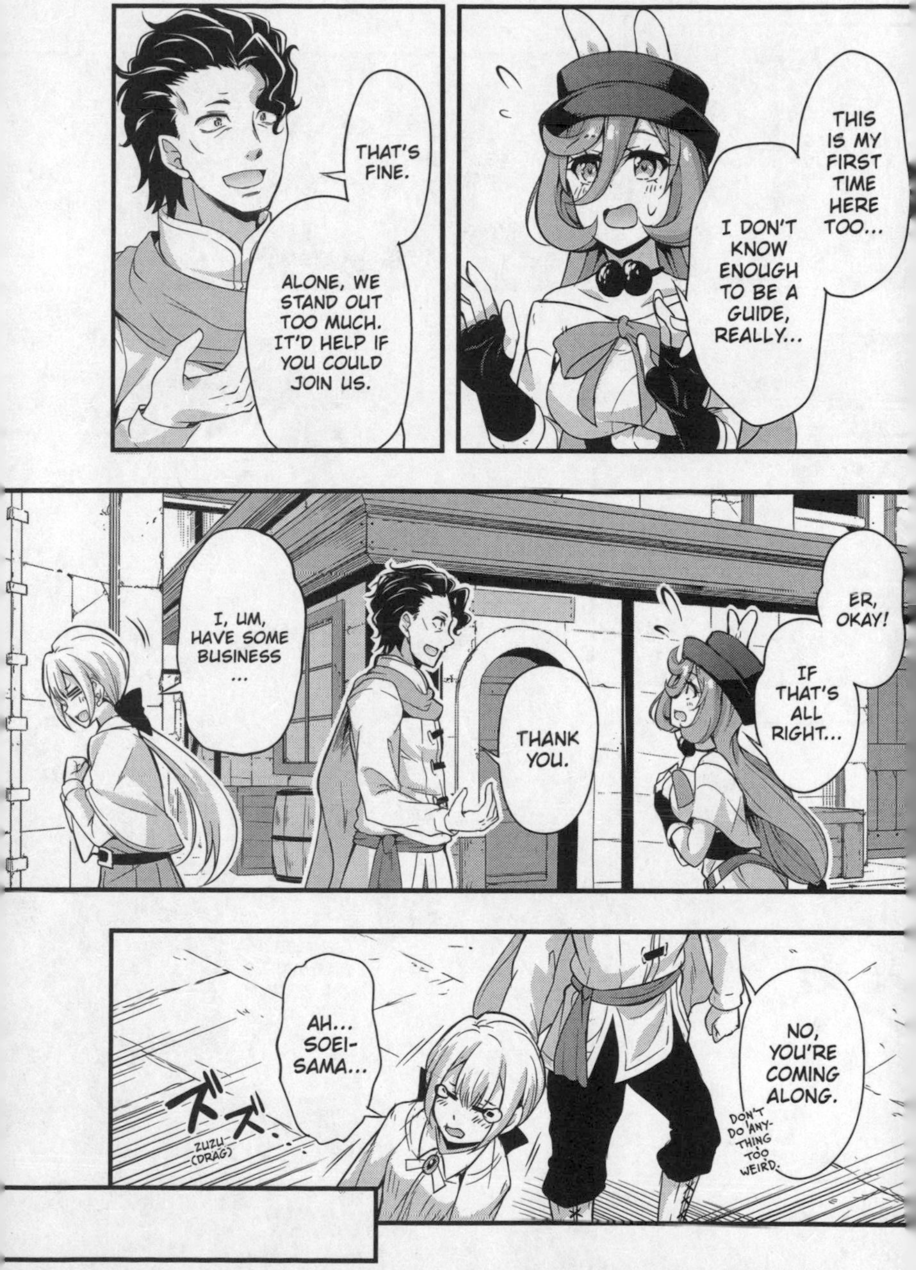
THIS IS MY FIRST TIME HERE TOO...
I DON'T KNOW ENOUGH TO BE A GUIDE, REALLY...
THAT'S FINE.
ALONE, WE STAND OUT TOO MUCH. IT'D HELP IF YOU COULD JOIN US.
ER, OKAY!
IF THAT'S ALL RIGHT...
THANK YOU.
I, UM, HAVE SOME BUSINESS ...
NO, YOU'RE COMING ALONG.
DON'T DO ANYTHING TOO WEIRD.
AH... SOEI-SAMA...
ZUZU (DRAG)

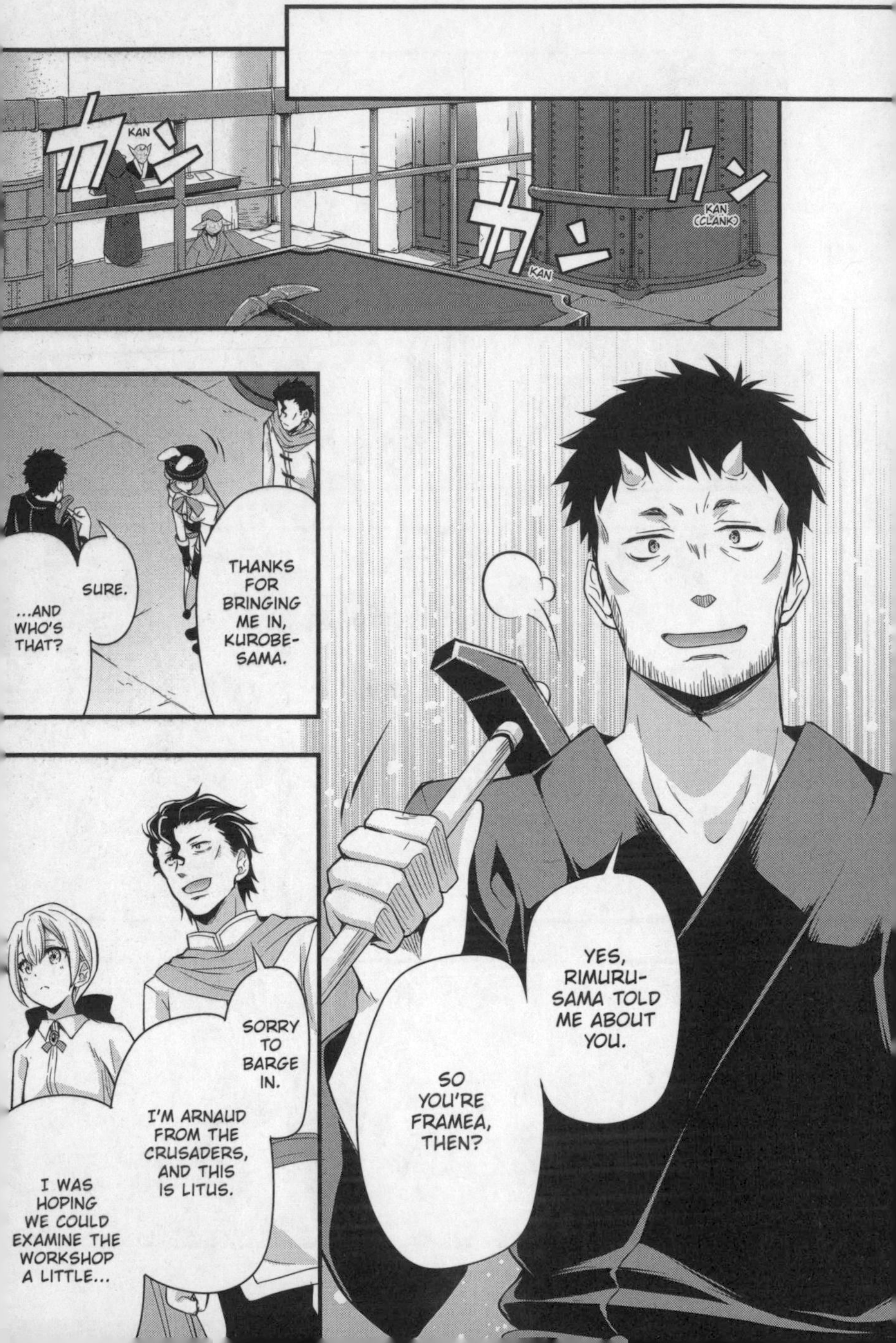
カン
KAN (CLANK)
カン
KAN
カン
KAN
YES, RIMURU-SAMA TOLD ME ABOUT YOU.
SO YOU'RE FRAMEA, THEN?
THANKS FOR BRINGING ME IN, KUROBE-SAMA.
SURE.
...AND WHO'S THAT?
SORRY TO BARGE IN.
I'M ARNAUD FROM THE CRUSADERS, AND THIS IS LITUS.
I WAS HOPING WE COULD EXAMINE THE WORKSHOP A LITTLE...

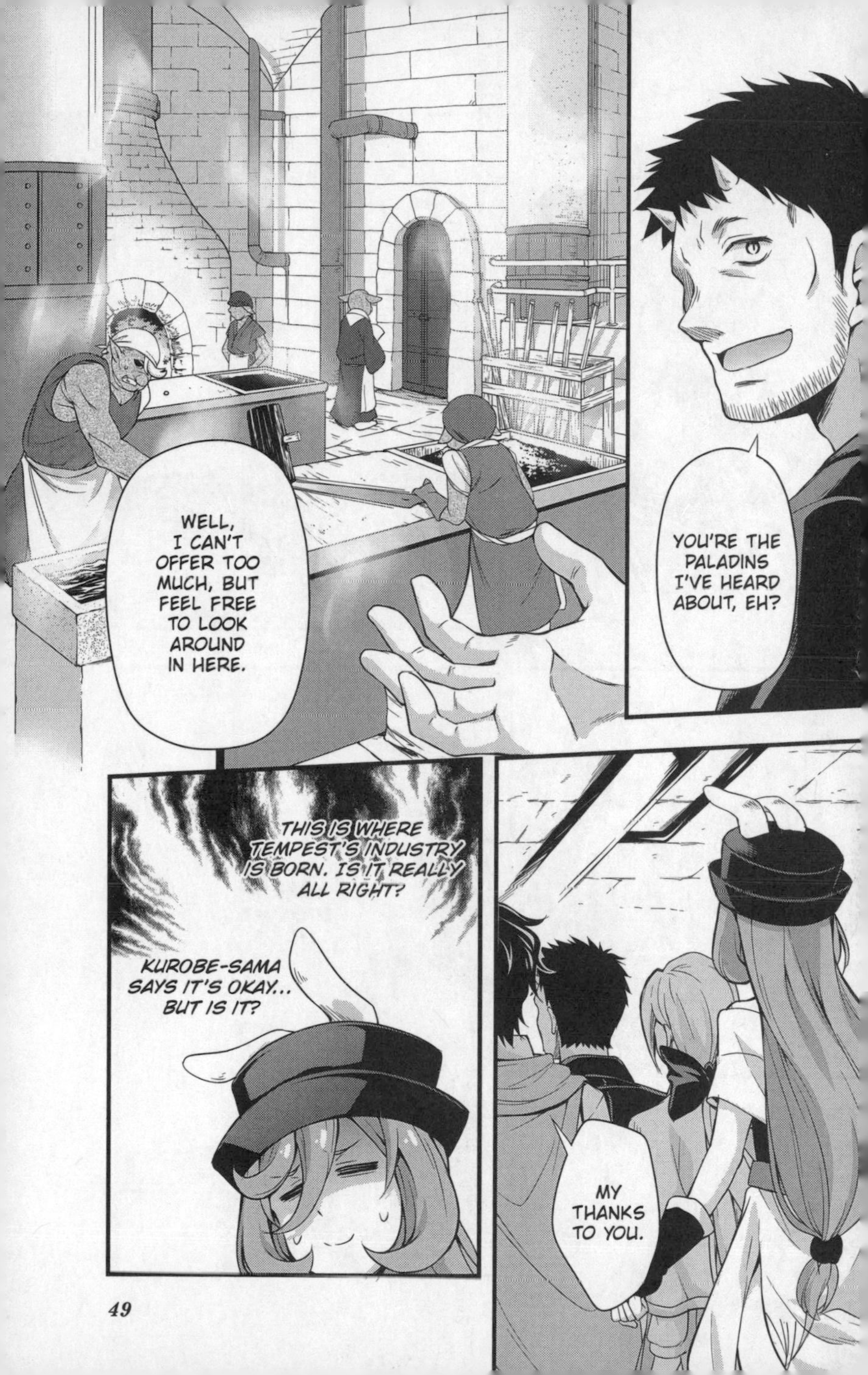
YOU'RE THE PALADINS I'VE HEARD ABOUT, EH?
WELL, I CAN'T OFFER TOO MUCH, BUT FEEL FREE TO LOOK AROUND IN HERE.
MY THANKS TO YOU.
THIS IS WHERE TEMPEST'S INDUSTRY IS BORN. IS IT REALLY ALL RIGHT?
KUROBE-SAMA SAYS IT'S OKAY... BUT IS IT?

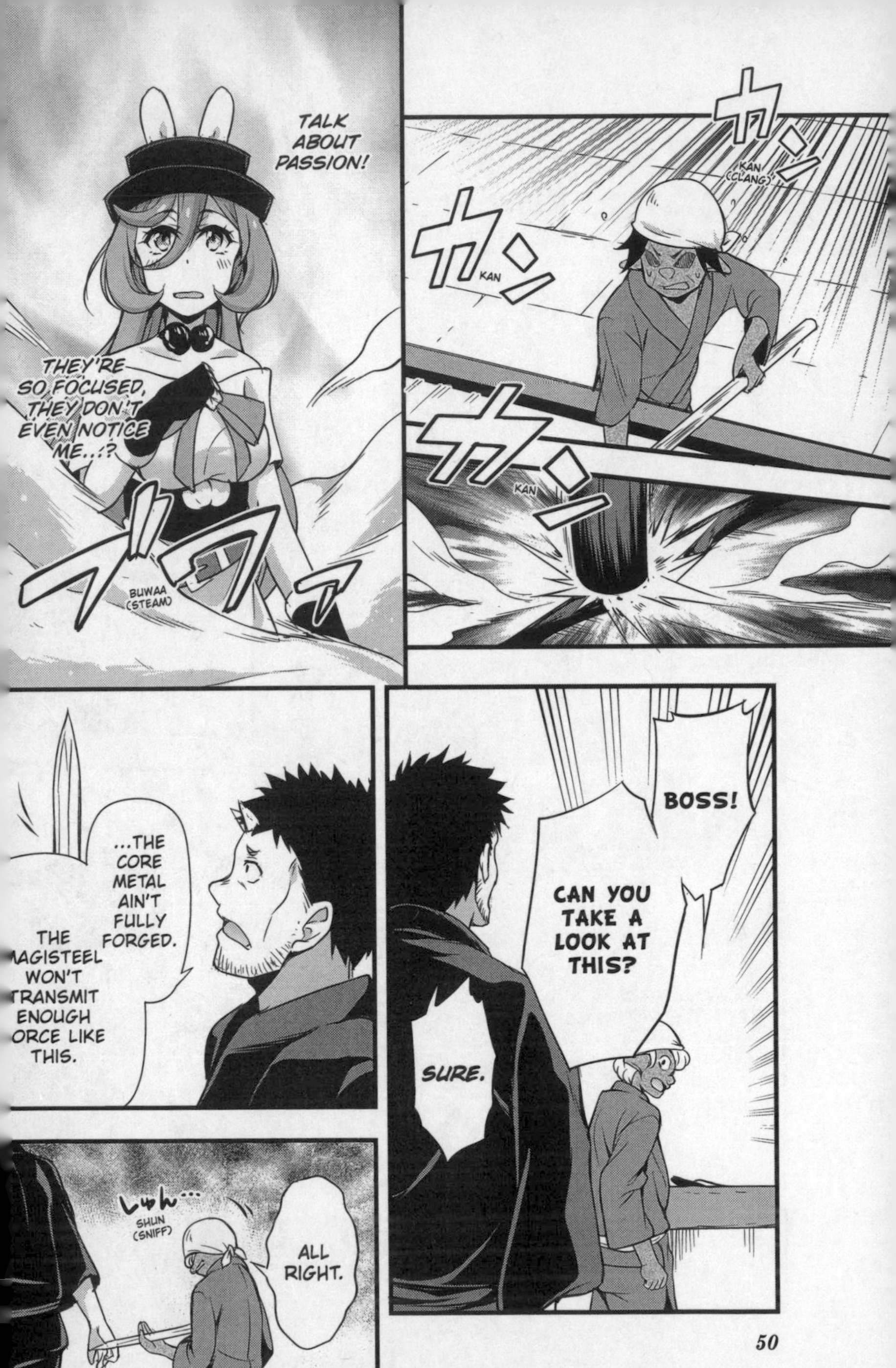
KAN (CLANG)
KAN
KAN
TALK ABOUT PASSION!
THEY'RE SO FOCUSED, THEY DON'T EVEN NOTICE ME...?
BUWAA (STEAM)
BOSS!
CAN YOU TAKE A LOOK AT THIS?
SURE.
...THE CORE METAL AIN'T FULLY FORGED.
THE MAGISTEEL WON'T TRANSMIT ENOUGH FORCE LIKE THIS.
ALL RIGHT.
SHUN (SNIFF)

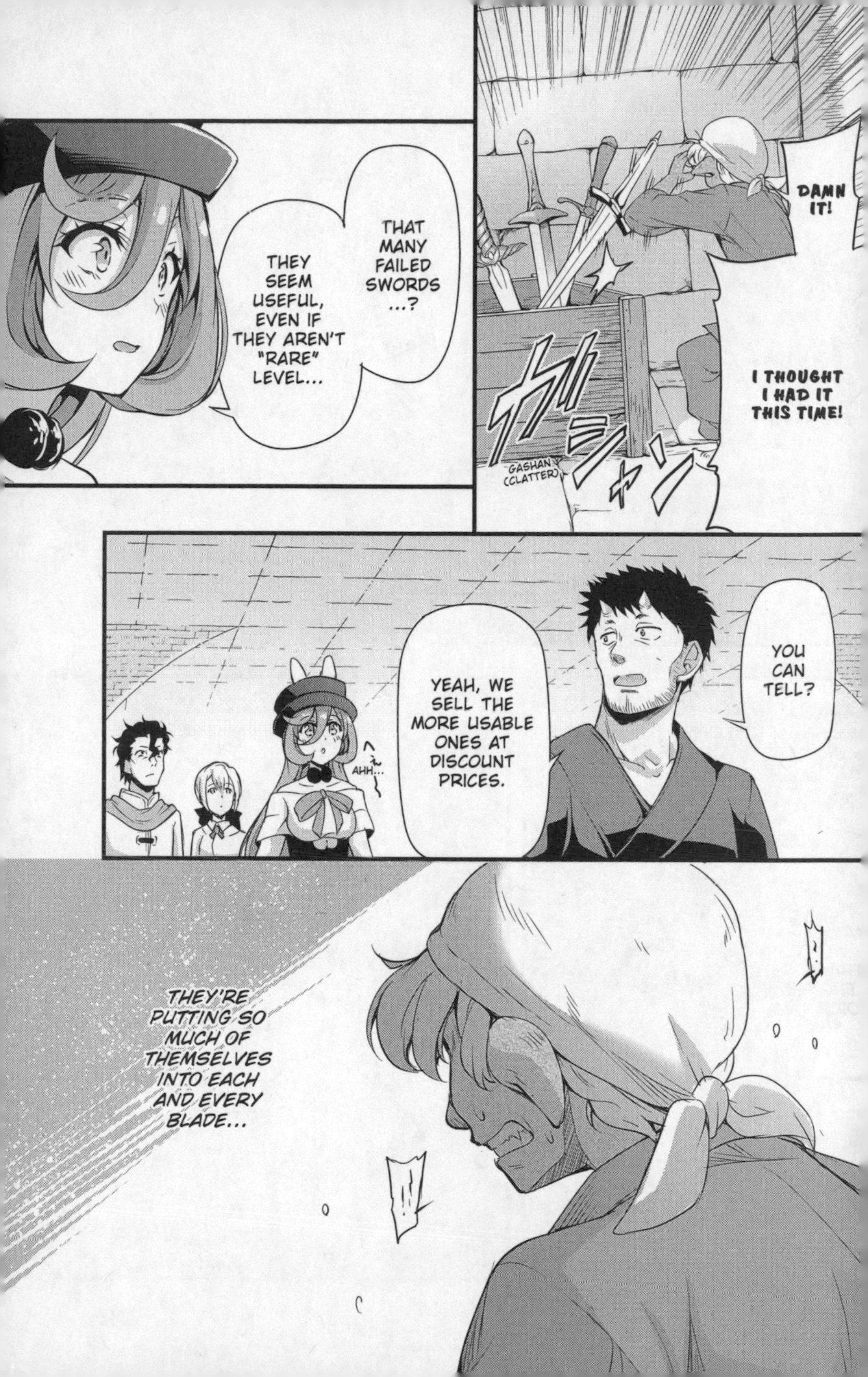
DAMN IT!
I THOUGHT I HAD IT THIS TIME!
GASHAN (CLATTER)
THAT MANY FAILED SWORDS ...?
THEY SEEM USEFUL, EVEN IF THEY AREN'T "RARE" LEVEL...
YOU CAN TELL?
YEAH, WE SELL THE MORE USABLE ONES AT DISCOUNT PRICES.
AHH...
THEY'RE PUTTING SO MUCH OF THEMSELVES INTO EACH AND EVERY BLADE...

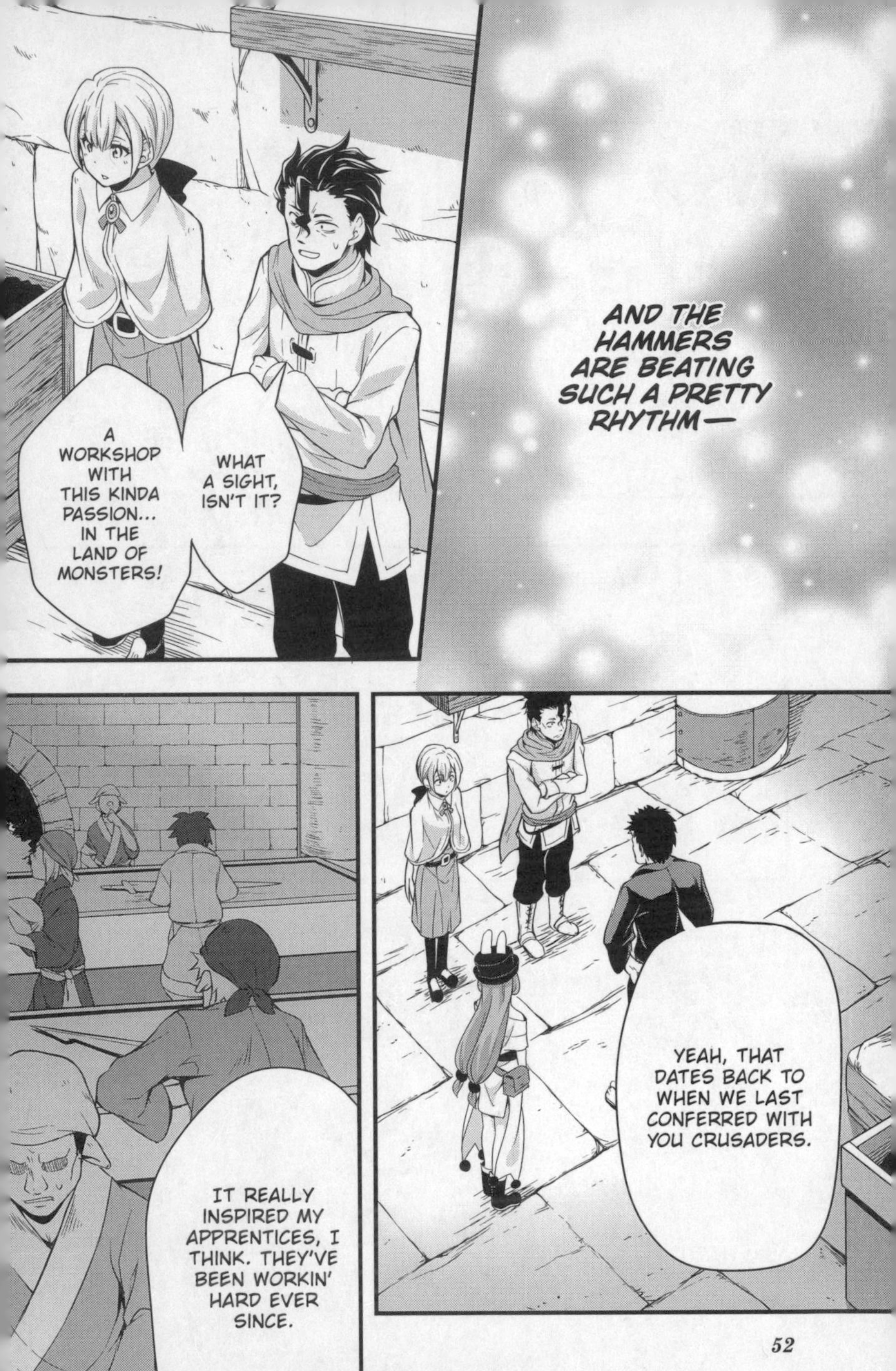
AND THE HAMMERS ARE BEATING SUCH A PRETTY RHYTHM—
WHAT A SIGHT, ISN'T IT?
A WORKSHOP WITH THIS KINDA PASSION... IN THE LAND OF MONSTERS!
YEAH, THAT DATES BACK TO WHEN WE LAST CONFERRED WITH YOU CRUSADERS.
IT REALLY INSPIRED MY APPRENTICES, I THINK. THEY'VE BEEN WORKIN' HARD EVER SINCE.

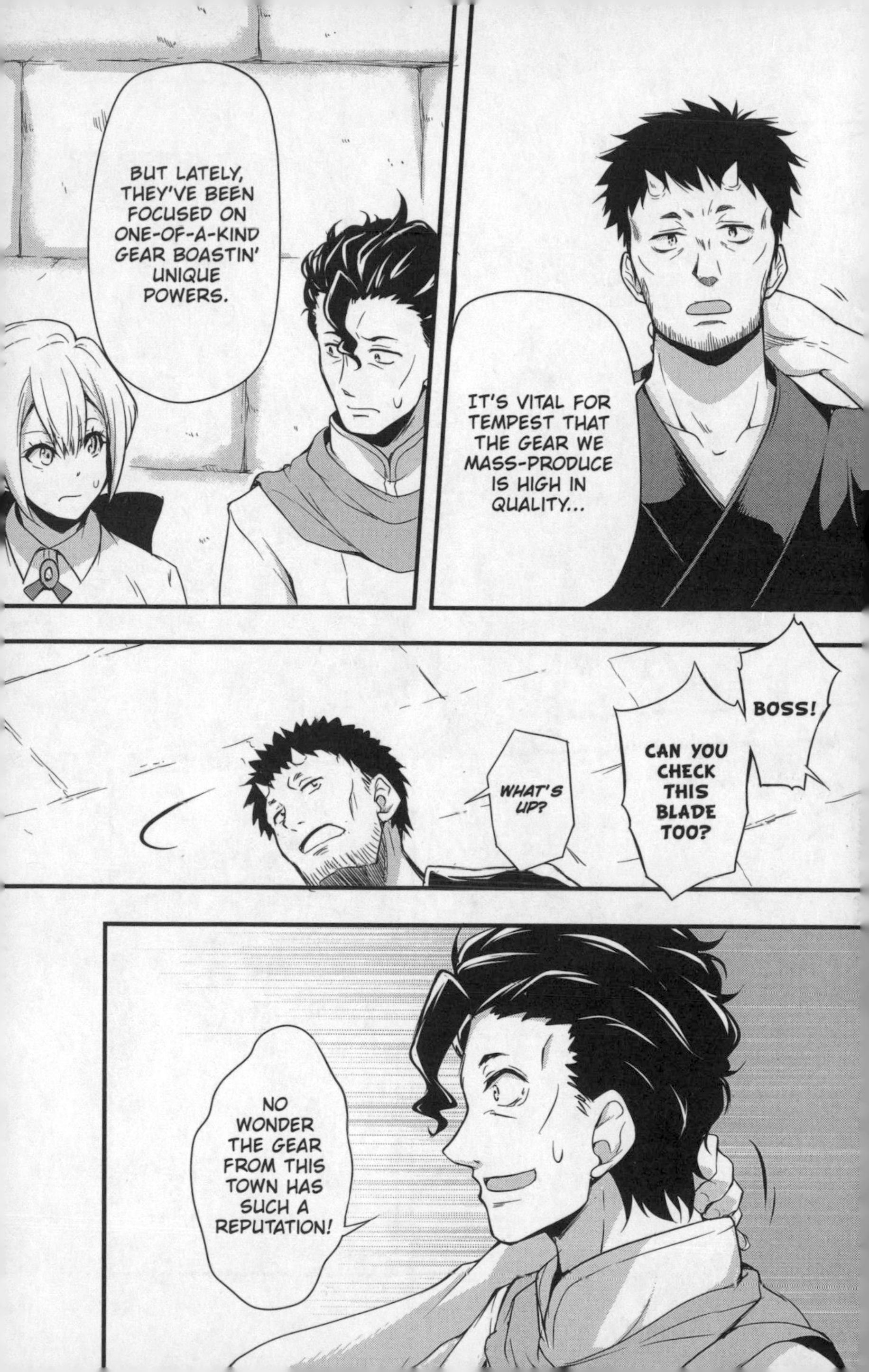
IT'S VITAL FOR TEMPEST THAT THE GEAR WE MASS-PRODUCE IS HIGH IN QUALITY...
BUT LATELY, THEY'VE BEEN FOCUSED ON ONE-OF-A-KIND GEAR BOASTIN' UNIQUE POWERS.
BOSS!
CAN YOU CHECK THIS BLADE TOO?
WHAT'S UP?
NO WONDER THE GEAR FROM THIS TOWN HAS SUCH A REPUTATION!

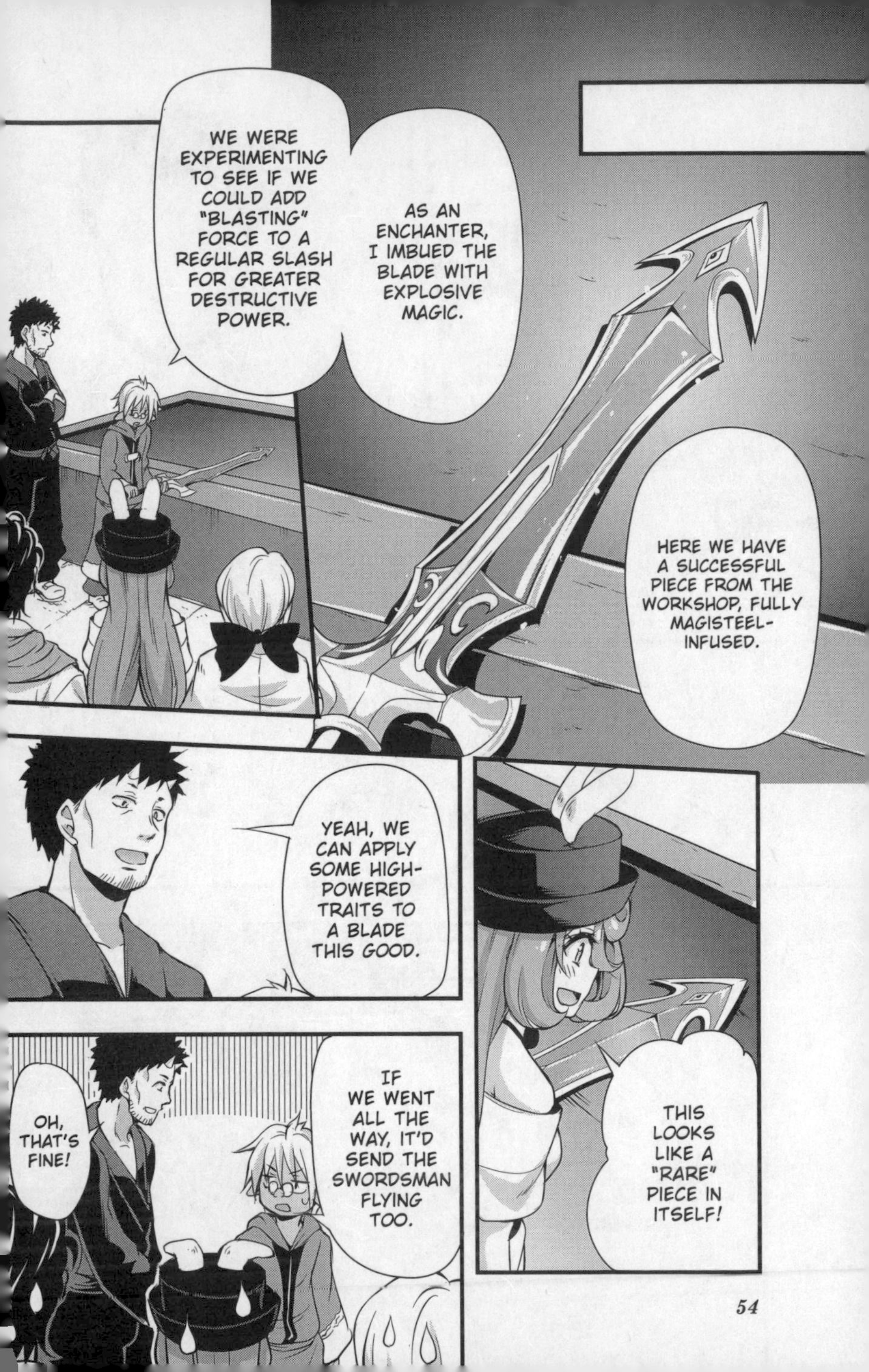
HERE WE HAVE A SUCCESSFUL PIECE FROM THE WORKSHOP, FULLY MAGISTEEL-INFUSED.
AS AN ENCHANTER, I IMBUED THE BLADE WITH EXPLOSIVE MAGIC.
WE WERE EXPERIMENTING TO SEE IF WE COULD ADD "BLASTING" FORCE TO A REGULAR SLASH FOR GREATER DESTRUCTIVE POWER.
THIS LOOKS LIKE A "RARE" PIECE IN ITSELF!
YEAH, WE CAN APPLY SOME HIGH-POWERED TRAITS TO A BLADE THIS GOOD.
IF WE WENT ALL THE WAY, IT'D SEND THE SWORDSMAN FLYING TOO.
OH, THAT'S FINE!

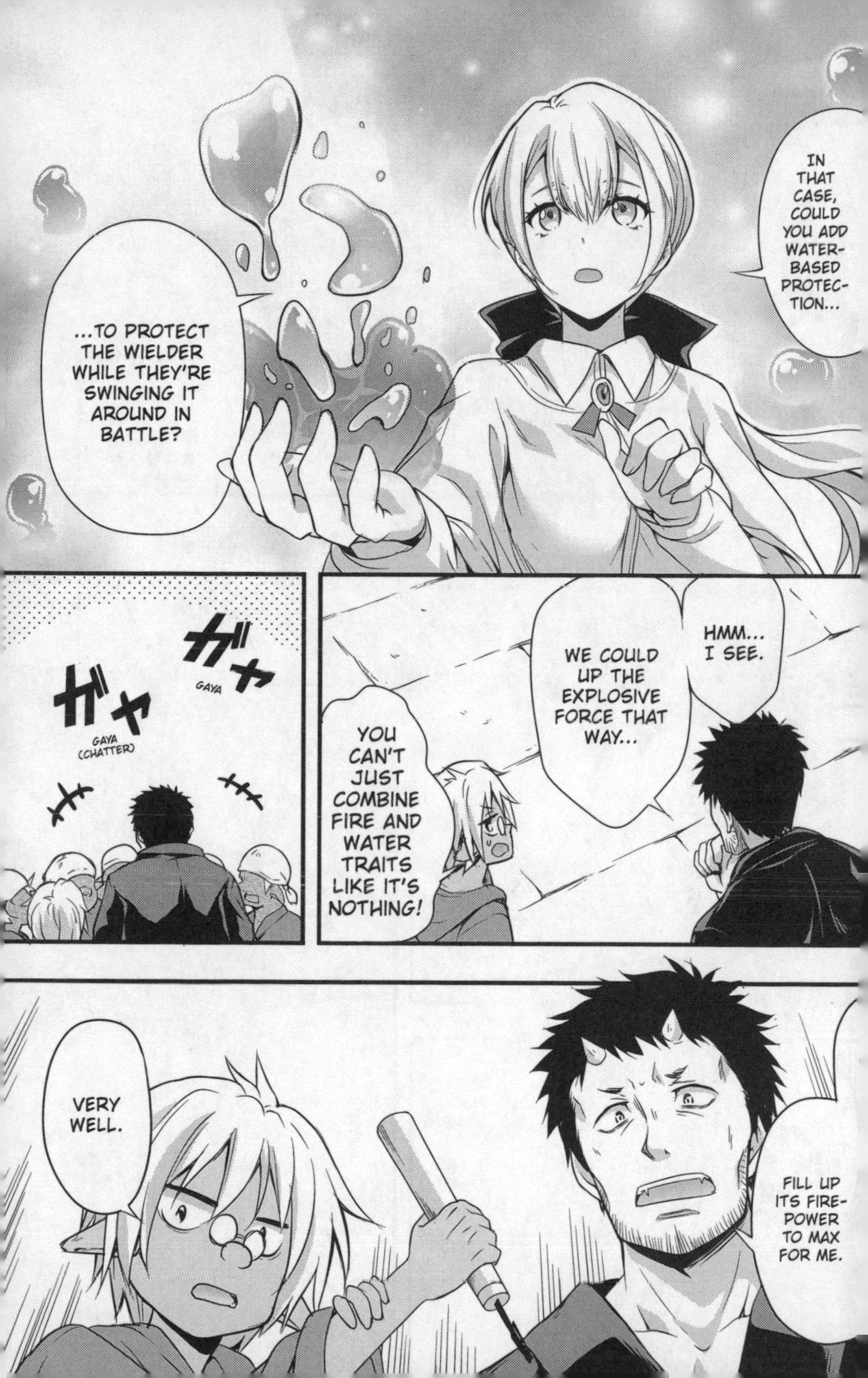
IN THAT CASE, COULD YOU ADD WATER-BASED PROTECTION...
...TO PROTECT THE WIELDER WHILE THEY'RE SWINGING IT AROUND IN BATTLE?
HMM... I SEE.
WE COULD UP THE EXPLOSIVE FORCE THAT WAY...
YOU CAN'T JUST COMBINE FIRE AND WATER TRAITS LIKE IT'S NOTHING!
ガヤ
GAYA
ガヤ
GAYA (CHATTER)
FILL UP ITS FIRE-POWER TO MAX FOR ME.
VERY WELL.

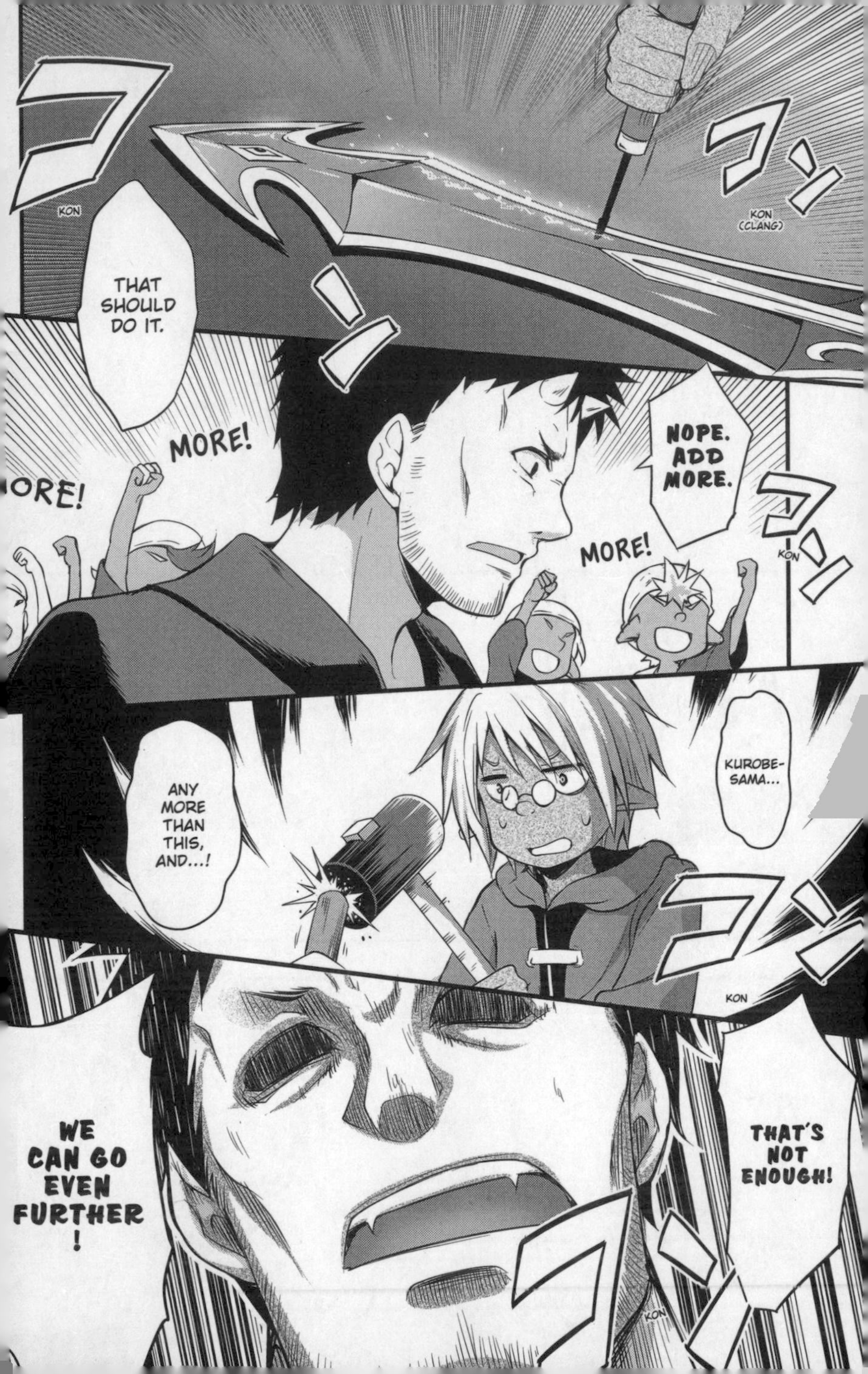
KON (CLANG)
THAT SHOULD DO IT.
KON
KON
NOPE. ADD MORE.
MORE!
MORE!
ORE!
KUROBE-SAMA...
ANY MORE THAN THIS, AND...!
KON
THAT'S NOT ENOUGH!
WE CAN GO EVEN FURTHER!
KON

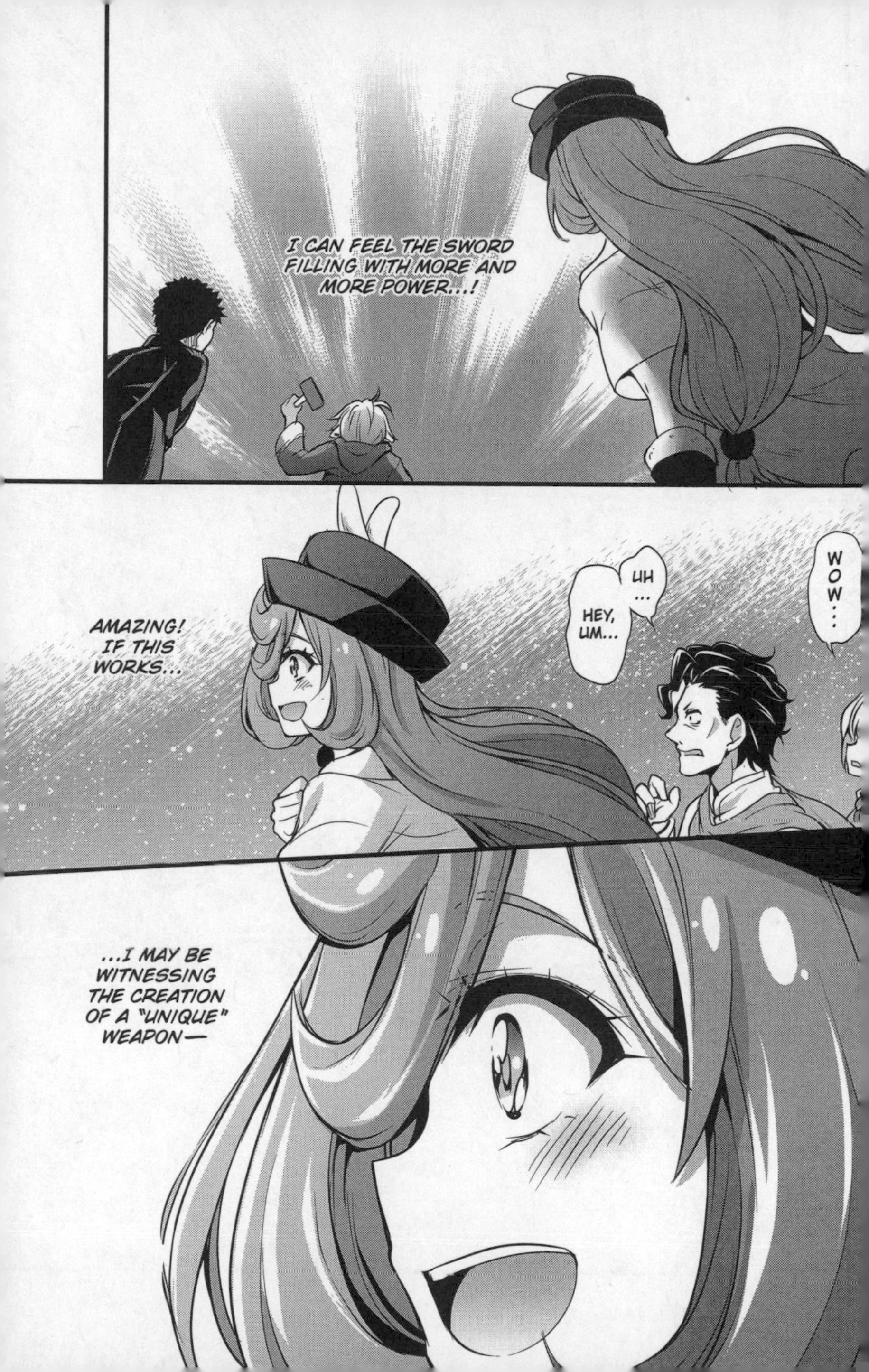
I CAN FEEL THE SWORD FILLING WITH MORE AND MORE POWER...!
WOW...
UH...
HEY, UM...
AMAZING! IF THIS WORKS...
...I MAY BE WITNESSING THE CREATION OF A "UNIQUE" WEAPON—

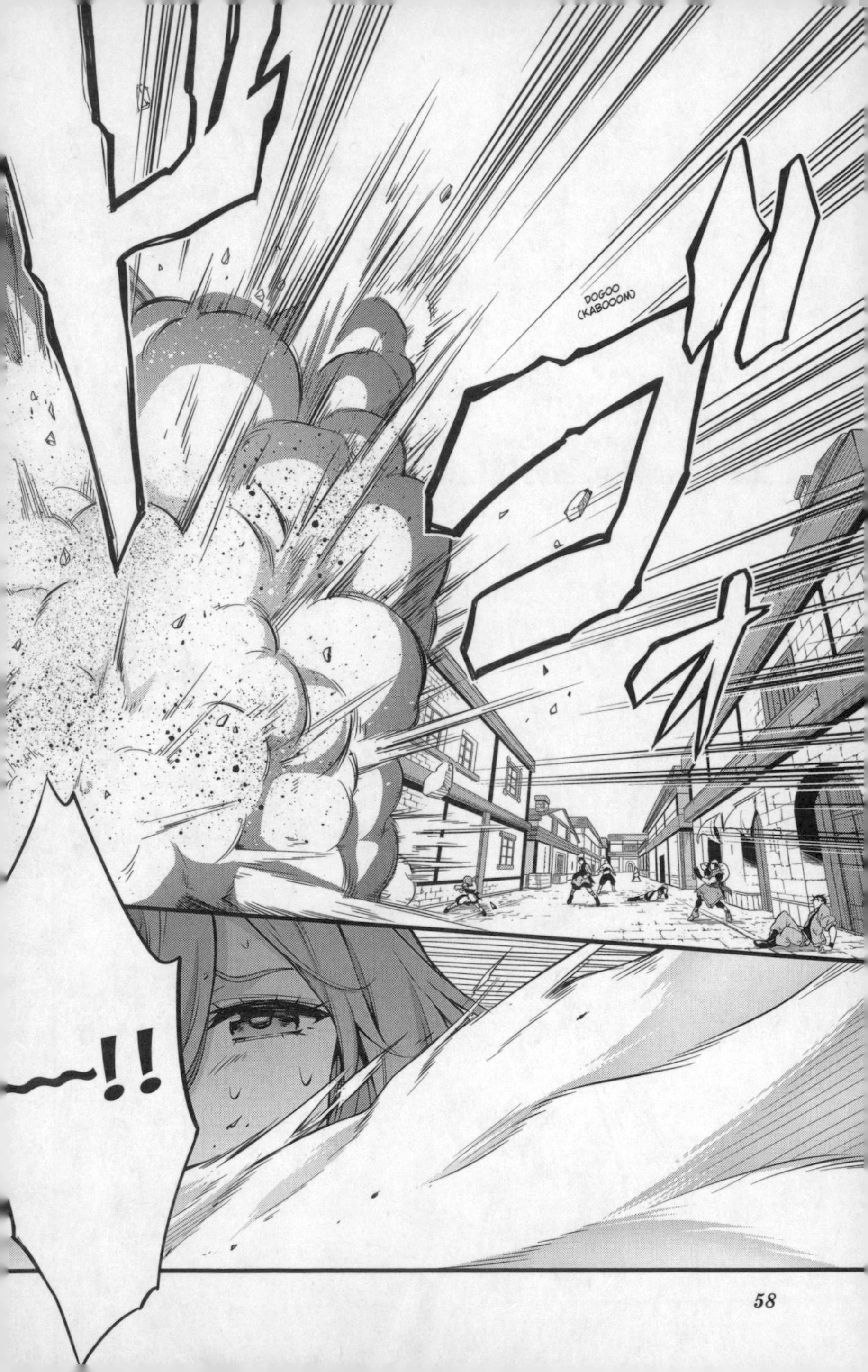
DOGOO
(KABOOOM)
—!!

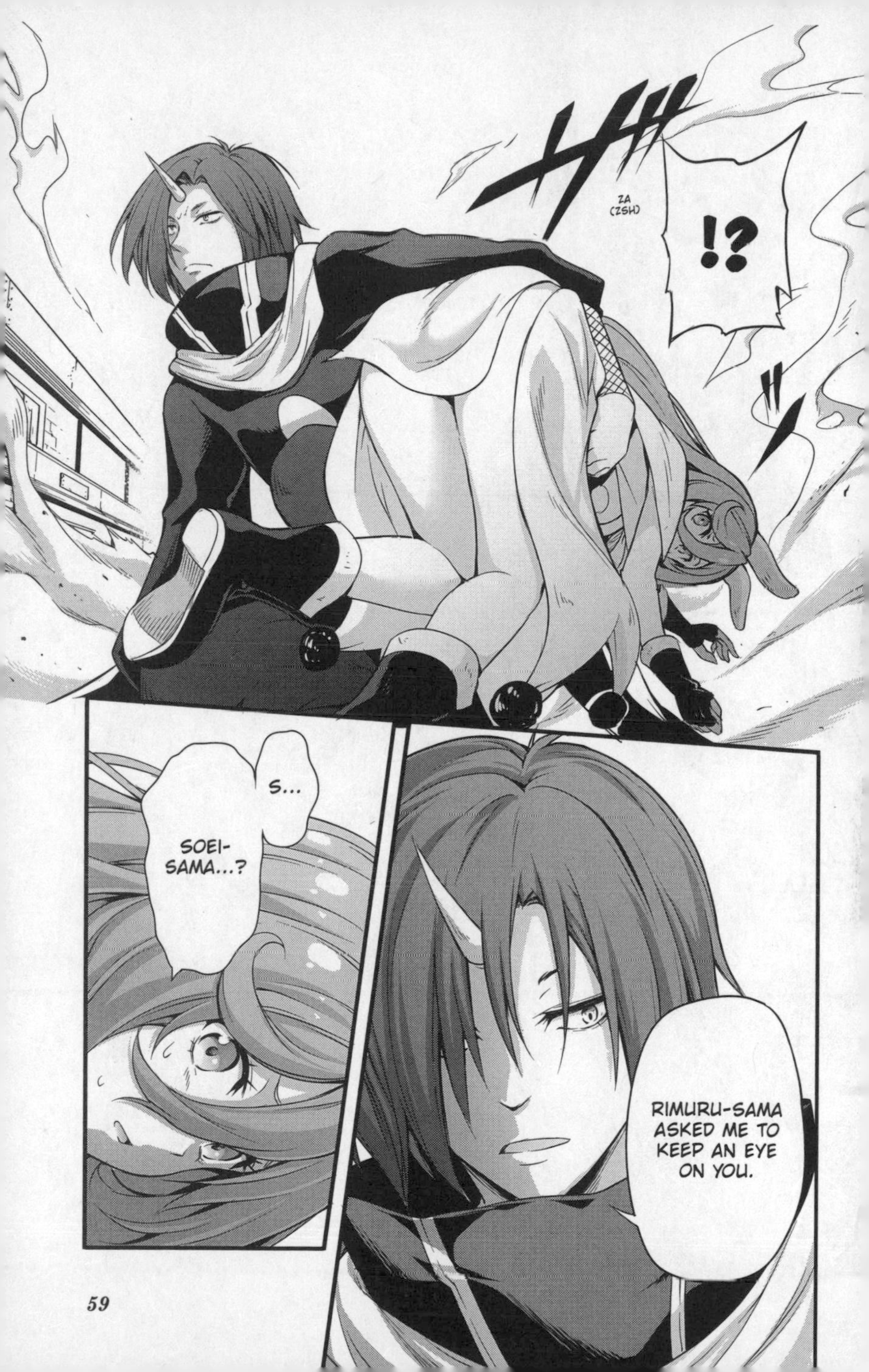
ZA
(ZSH)
!?
RIMURU-SAMA ASKED ME TO KEEP AN EYE ON YOU.
S...
SOEI-SAMA...?

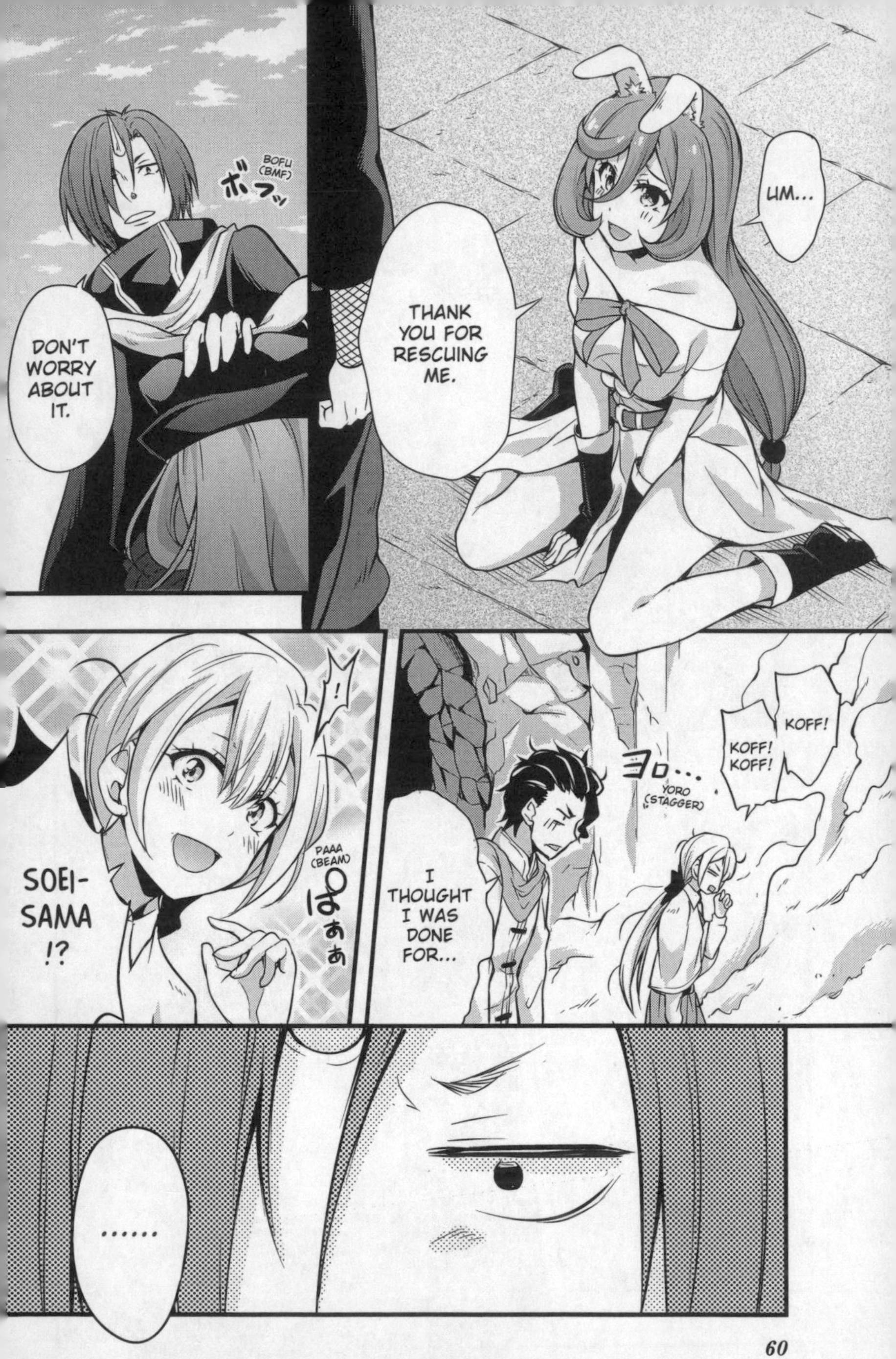
UM...
THANK YOU FOR RESCUING ME.
BOFU (BMF)
ボフッ
DON'T WORRY ABOUT IT.
KOFF!
KOFF! KOFF!
ヨロ...
YORO (STAGGER)
I THOUGHT I WAS DONE FOR...
!
PAAA (BEAM)
ぱぁぁ
SOEI-SAMA!?
......

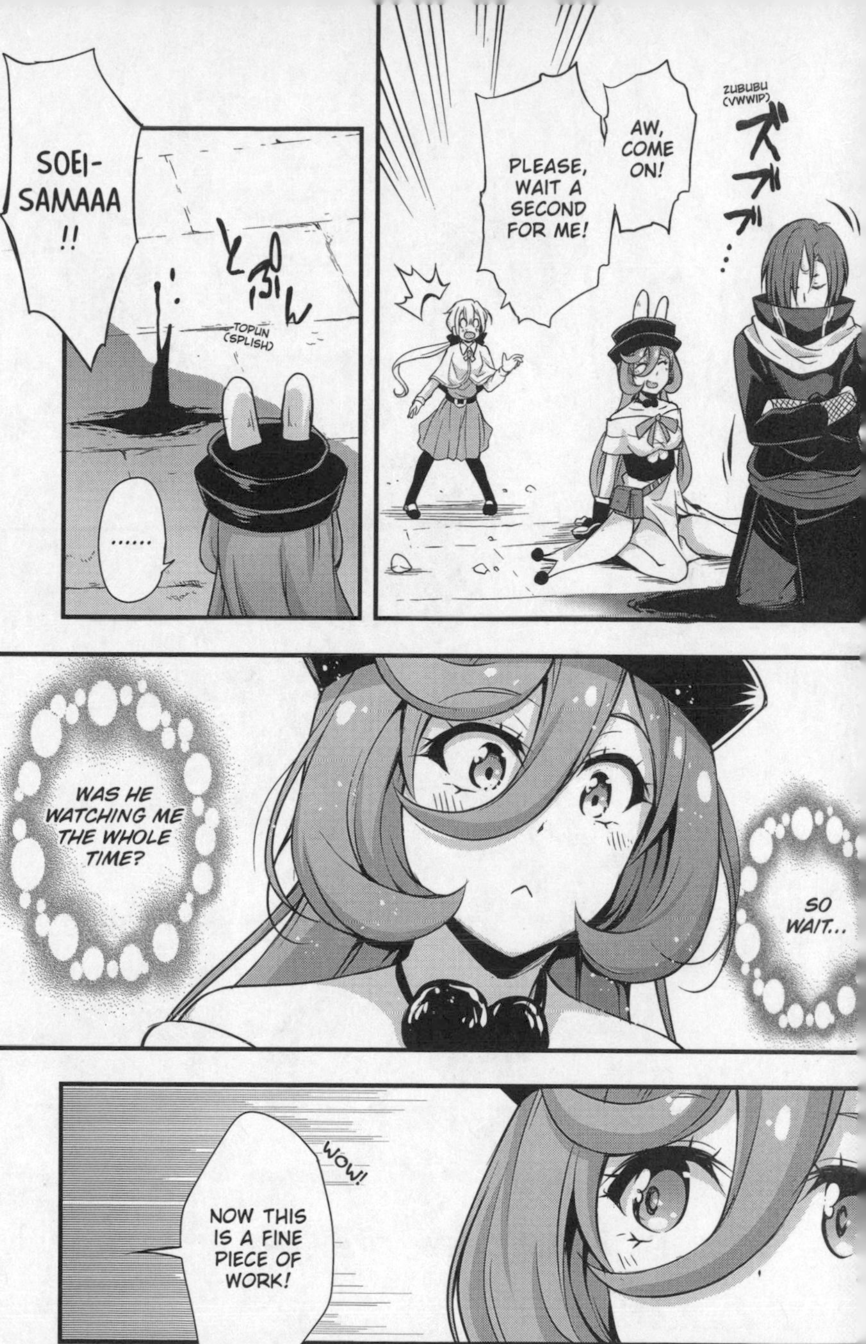
ZUBUBU (VWWIP)
ズブブ…
AW, COME ON!
PLEASE, WAIT A SECOND FOR ME!
SOEI-SAMAAA!!
とぷん
TOPUN (SPLISH)
......
SO WAIT...
WAS HE WATCHING ME THE WHOLE TIME?
WOW!
NOW THIS IS A FINE PIECE OF WORK!

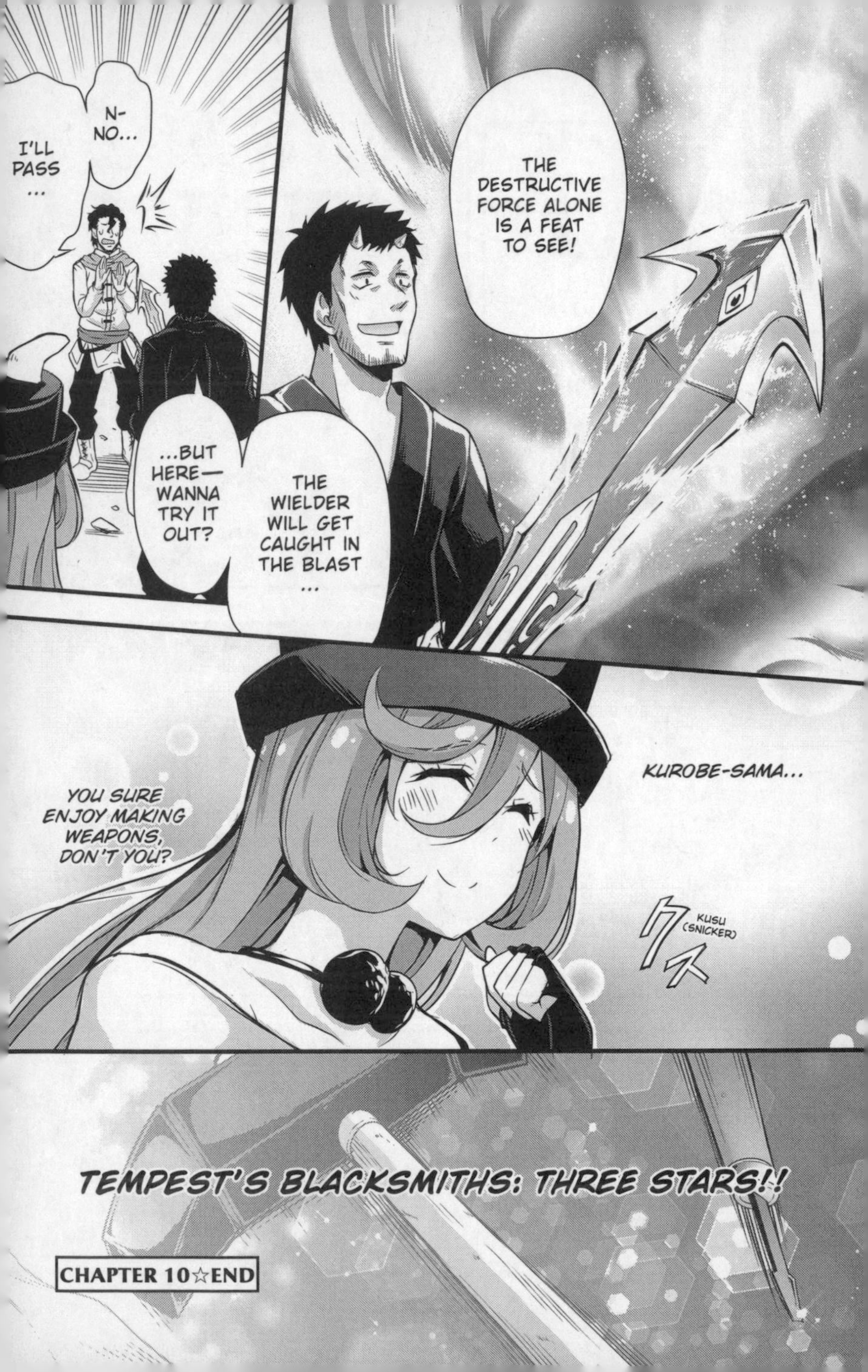
THE DESTRUCTIVE FORCE ALONE IS A FEAT TO SEE!
THE WIELDER WILL GET CAUGHT IN THE BLAST ...
...BUT HERE— WANNA TRY IT OUT?
N- NO...
I'LL PASS ...
KUROBE-SAMA...
YOU SURE ENJOY MAKING WEAPONS, DON'T YOU?
クス
KUSU (SNICKER)
TEMPEST'S BLACKSMITHS: THREE STARS!!
CHAPTER 10☆END

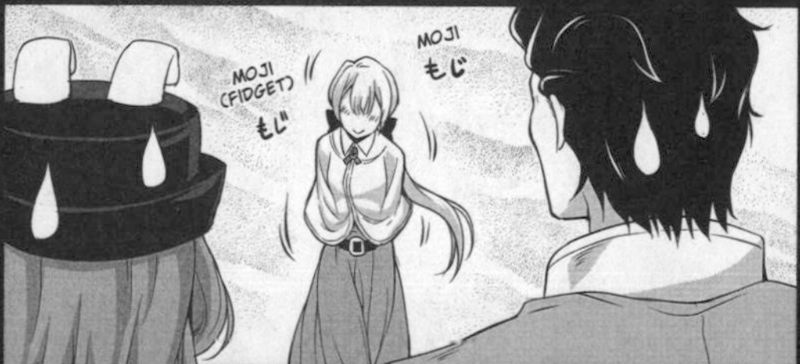
MOJI
もじ
MOJI
(FIDGET)
もじ

That Time I Got Reìncarnated as a SLIME

The Ways of the Monster Nation

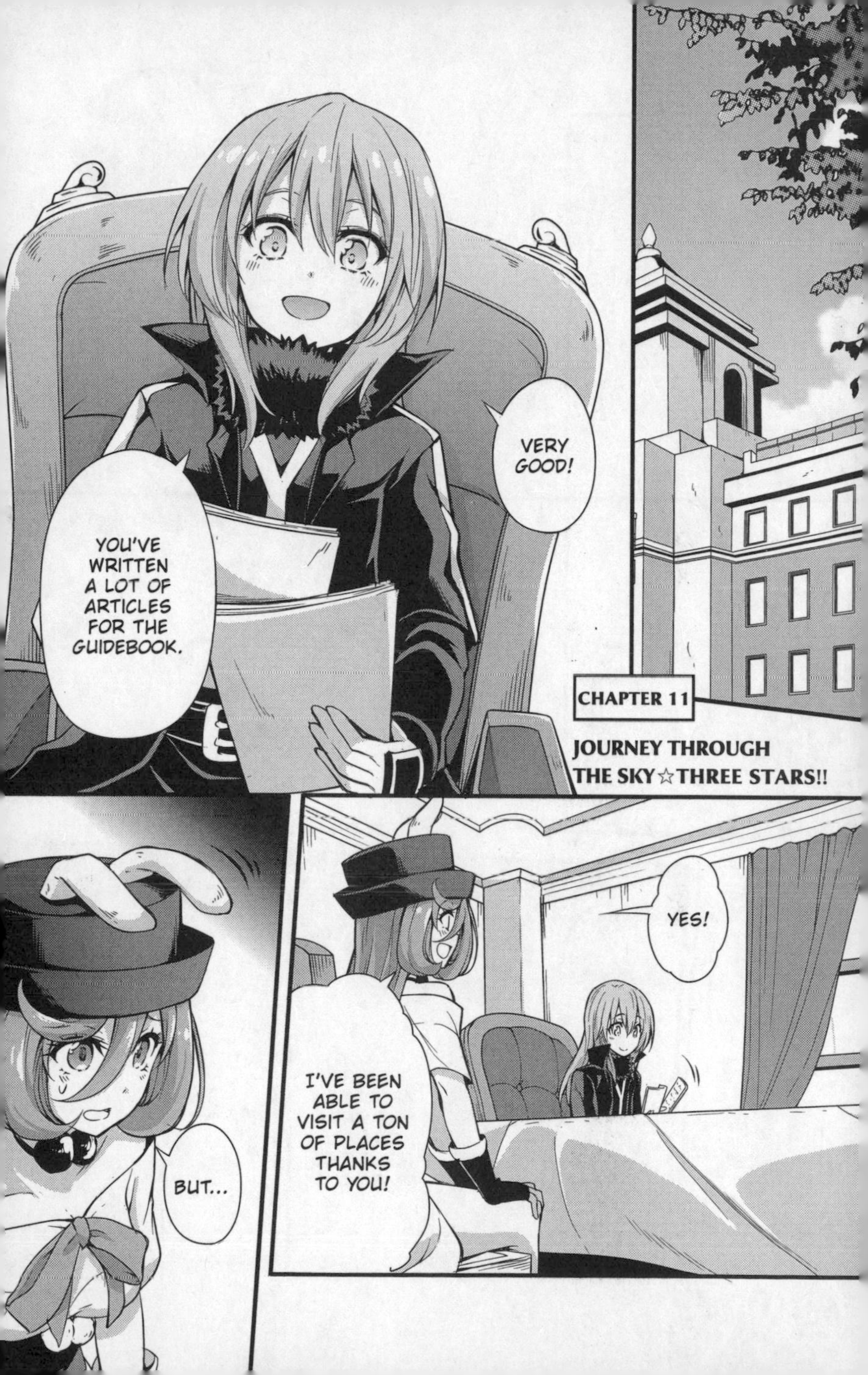
CHAPTER 11
JOURNEY THROUGH THE SKY☆THREE STARS!!
VERY GOOD!
YOU'VE WRITTEN A LOT OF ARTICLES FOR THE GUIDEBOOK.
YES!
I'VE BEEN ABLE TO VISIT A TON OF PLACES THANKS TO YOU!
BUT...

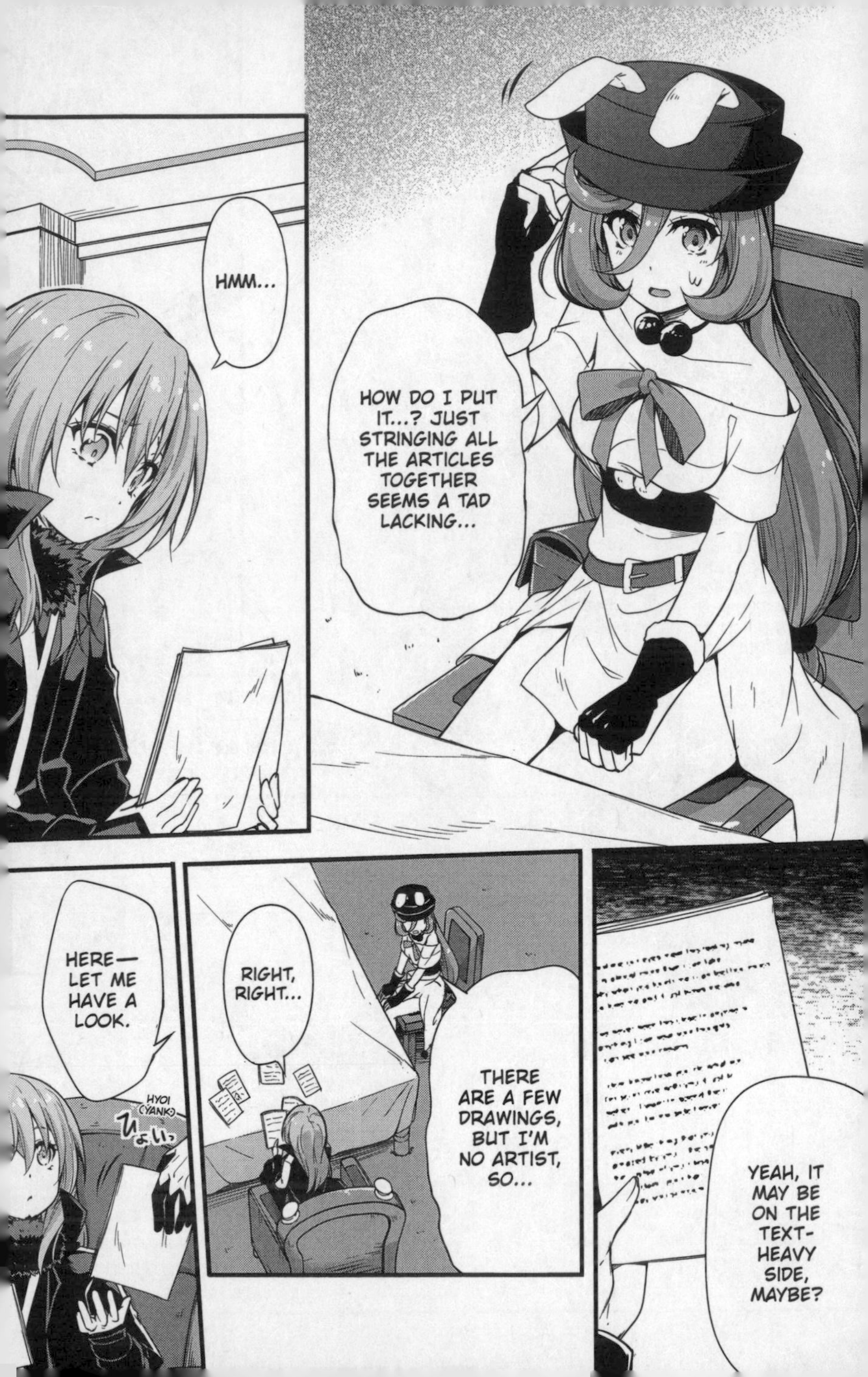
HOW DO I PUT IT...? JUST STRINGING ALL THE ARTICLES TOGETHER SEEMS A TAD LACKING...
HMM...
YEAH, IT MAY BE ON THE TEXT-HEAVY SIDE, MAYBE?
THERE ARE A FEW DRAWINGS, BUT I'M NO ARTIST, SO...
RIGHT, RIGHT...
HERE— LET ME HAVE A LOOK.
HYOI (YANK)
ひょいっ

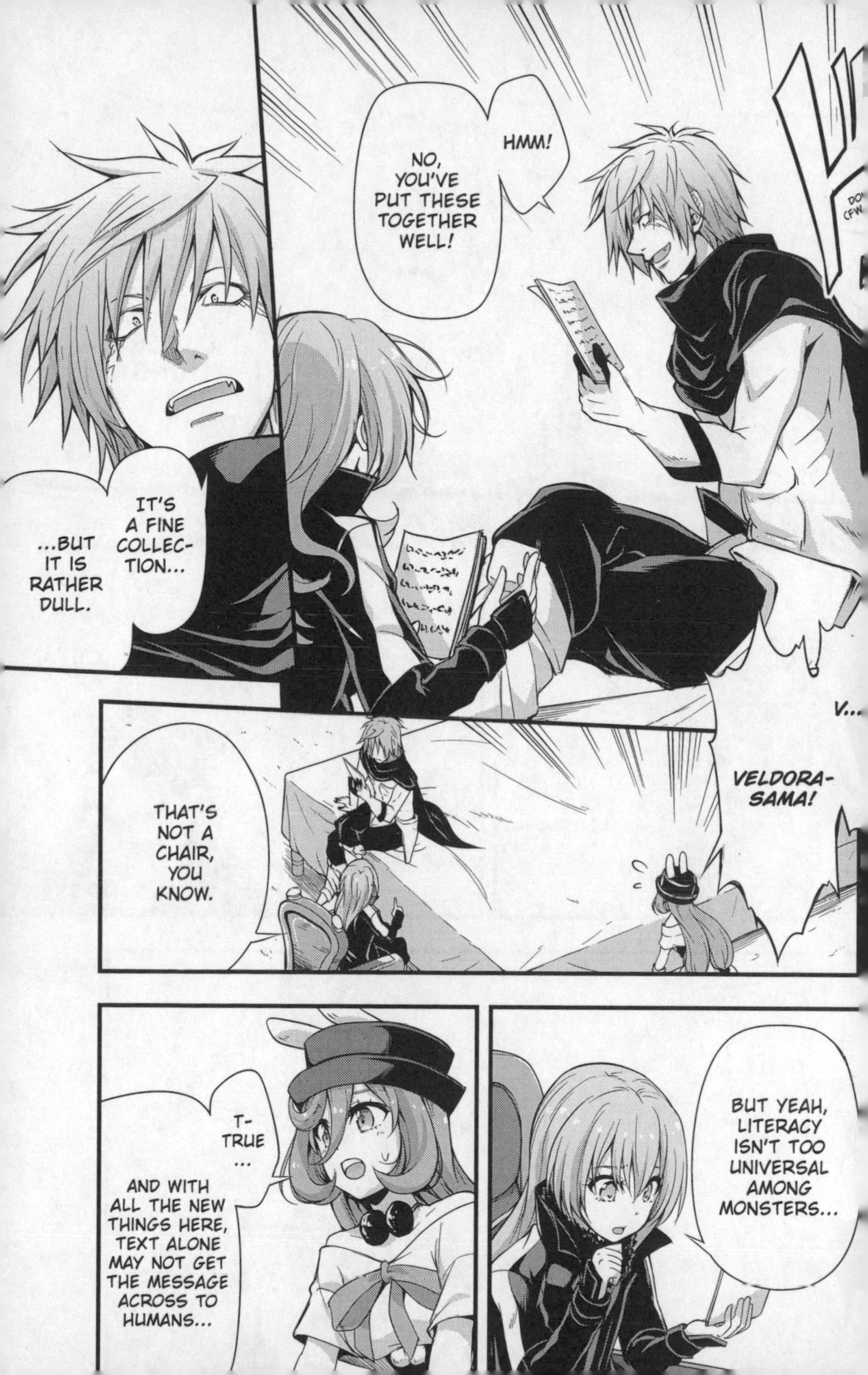
HMM!
NO, YOU'VE PUT THESE TOGETHER WELL!
IT'S A FINE COLLECTION...
...BUT IT IS RATHER DULL.
V...
VELDORA-SAMA!
THAT'S NOT A CHAIR, YOU KNOW.
BUT YEAH, LITERACY ISN'T TOO UNIVERSAL AMONG MONSTERS...
T-TRUE...
AND WITH ALL THE NEW THINGS HERE, TEXT ALONE MAY NOT GET THE MESSAGE ACROSS TO HUMANS...

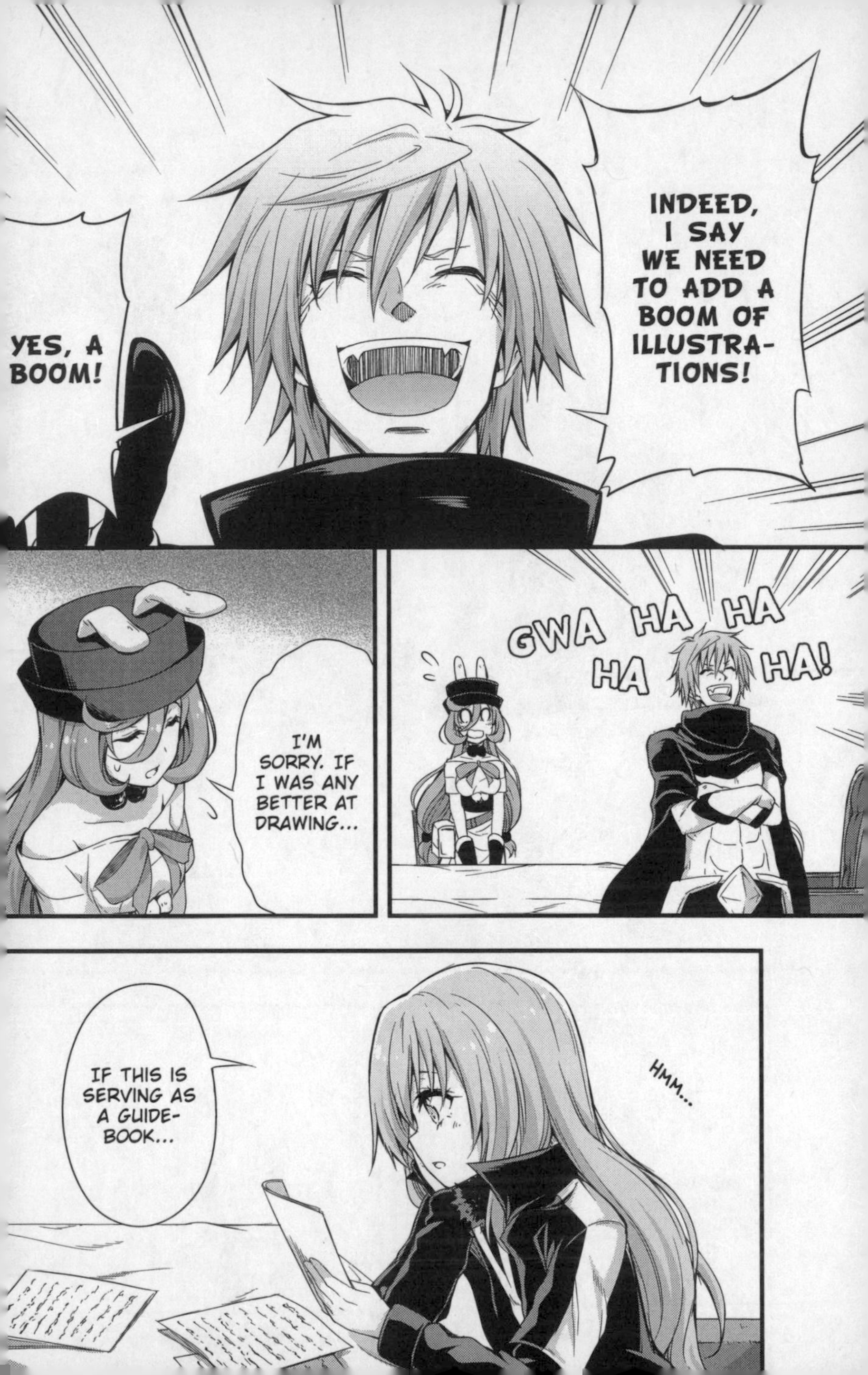
INDEED, I SAY WE NEED TO ADD A BOOM OF ILLUSTRA-TIONS!
YES, A BOOM!
GWA HA HA HA HA!
I'M SORRY. IF I WAS ANY BETTER AT DRAWING...
HMM...
IF THIS IS SERVING AS A GUIDE-BOOK...

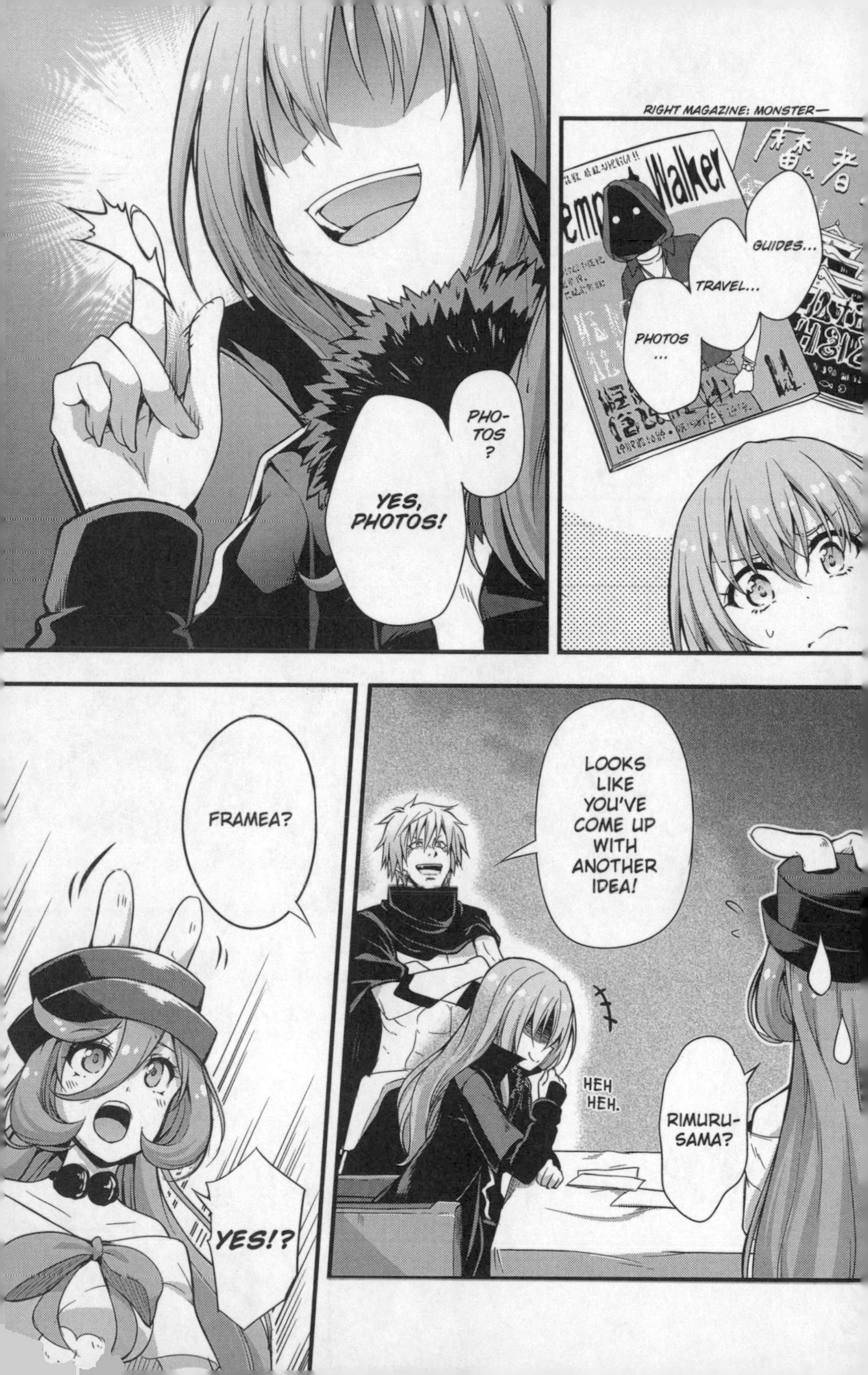
RIGHT MAGAZINE: MONSTER—
GUIDES...
TRAVEL...
PHOTOS ...
PHOTOS?
YES, PHOTOS!
LOOKS LIKE YOU'VE COME UP WITH ANOTHER IDEA!
RIMURU-SAMA?
HEH HEH.
FRAMEA?
YES!?

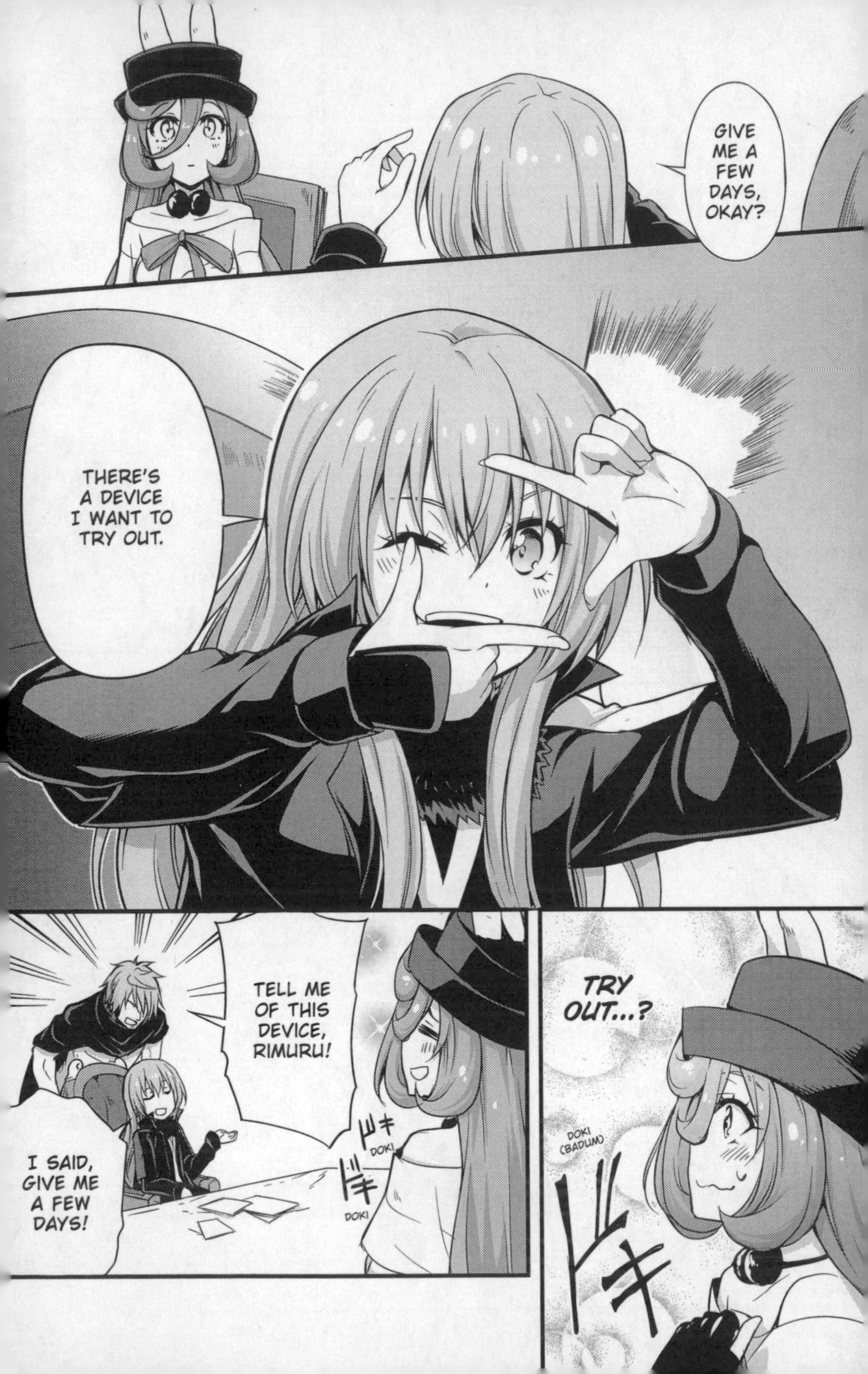
GIVE ME A FEW DAYS, OKAY?
THERE'S A DEVICE I WANT TO TRY OUT.
TRY OUT...?
DOKI (BADUM)
ドキ
TELL ME OF THIS DEVICE, RIMURU!
ドキ
DOKI
ドキ
DOKI
I SAID, GIVE ME A FEW DAYS!

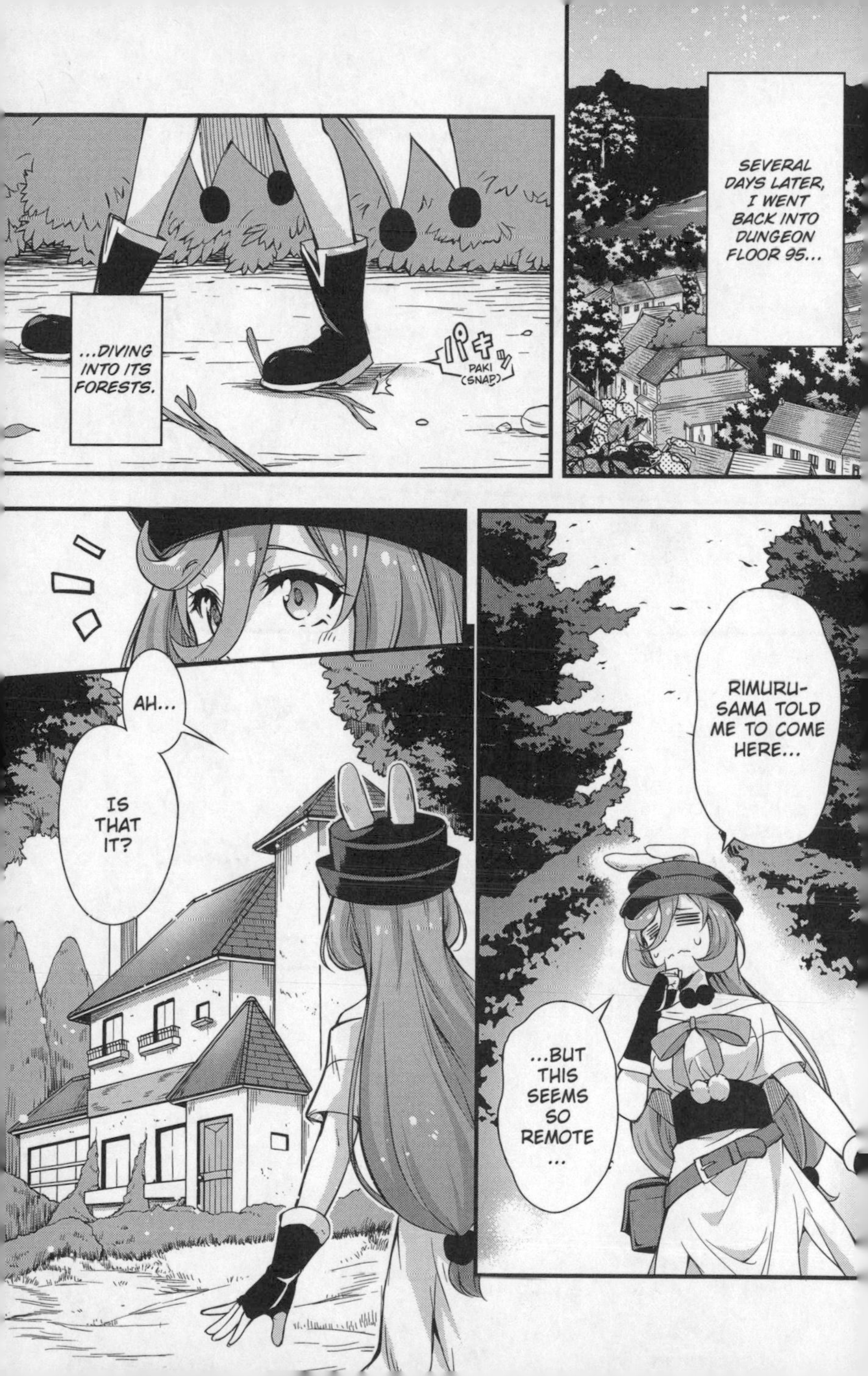
SEVERAL DAYS LATER, I WENT BACK INTO DUNGEON FLOOR 95...
...DIVING INTO ITS FORESTS.
パキッ
PAKI (SNAP)
RIMURU-SAMA TOLD ME TO COME HERE...
...BUT THIS SEEMS SO REMOTE...
AH...
IS THAT IT?

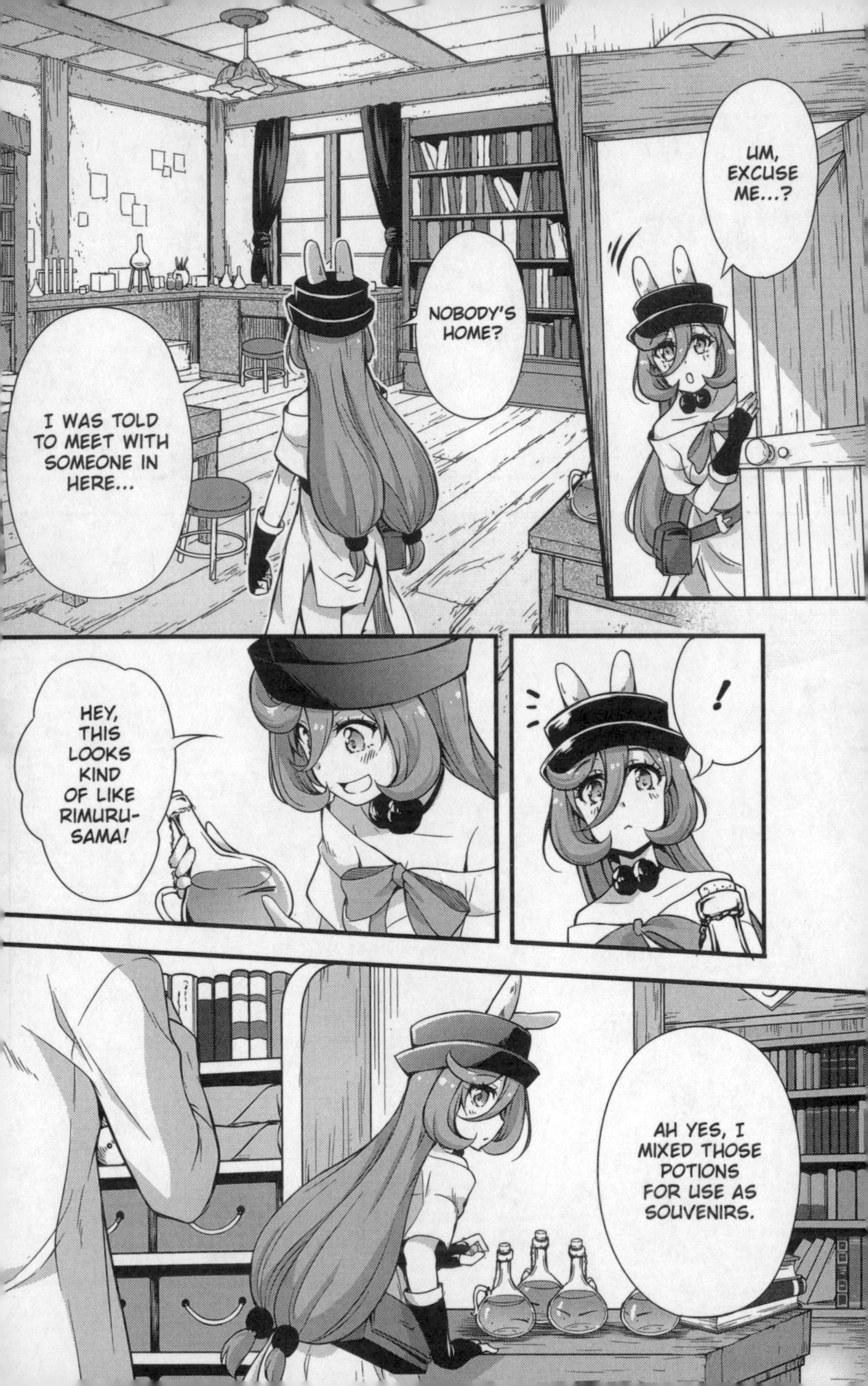
UM, EXCUSE ME...?
NOBODY'S HOME?
I WAS TOLD TO MEET WITH SOMEONE IN HERE...
!
HEY, THIS LOOKS KIND OF LIKE RIMURU-SAMA!
AH YES, I MIXED THOSE POTIONS FOR USE AS SOUVENIRS.

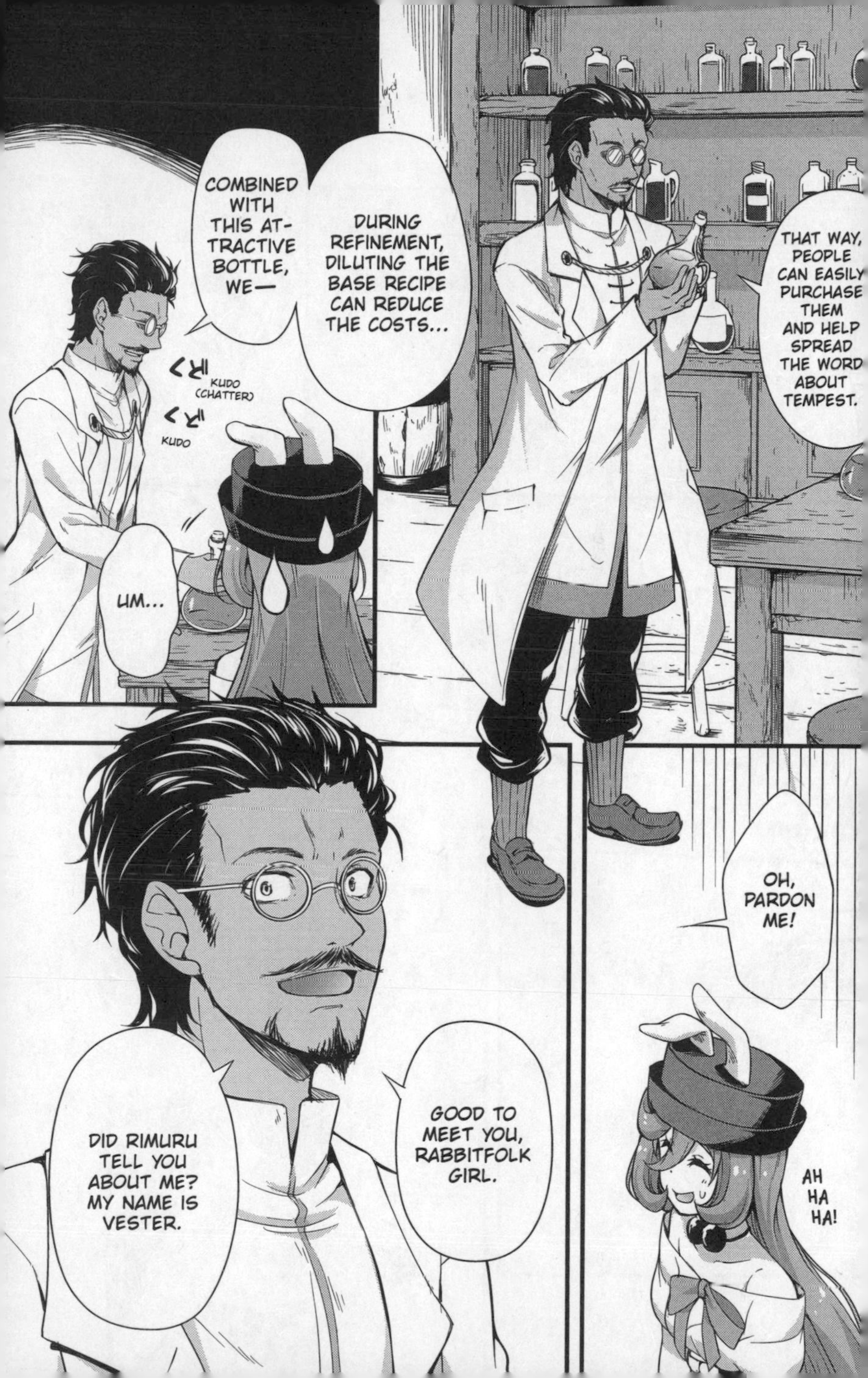
THAT WAY, PEOPLE CAN EASILY PURCHASE THEM AND HELP SPREAD THE WORD ABOUT TEMPEST.
DURING REFINEMENT, DILUTING THE BASE RECIPE CAN REDUCE THE COSTS...
COMBINED WITH THIS AT-TRACTIVE BOTTLE, WE—
くど KUDO (CHATTER)
くど KUDO
UM...
OH, PARDON ME!
AH HA HA!
GOOD TO MEET YOU, RABBITFOLK GIRL.
DID RIMURU TELL YOU ABOUT ME? MY NAME IS VESTER.

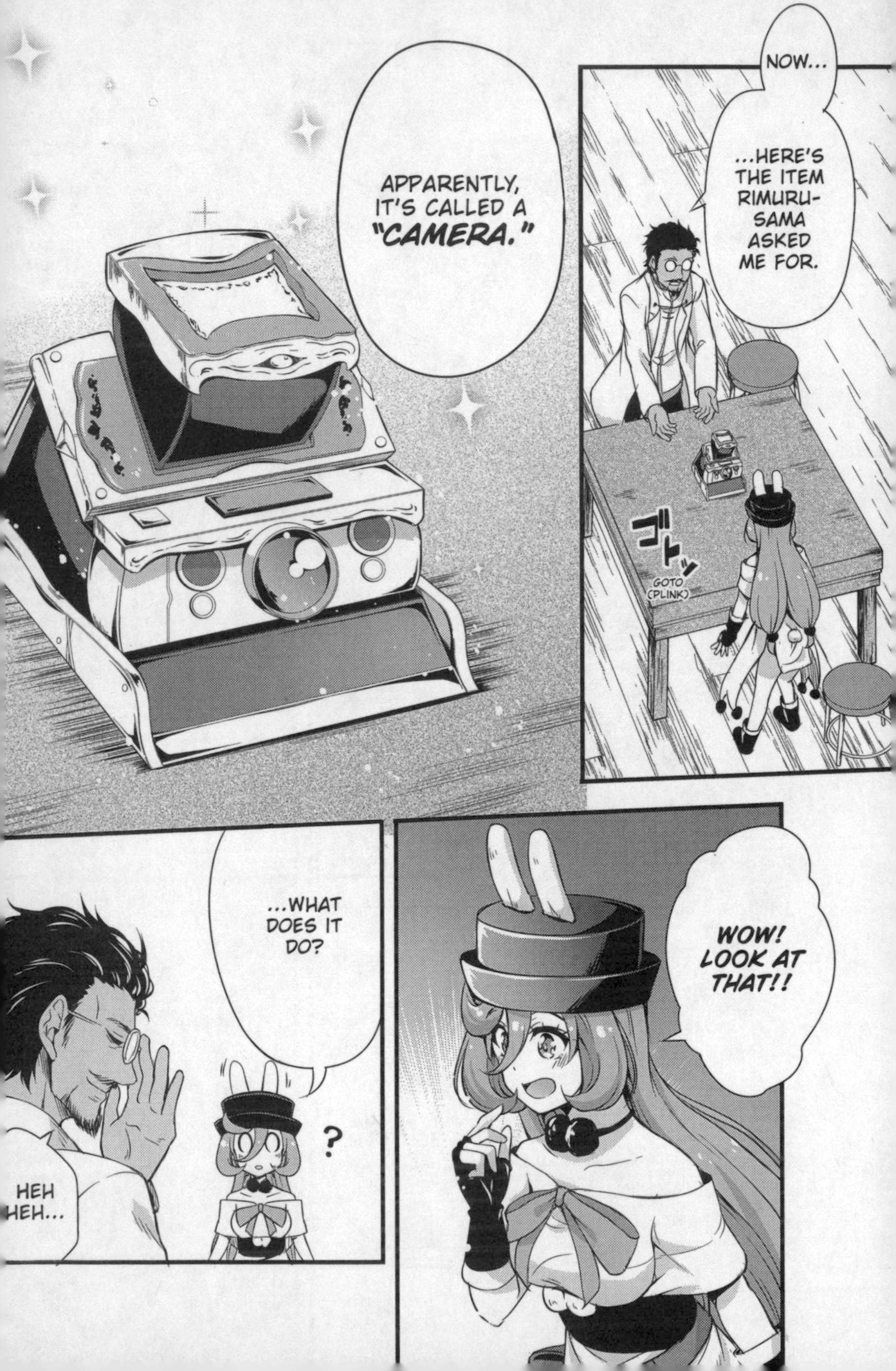
NOW...
...HERE'S THE ITEM RIMURU-SAMA ASKED ME FOR.
ゴトッ
GOTO (PLINK)
APPARENTLY, IT'S CALLED A "CAMERA."
WOW! LOOK AT THAT!!
...WHAT DOES IT DO?
?
HEH HEH...

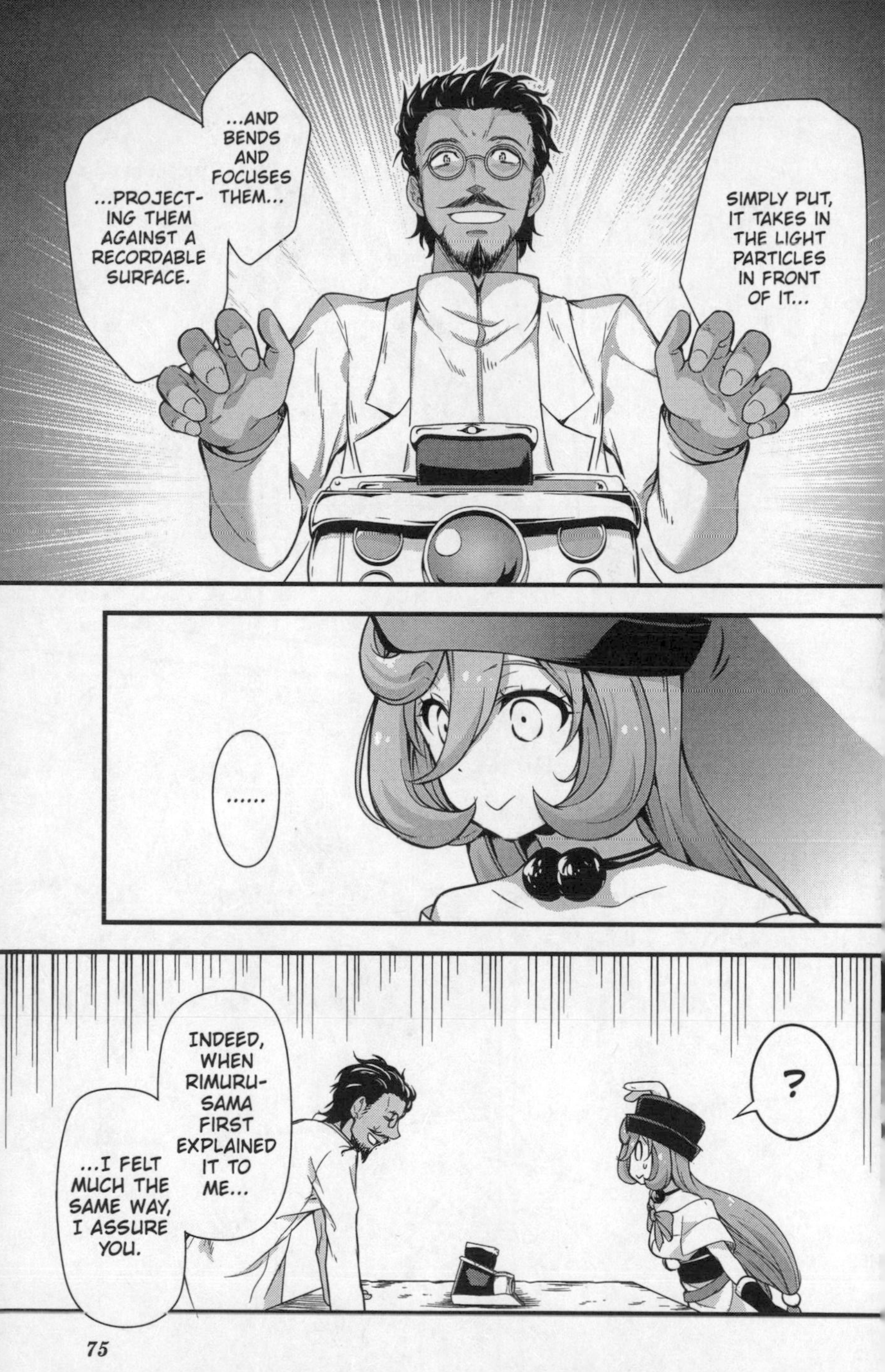
SIMPLY PUT, IT TAKES IN THE LIGHT PARTICLES IN FRONT OF IT...
...AND BENDS AND FOCUSES THEM...
...PROJECTING THEM AGAINST A RECORDABLE SURFACE.
......
?
INDEED, WHEN RIMURU-SAMA FIRST EXPLAINED IT TO ME...
...I FELT MUCH THE SAME WAY, I ASSURE YOU.

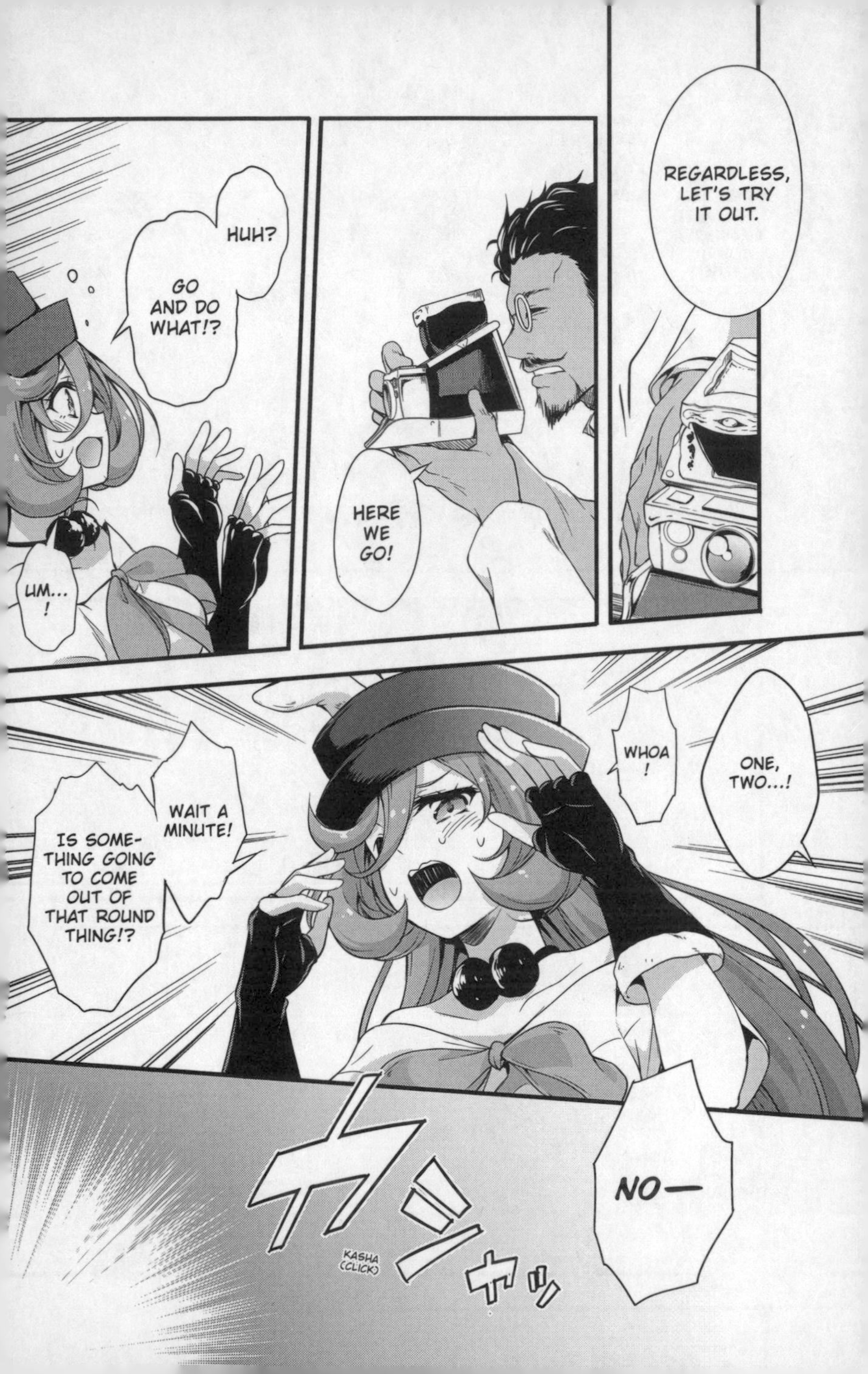
REGARDLESS, LET'S TRY IT OUT.
HERE WE GO!
HUH?
GO AND DO WHAT!?
UM... !
ONE, TWO...!
WHOA !
WAIT A MINUTE!
IS SOME-THING GOING TO COME OUT OF THAT ROUND THING!?
NO—
KASHA (CLICK)

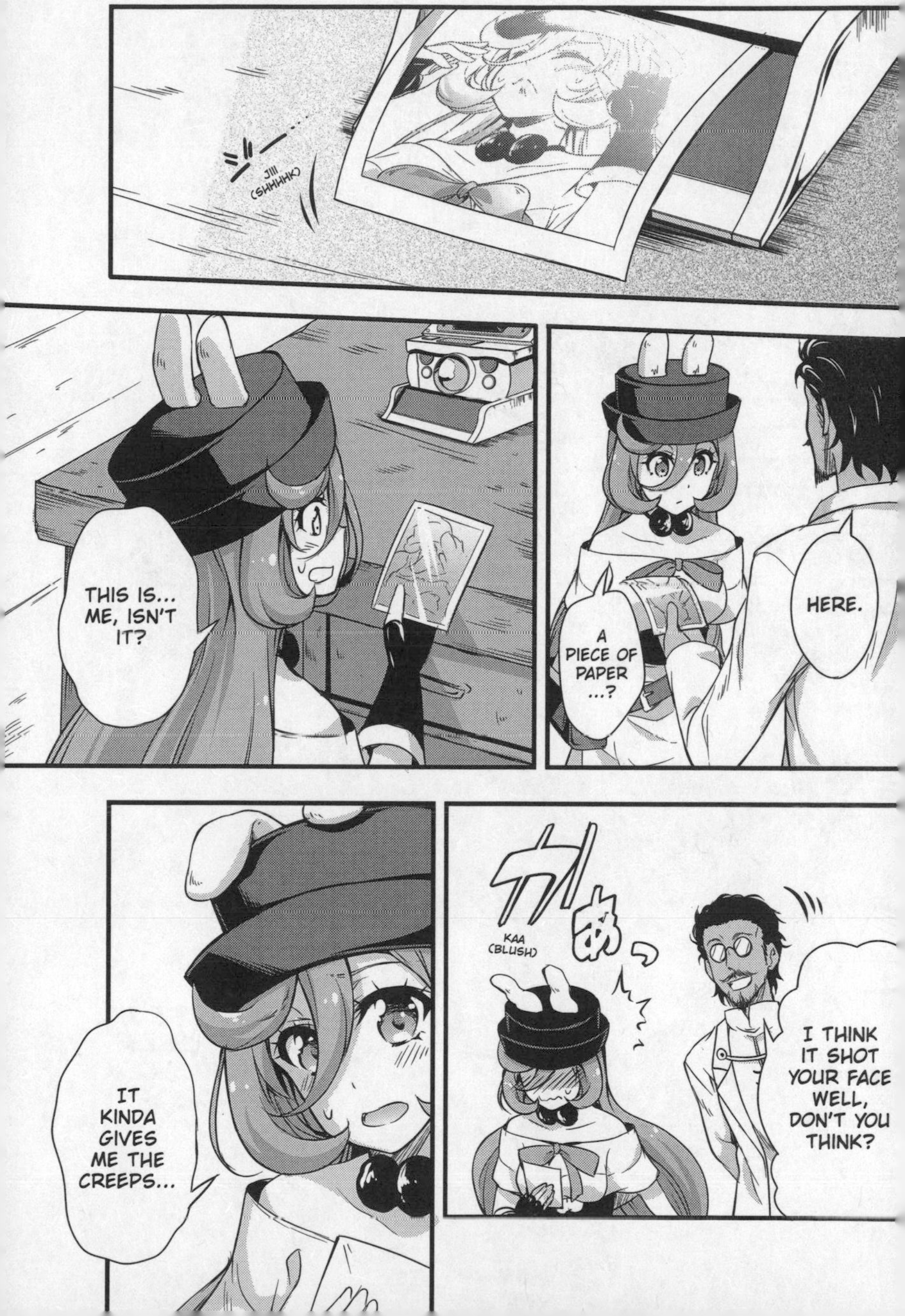
JIII
(SHHHHK)
HERE.
A PIECE OF PAPER ...?
THIS IS... ME, ISN'T IT?
I THINK IT SHOT YOUR FACE WELL, DON'T YOU THINK?
KAA
(BLUSH)
IT KINDA GIVES ME THE CREEPS...

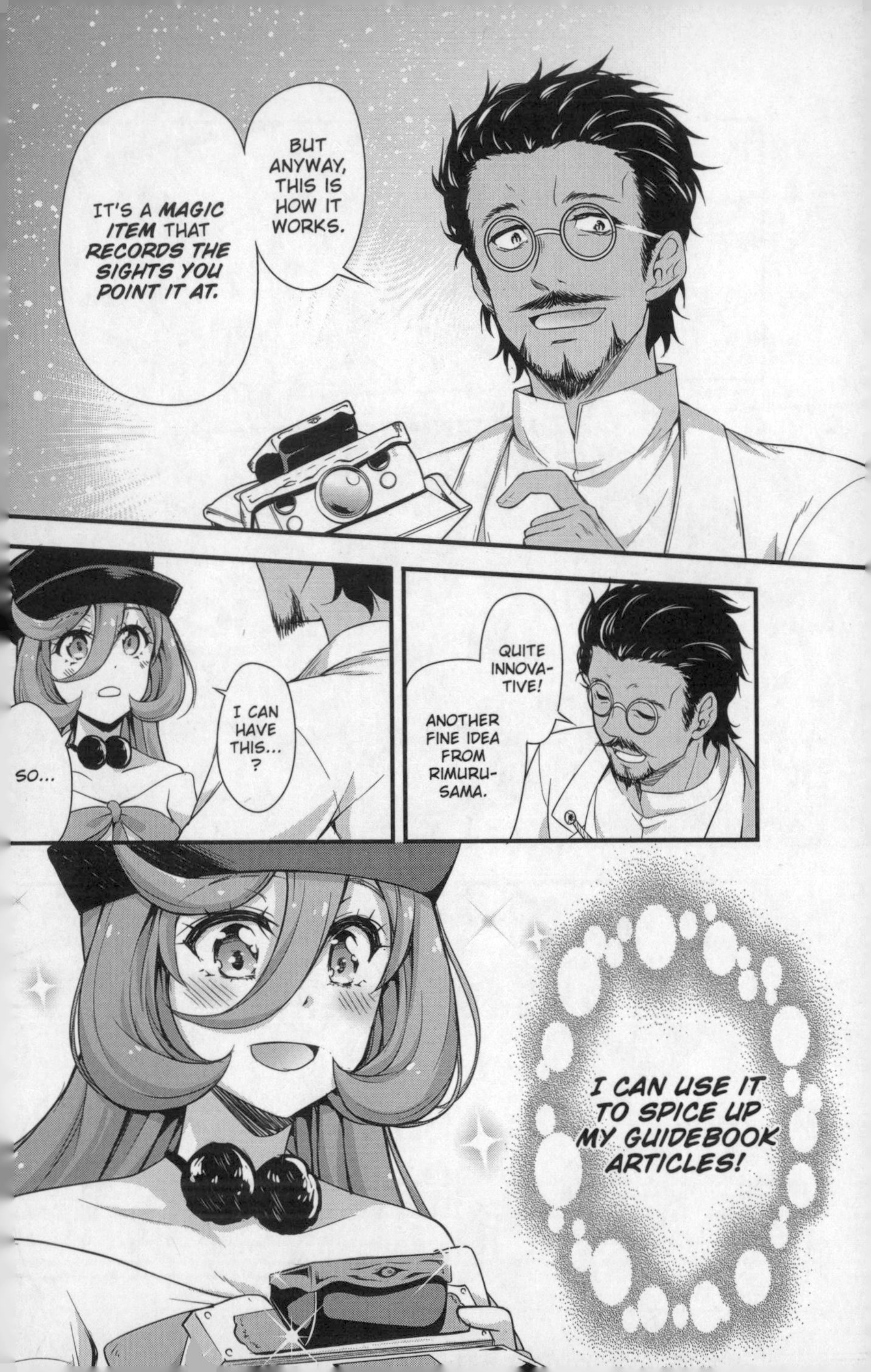
BUT ANYWAY, THIS IS HOW IT WORKS.
IT'S A ***MAGIC ITEM*** THAT ***RECORDS THE SIGHTS YOU POINT IT AT.***
QUITE INNOVA-TIVE!
ANOTHER FINE IDEA FROM RIMURU-SAMA.
I CAN HAVE THIS... ?
SO...
I CAN USE IT TO SPICE UP MY GUIDEBOOK ARTICLES!

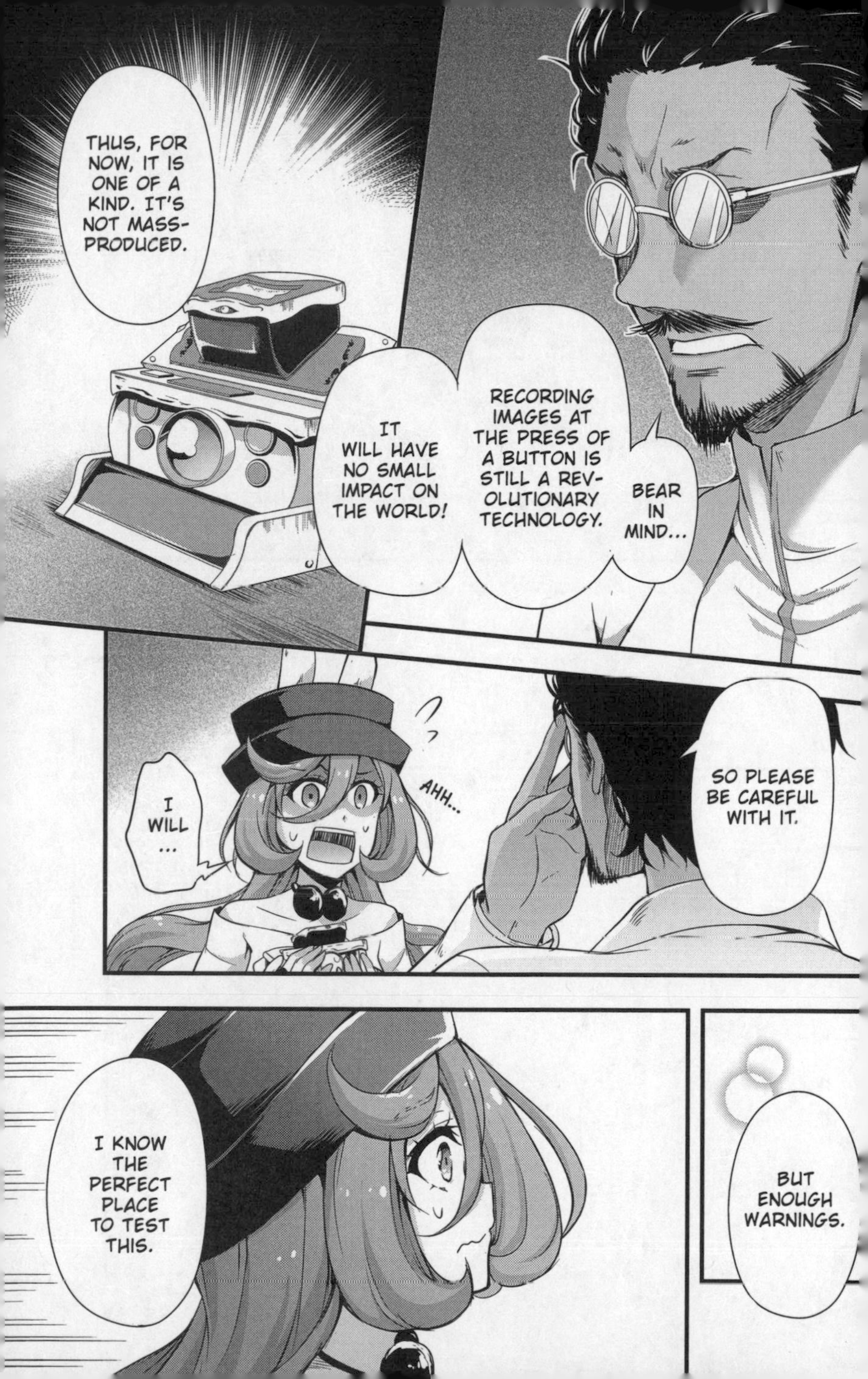
BEAR IN MIND...
RECORDING IMAGES AT THE PRESS OF A BUTTON IS STILL A REVOLUTIONARY TECHNOLOGY.
IT WILL HAVE NO SMALL IMPACT ON THE WORLD!
THUS, FOR NOW, IT IS ONE OF A KIND. IT'S NOT MASS-PRODUCED.
SO PLEASE BE CAREFUL WITH IT.
AHH...
I WILL ...
BUT ENOUGH WARNINGS.
I KNOW THE PERFECT PLACE TO TEST THIS.

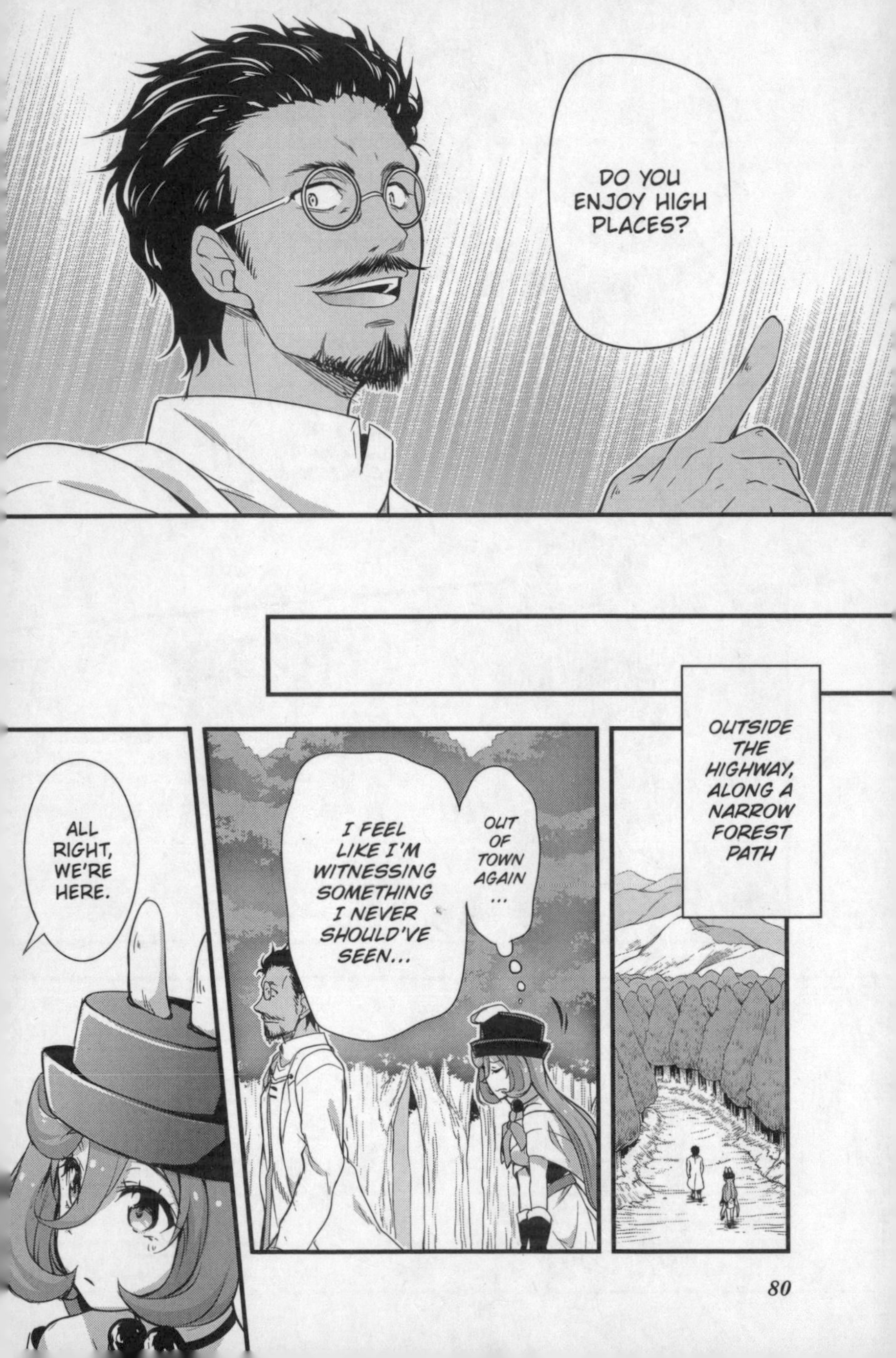
DO YOU ENJOY HIGH PLACES?
OUTSIDE THE HIGHWAY, ALONG A NARROW FOREST PATH
OUT OF TOWN AGAIN...
I FEEL LIKE I'M WITNESSING SOMETHING I NEVER SHOULD'VE SEEN...
ALL RIGHT, WE'RE HERE.

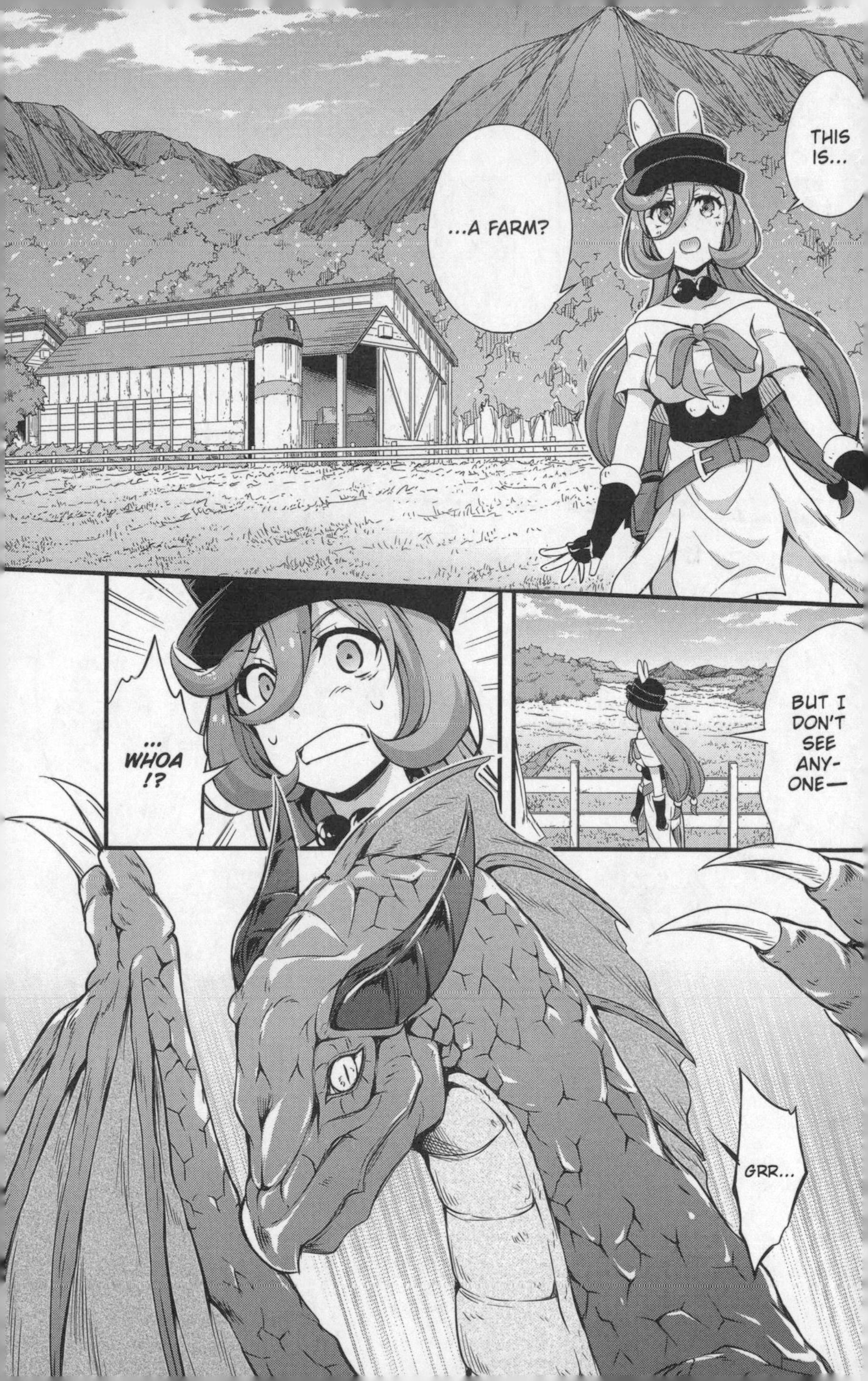
THIS IS...
...A FARM?
BUT I DON'T SEE ANY-ONE—
...WHOA!?
GRR...

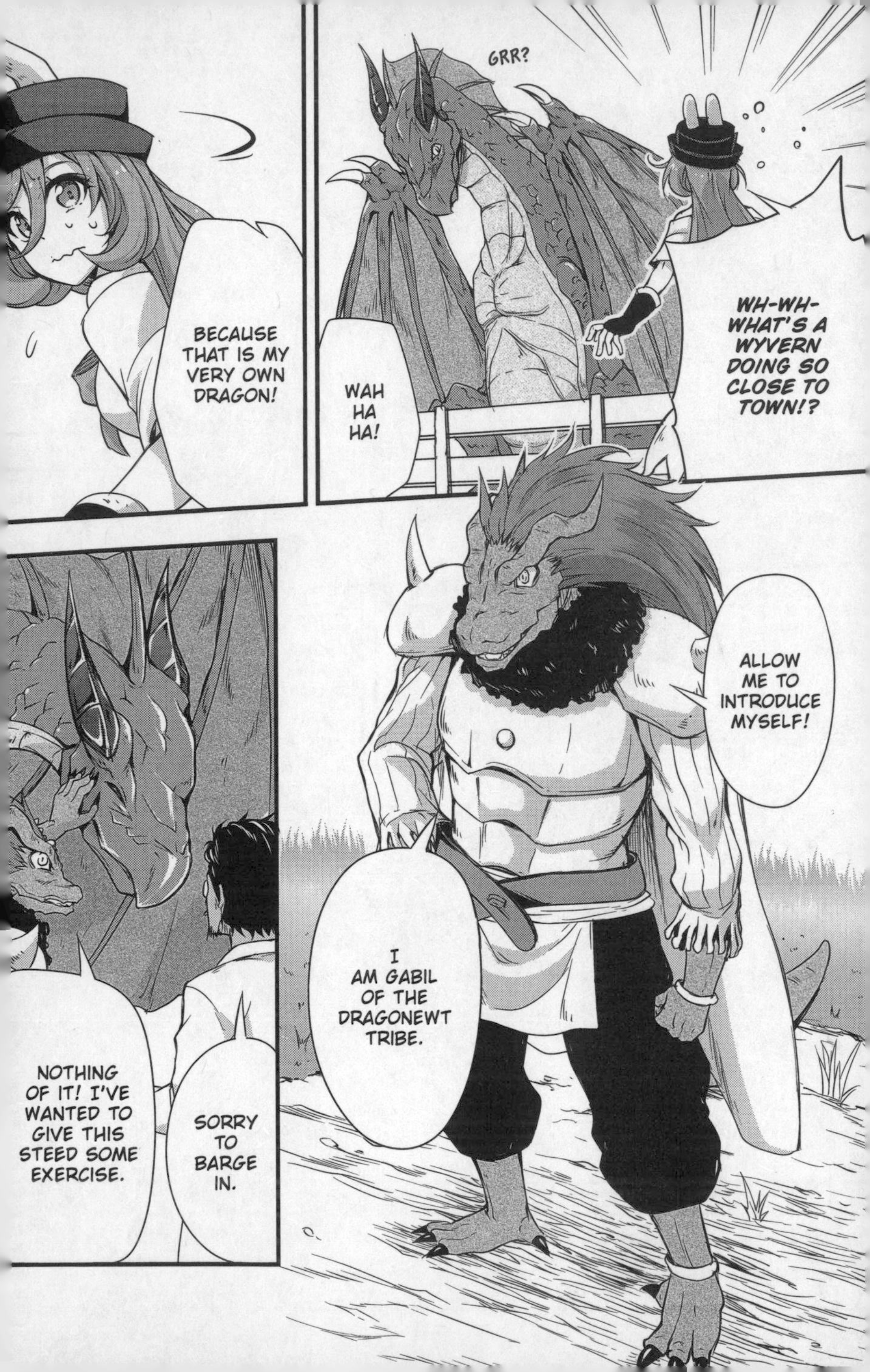
GRR?
WH-WH-WHAT'S A WYVERN DOING SO CLOSE TO TOWN!?
WAH HA HA!
BECAUSE THAT IS MY VERY OWN DRAGON!
ALLOW ME TO INTRODUCE MYSELF!
I AM GABIL OF THE DRAGONEWT TRIBE.
SORRY TO BARGE IN.
NOTHING OF IT! I'VE WANTED TO GIVE THIS STEED SOME EXERCISE.

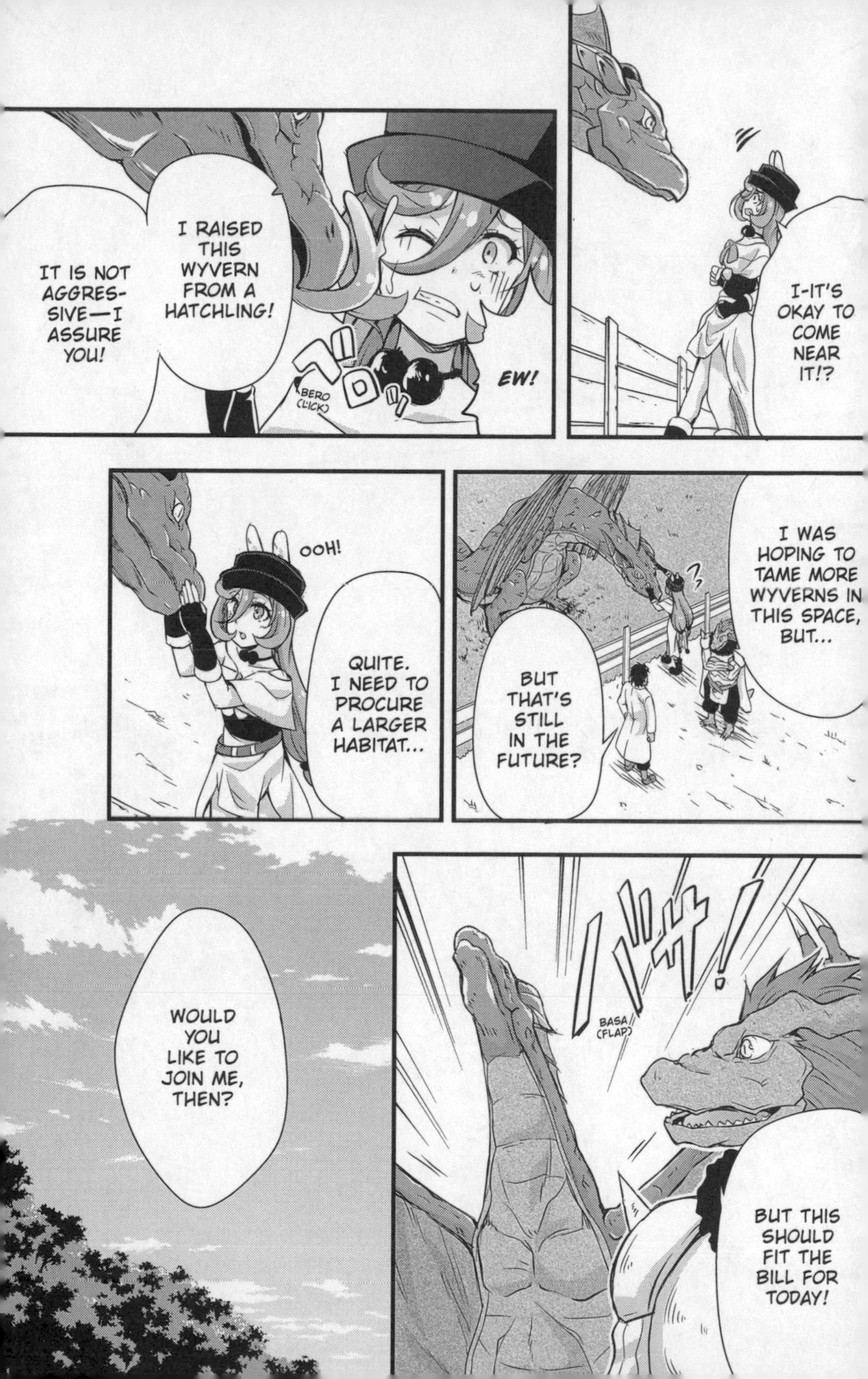
I-IT'S OKAY TO COME NEAR IT!?
I RAISED THIS WYVERN FROM A HATCHLING!
IT IS NOT AGGRES-SIVE—I ASSURE YOU!
EW!
BERO (LICK)
I WAS HOPING TO TAME MORE WYVERNS IN THIS SPACE, BUT...
BUT THAT'S STILL IN THE FUTURE?
OOH!
QUITE. I NEED TO PROCURE A LARGER HABITAT...
BASA (FLAP)
BUT THIS SHOULD FIT THE BILL FOR TODAY!
WOULD YOU LIKE TO JOIN ME, THEN?

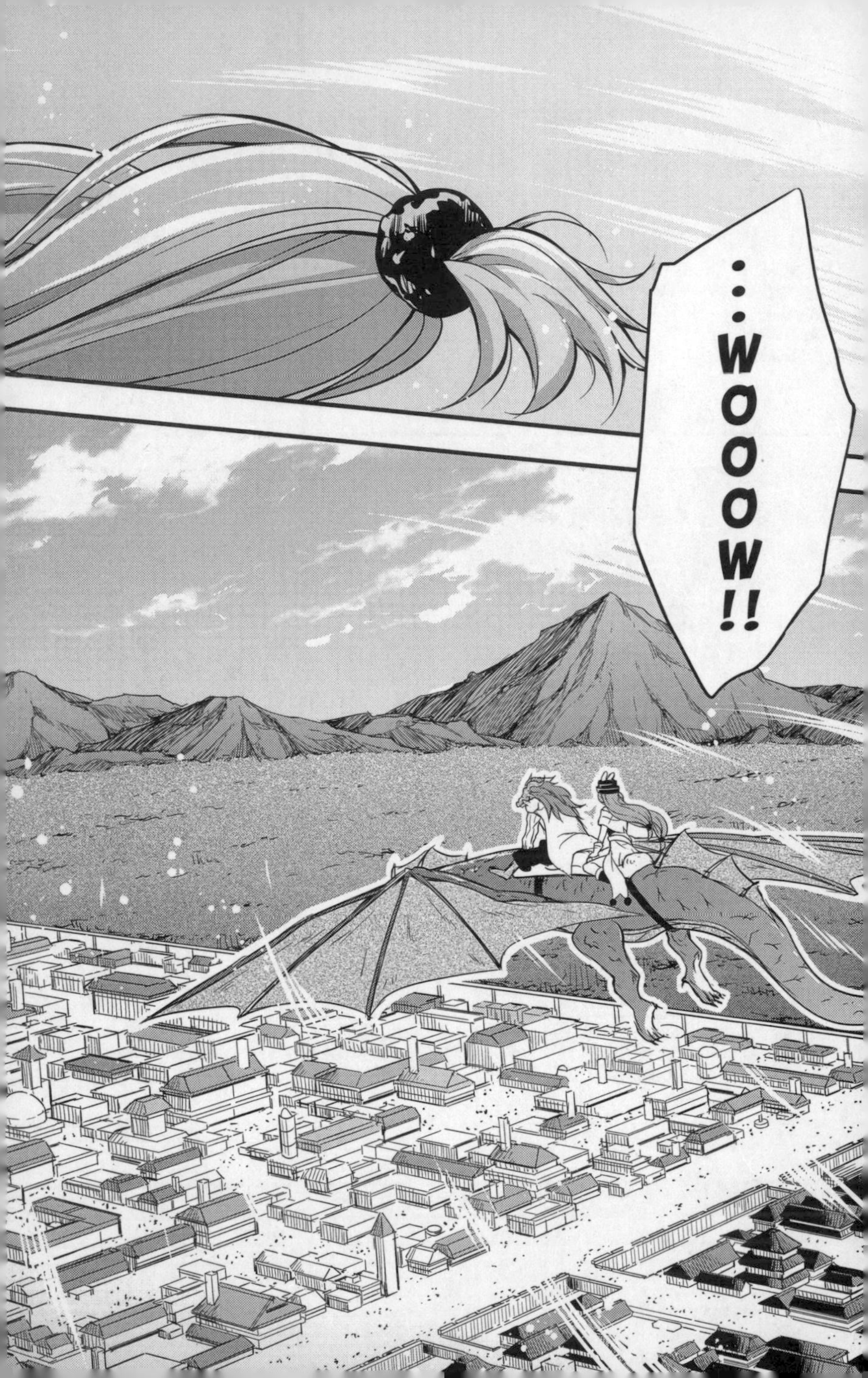
...WOOOW!!

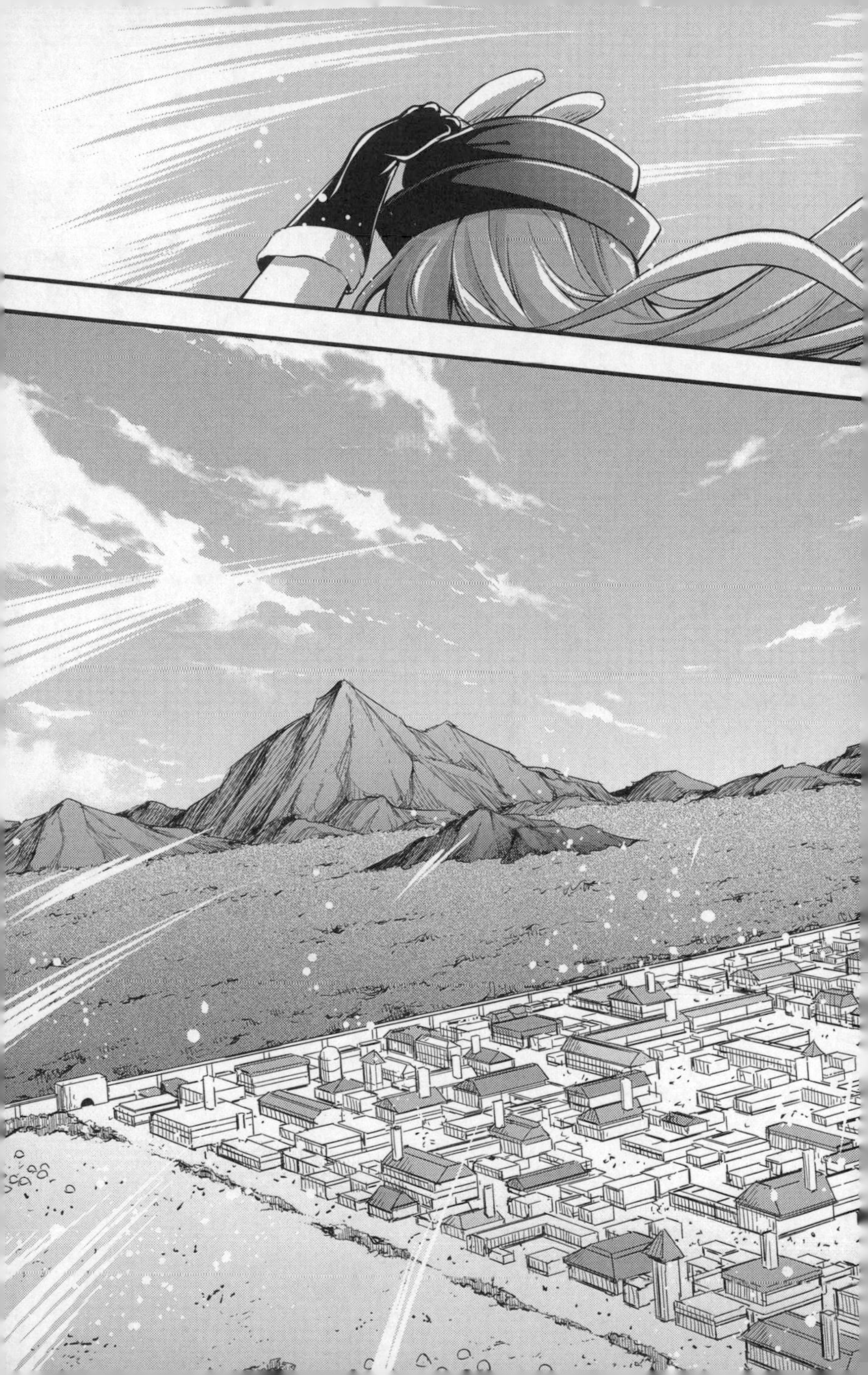

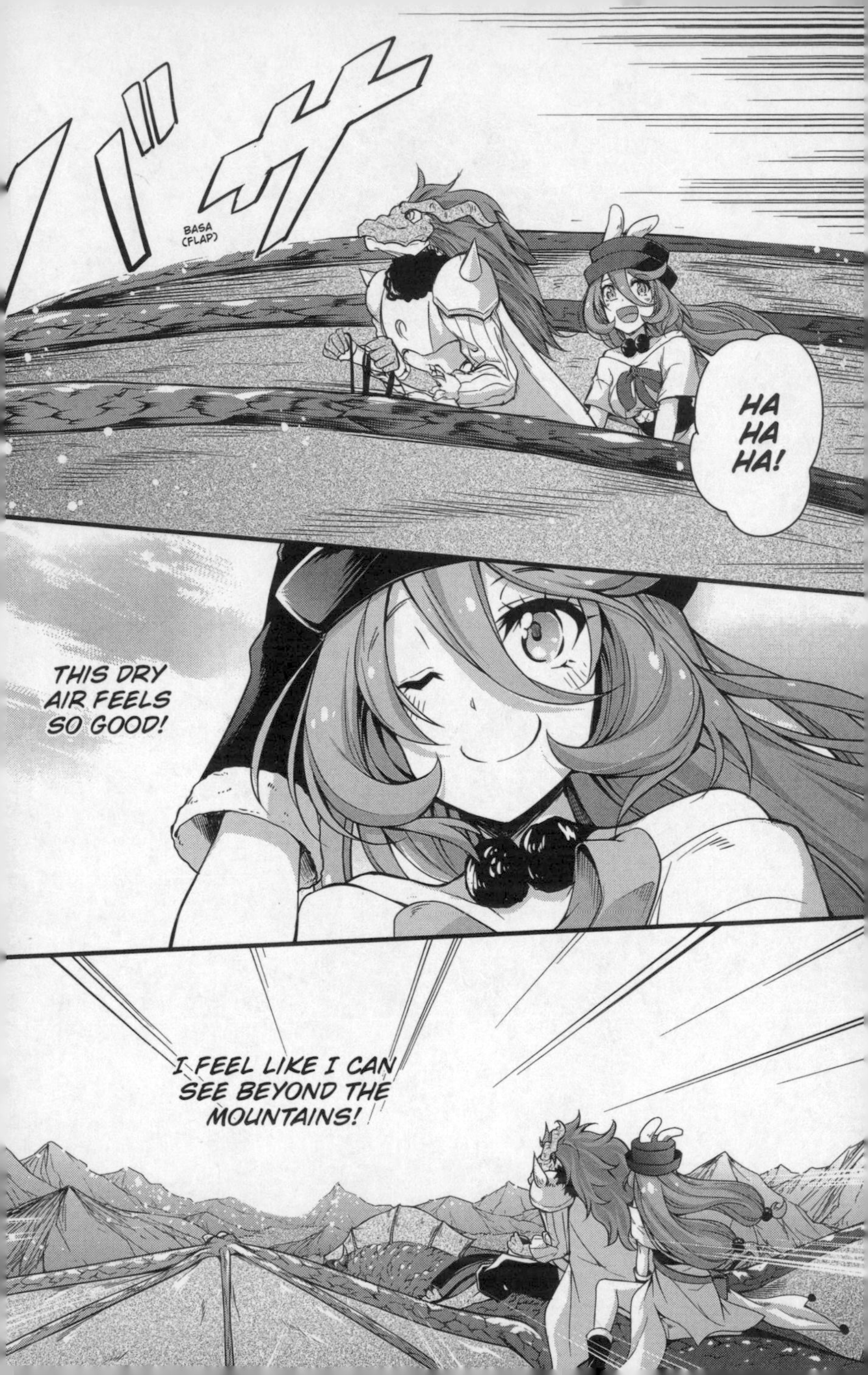
BASA (FLAP)
HA HA HA!
THIS DRY AIR FEELS SO GOOD!
I FEEL LIKE I CAN SEE BEYOND THE MOUNTAINS!

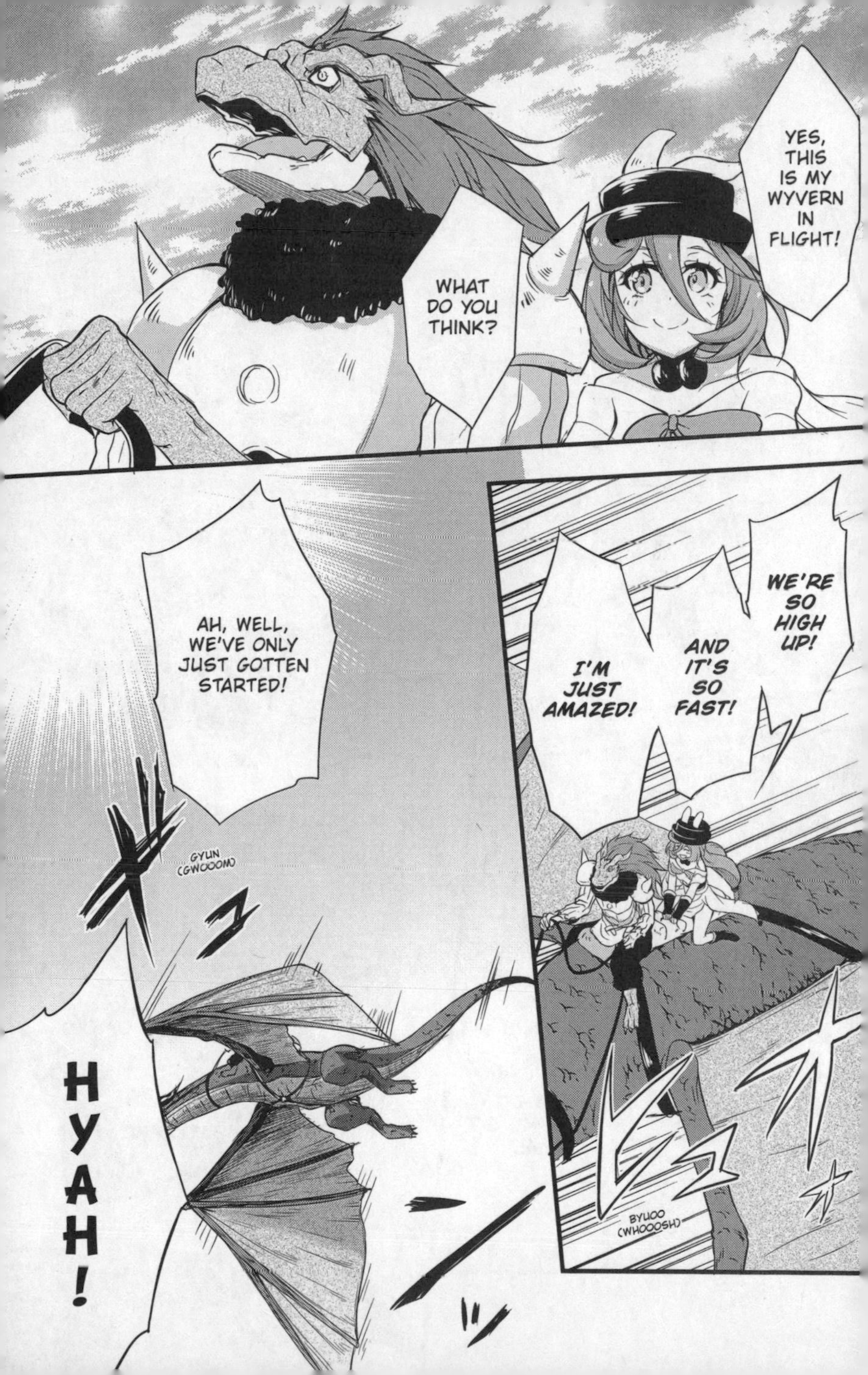
YES, THIS IS MY WYVERN IN FLIGHT!
WHAT DO YOU THINK?
WE'RE SO HIGH UP!
AND IT'S SO FAST!
I'M JUST AMAZED!
BYUOO (WHOOOSH)
AH, WELL, WE'VE ONLY JUST GOTTEN STARTED!
GYUN (GWOOOM)
HYAH!

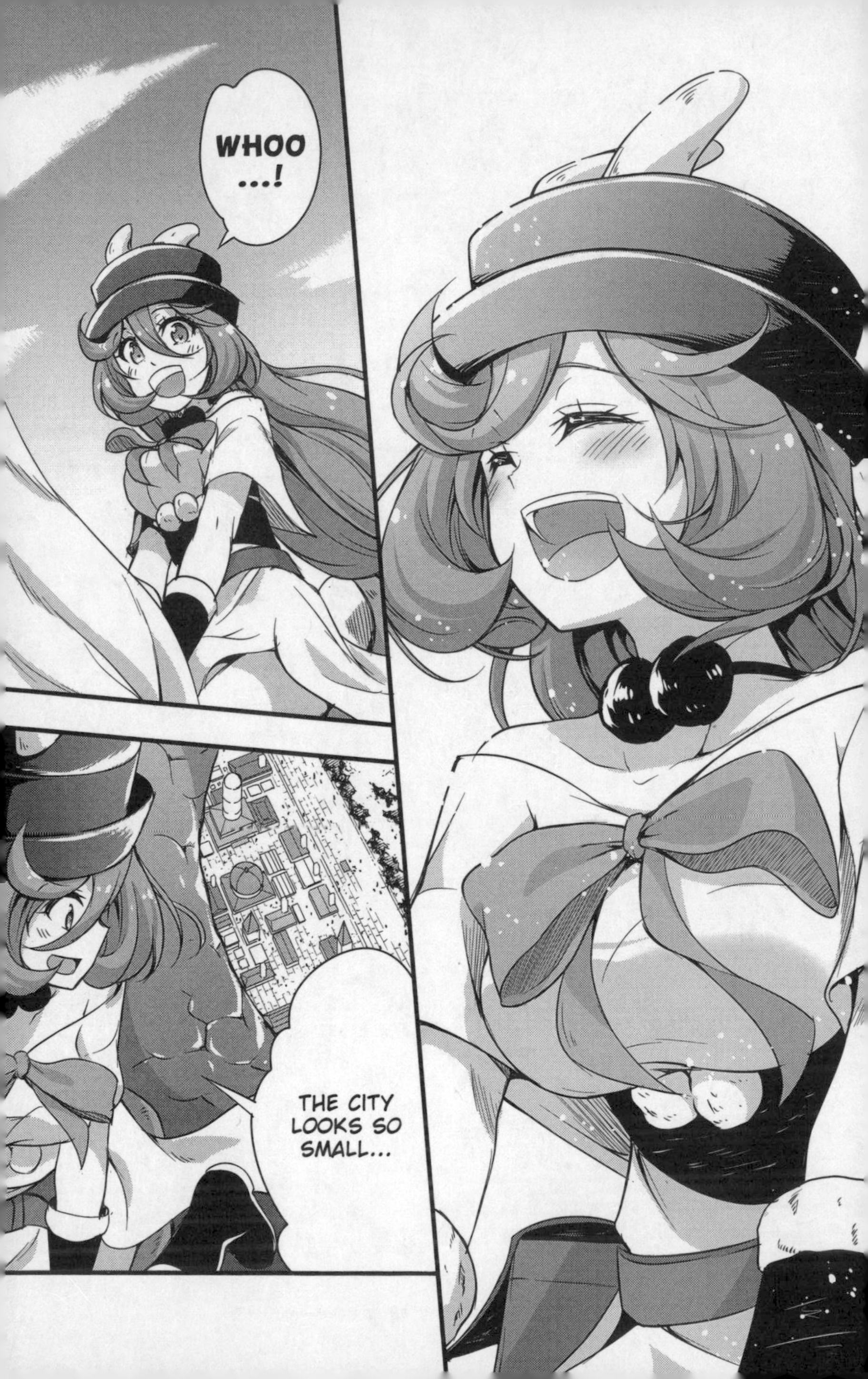
WHOO ...!
THE CITY LOOKS SO SMALL...

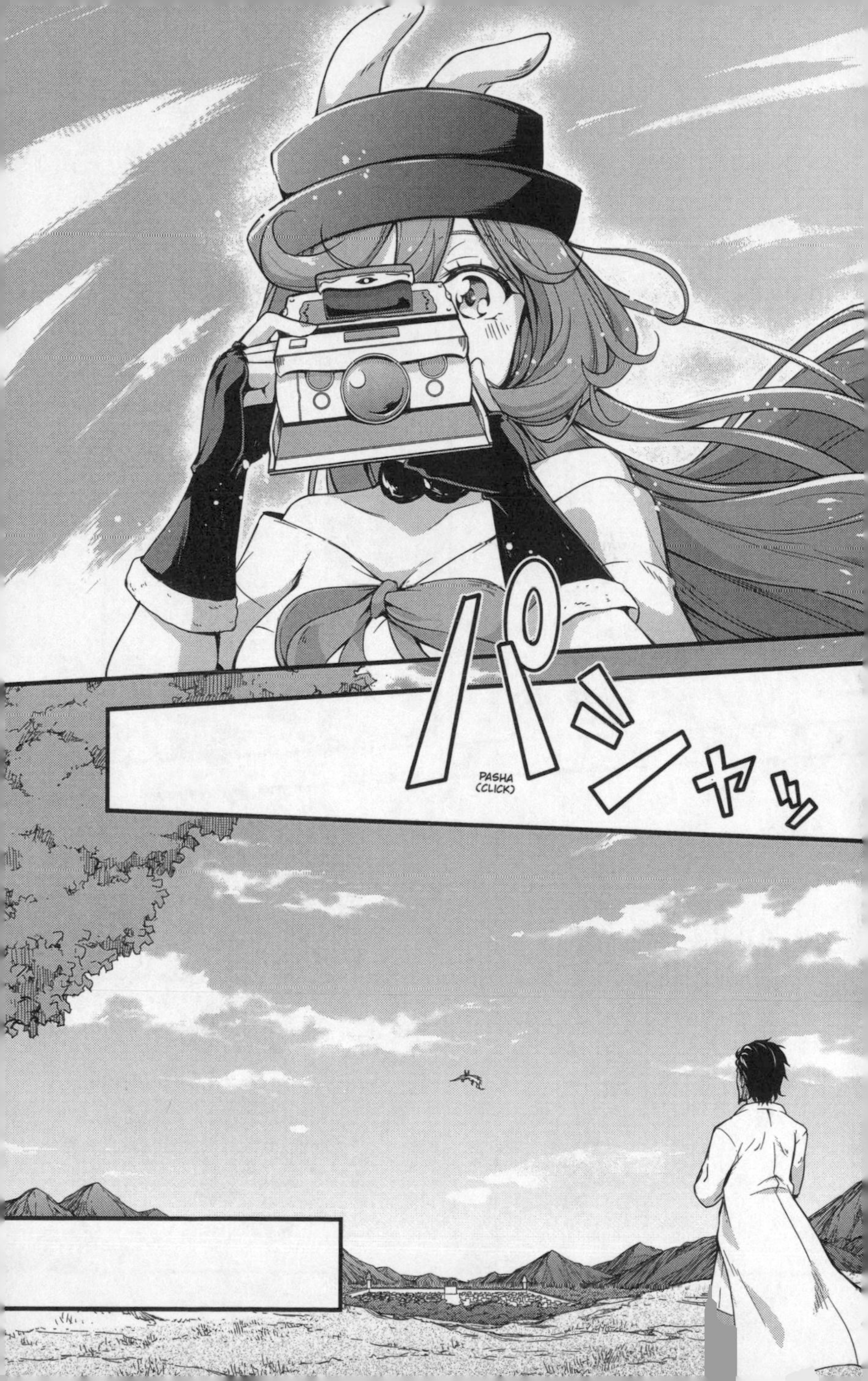
パシャッ
PASHA
(CLICK)

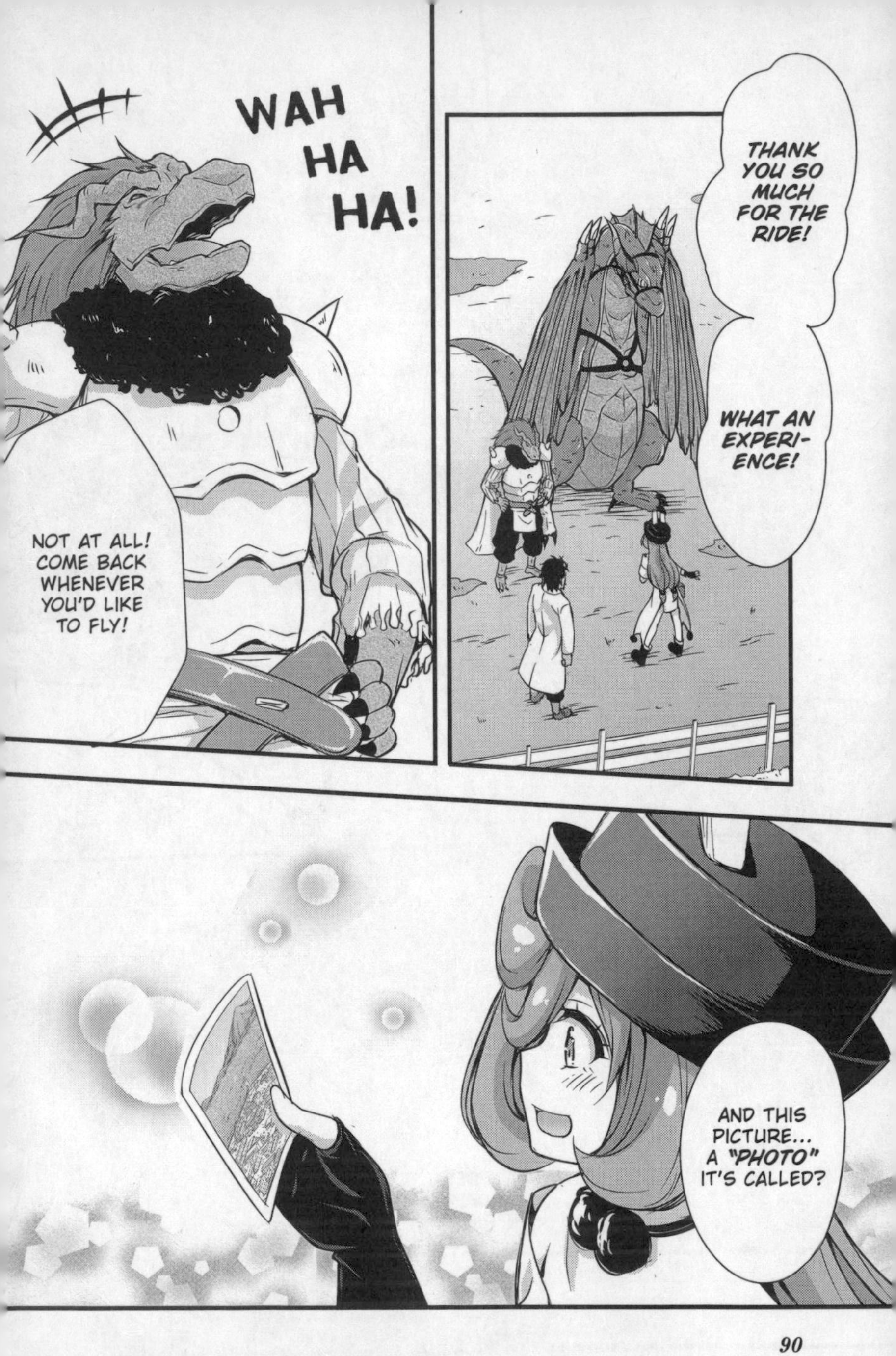
THANK YOU SO MUCH FOR THE RIDE!
WHAT AN EXPERI- ENCE!
WAH HA HA!
NOT AT ALL! COME BACK WHENEVER YOU'D LIKE TO FLY!
AND THIS PICTURE... A "PHOTO" IT'S CALLED?

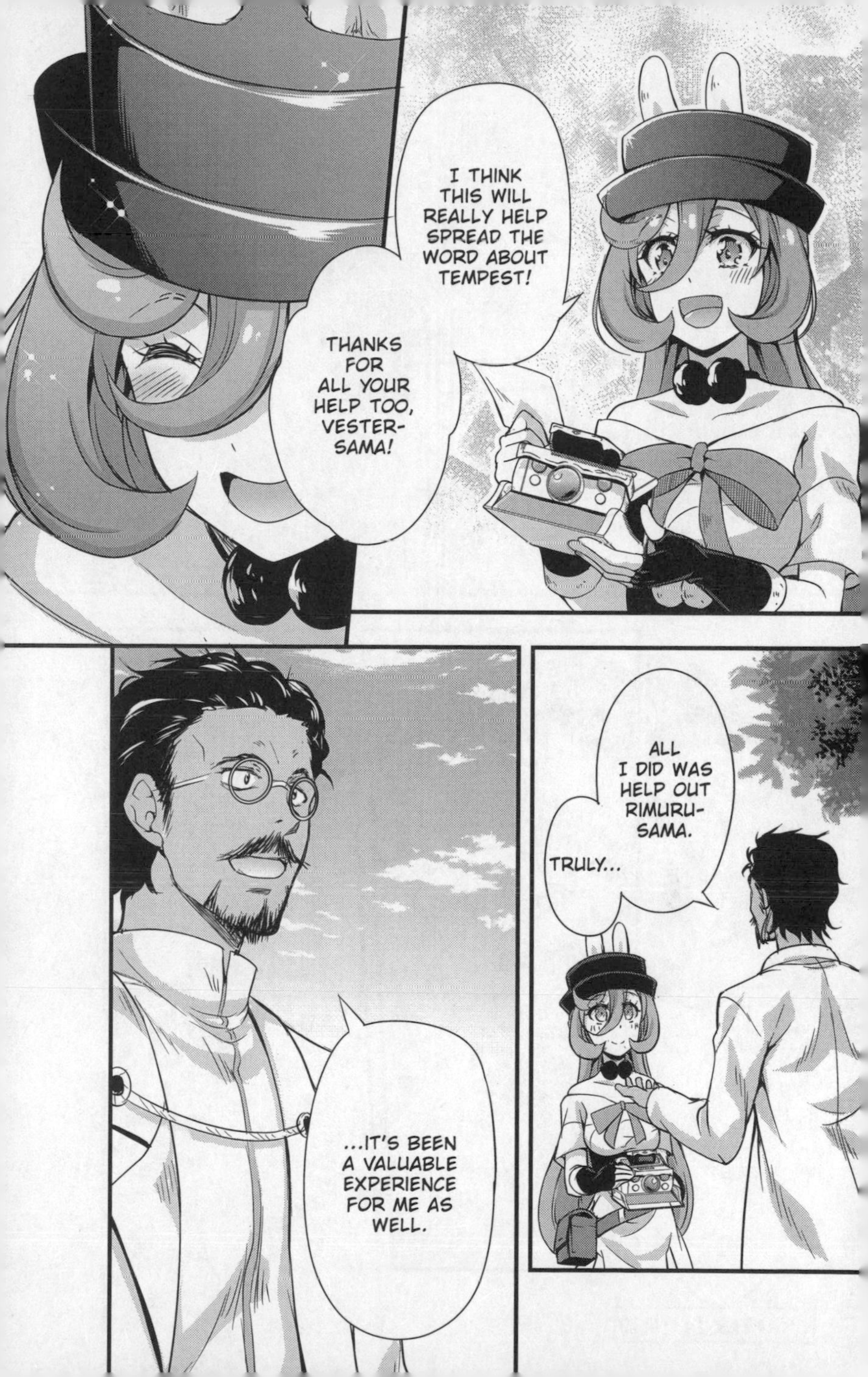
I THINK THIS WILL REALLY HELP SPREAD THE WORD ABOUT TEMPEST!
THANKS FOR ALL YOUR HELP TOO, VESTER-SAMA!
ALL I DID WAS HELP OUT RIMURU-SAMA.
TRULY...
...IT'S BEEN A VALUABLE EXPERIENCE FOR ME AS WELL.

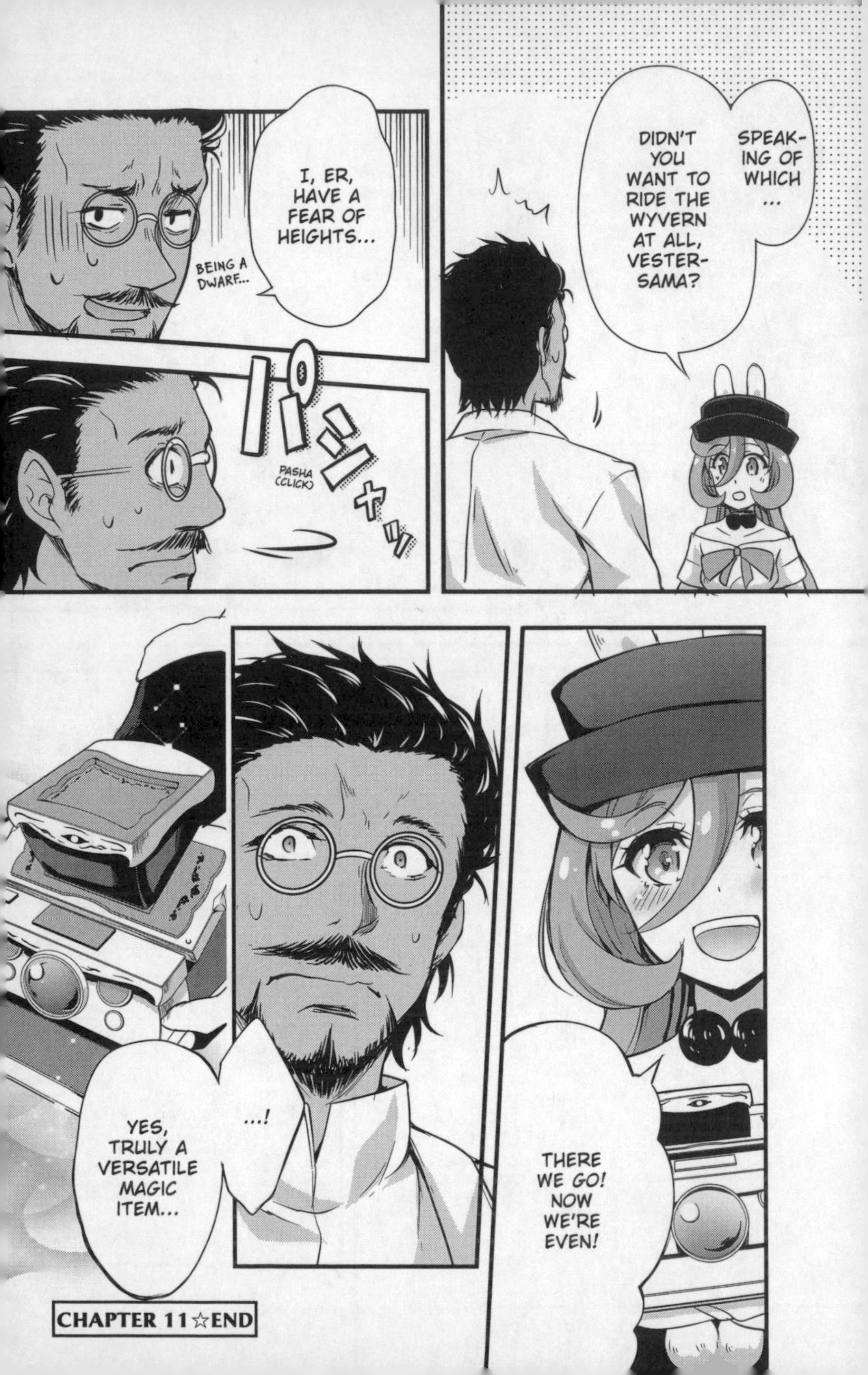
SPEAKING OF WHICH...
DIDN'T YOU WANT TO RIDE THE WYVERN AT ALL, VESTER-SAMA?
I, ER, HAVE A FEAR OF HEIGHTS...
BEING A DWARF...
パシャッ
PASHA (CLICK)
THERE WE GO! NOW WE'RE EVEN!
...!
YES, TRULY A VERSATILE MAGIC ITEM...
CHAPTER 11☆END

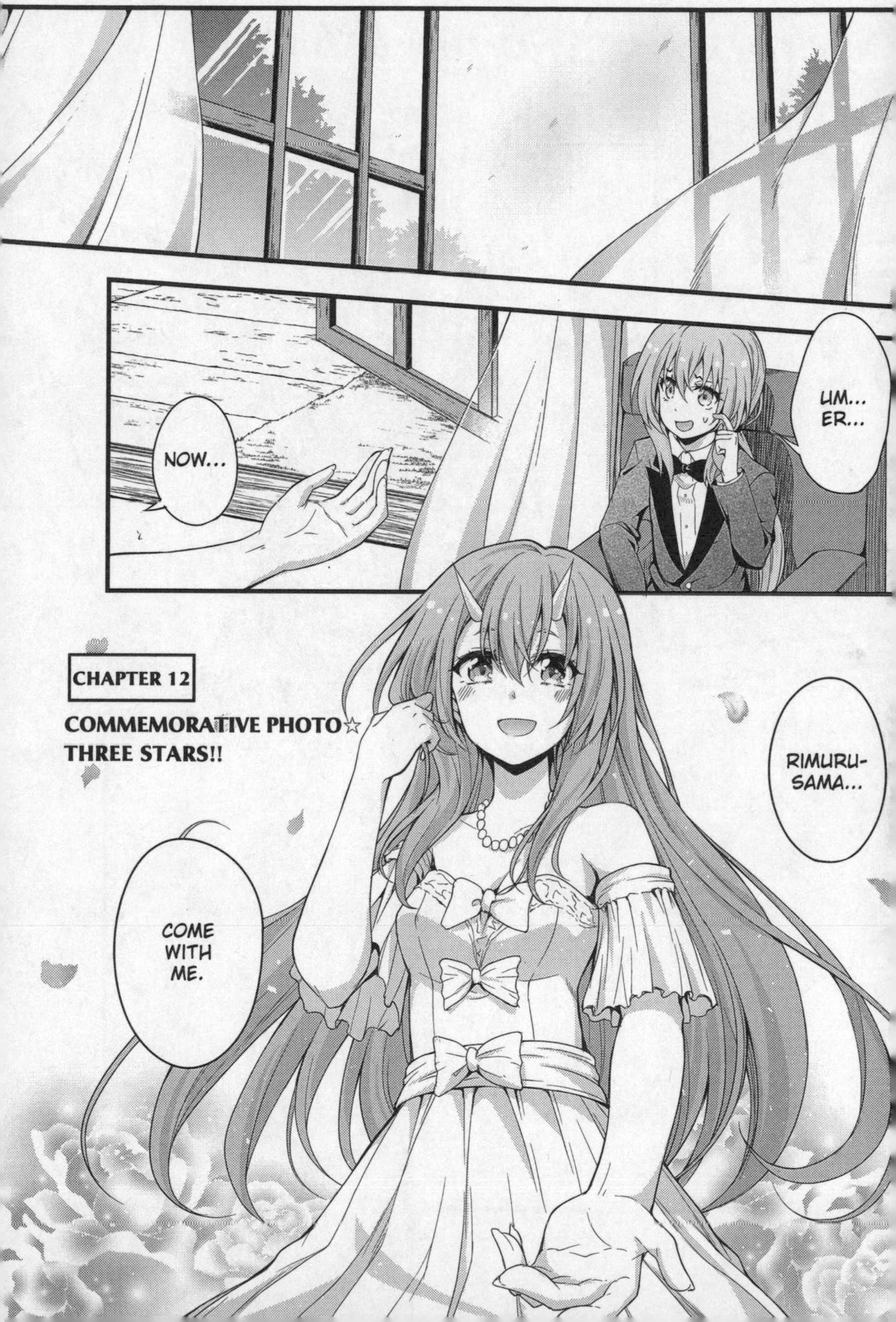
UM... ER...
NOW...
RIMURU-SAMA...
CHAPTER 12
COMMEMORATIVE PHOTO☆ THREE STARS!!
COME WITH ME.

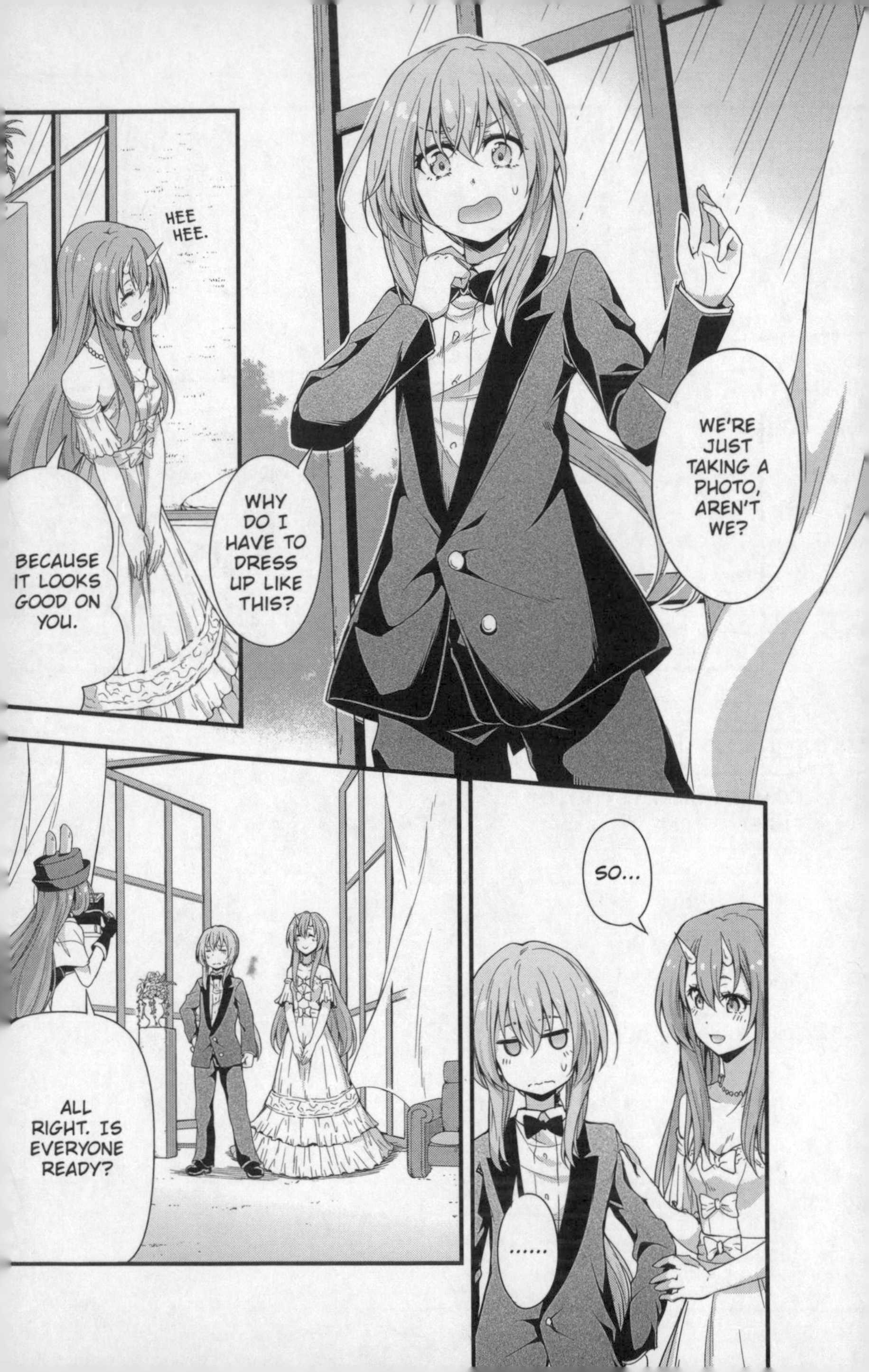
WE'RE JUST TAKING A PHOTO, AREN'T WE?
WHY DO I HAVE TO DRESS UP LIKE THIS?
HEE HEE.
BECAUSE IT LOOKS GOOD ON YOU.
SO...
....
ALL RIGHT. IS EVERYONE READY?

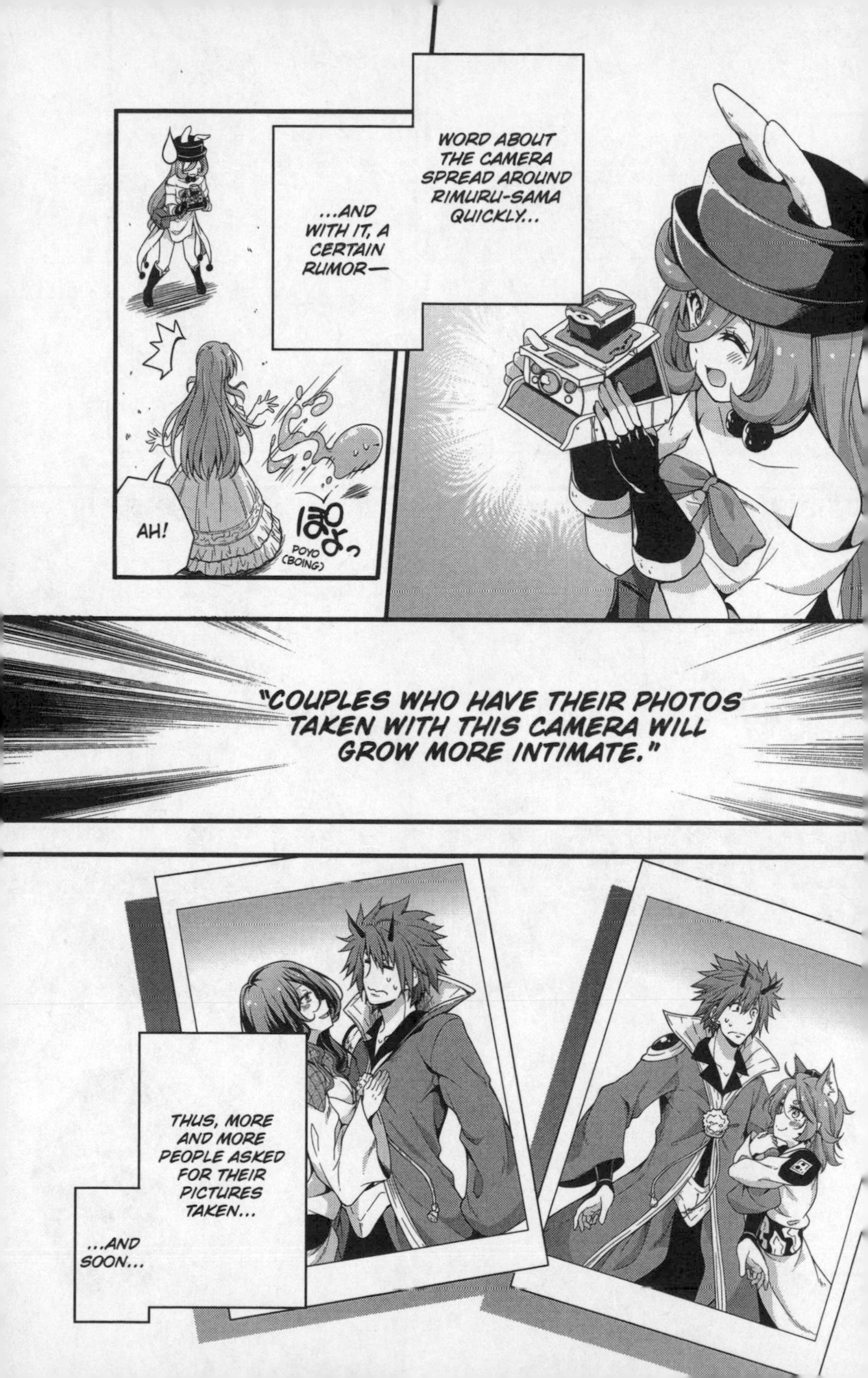
WORD ABOUT THE CAMERA SPREAD AROUND RIMURU-SAMA QUICKLY...
...AND WITH IT, A CERTAIN RUMOR—
AH!
ぽよっ
POYO (BOING)
"COUPLES WHO HAVE THEIR PHOTOS TAKEN WITH THIS CAMERA WILL GROW MORE INTIMATE."
THUS, MORE AND MORE PEOPLE ASKED FOR THEIR PICTURES TAKEN...
...AND SOON...

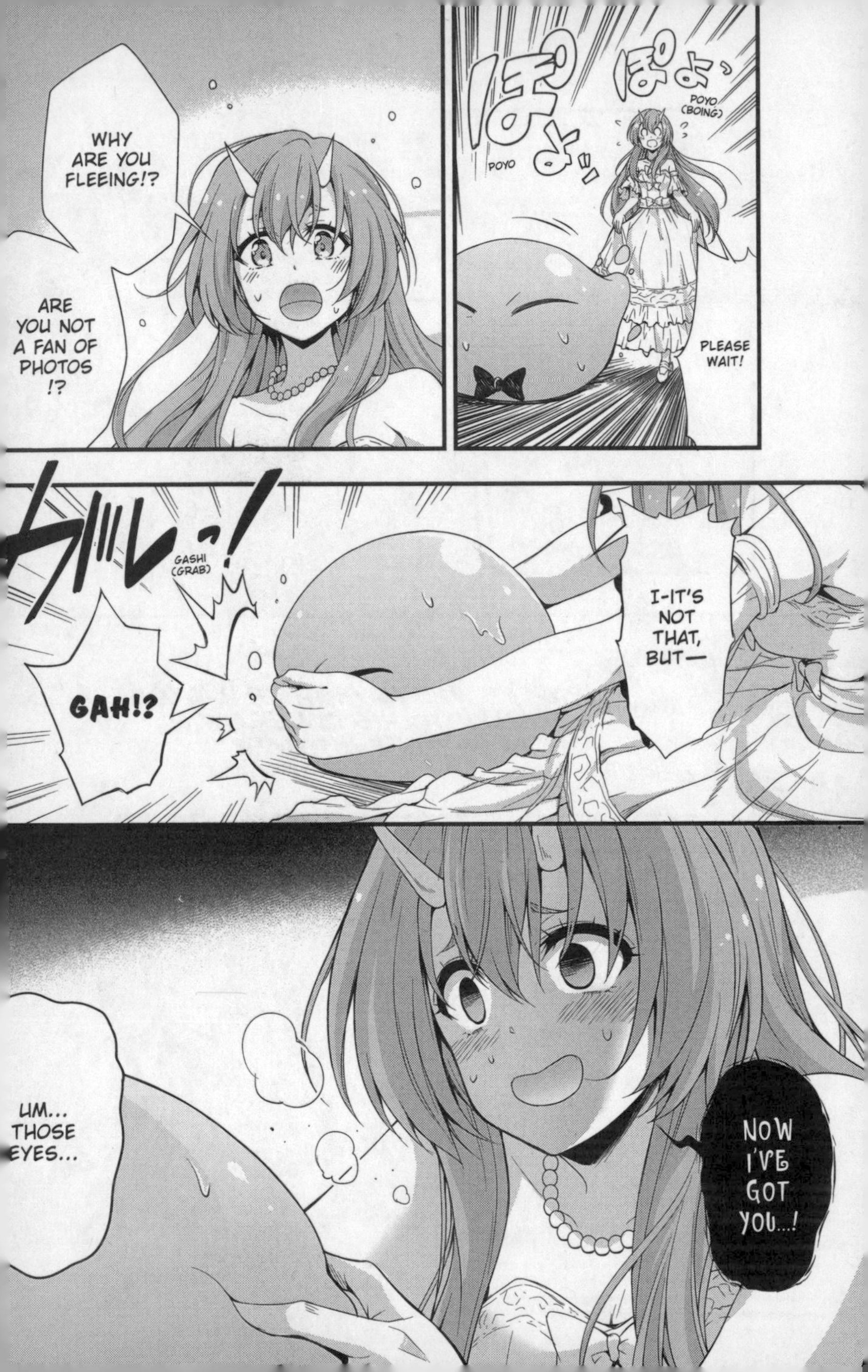

ぽよっ
POYO (BOING)
ぽよっ
POYO
PLEASE WAIT!
WHY ARE YOU FLEEING!?
ARE YOU NOT A FAN OF PHOTOS!?
I-IT'S NOT THAT, BUT—
ガシッ!
GASHI (GRAB)
GAH!?
NOW I'VE GOT YOU...!
UM... THOSE EYES...

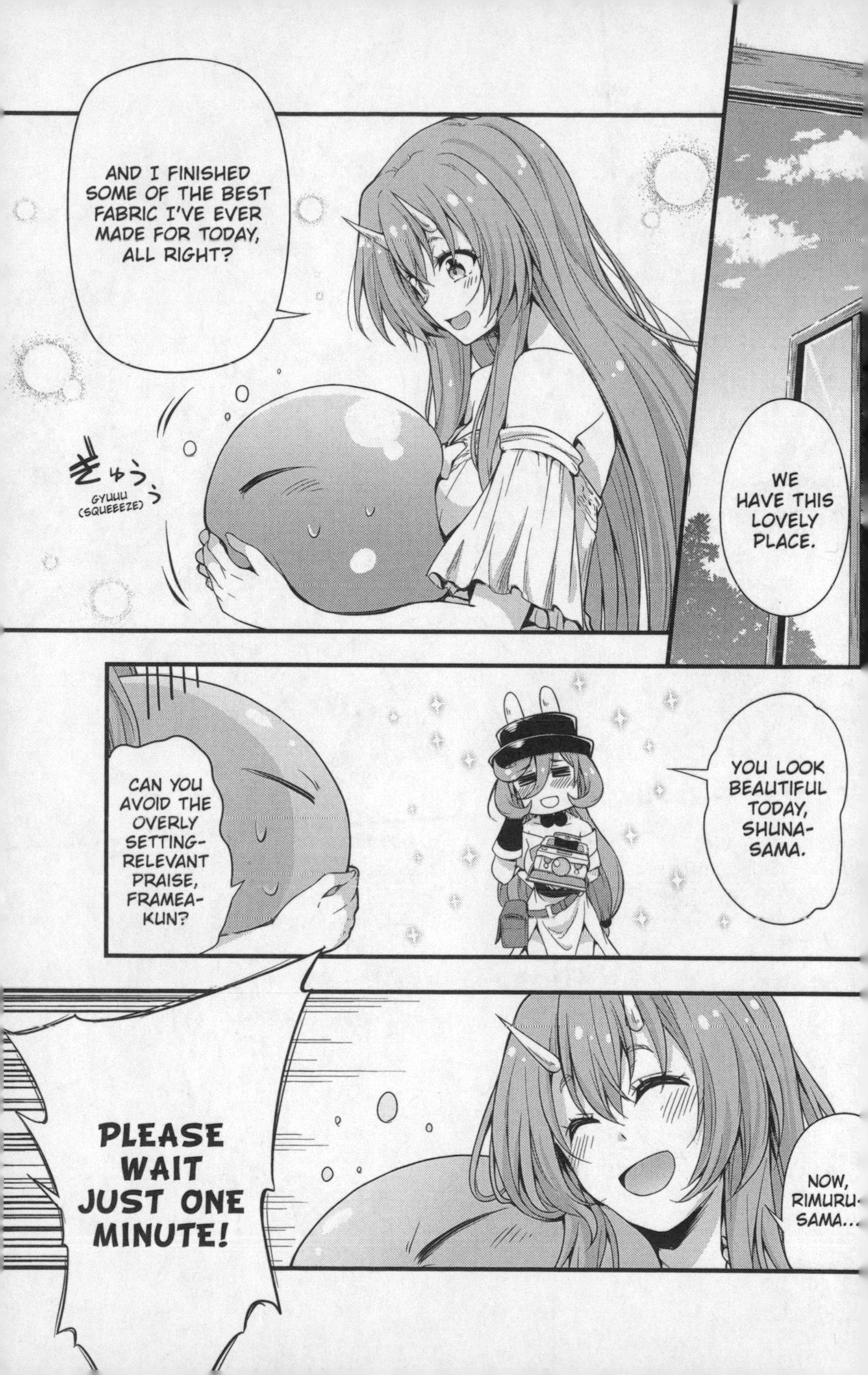
WE HAVE THIS LOVELY PLACE.
AND I FINISHED SOME OF THE BEST FABRIC I'VE EVER MADE FOR TODAY, ALL RIGHT?
ぎゅう
GYUUU (SQUEEEZE)
YOU LOOK BEAUTIFUL TODAY, SHUNA-SAMA.
CAN YOU AVOID THE OVERLY SETTING-RELEVANT PRAISE, FRAMEA-KUN?
NOW, RIMURU-SAMA...
PLEASE WAIT JUST ONE MINUTE!

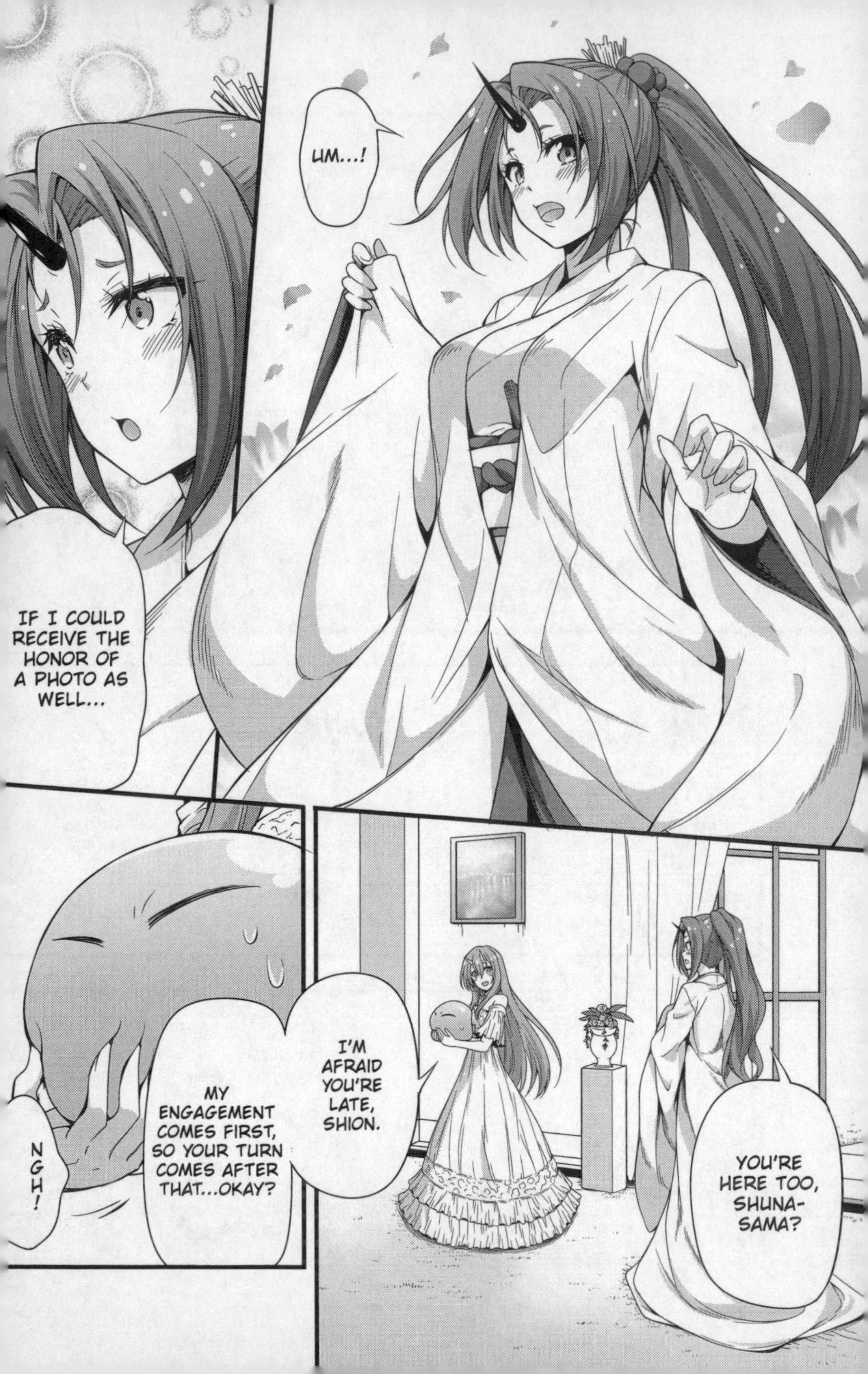
UM...!
IF I COULD RECEIVE THE HONOR OF A PHOTO AS WELL...
YOU'RE HERE TOO, SHUNA-SAMA?
I'M AFRAID YOU'RE LATE, SHION.
MY ENGAGEMENT COMES FIRST, SO YOUR TURN COMES AFTER THAT...OKAY?
NGH!

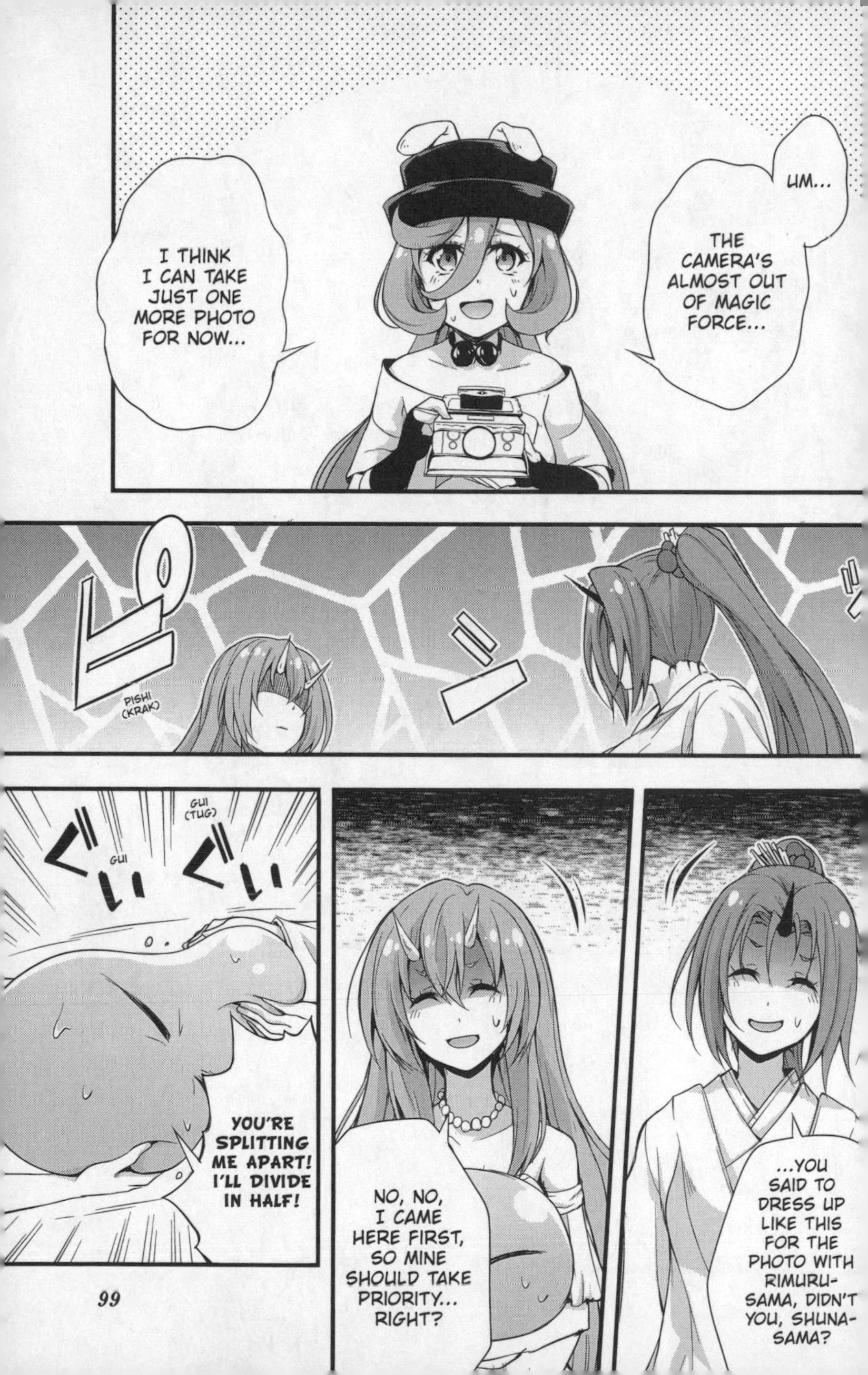

UM...
THE CAMERA'S ALMOST OUT OF MAGIC FORCE...
I THINK I CAN TAKE JUST ONE MORE PHOTO FOR NOW...
PISHI (KRAK)
...YOU SAID TO DRESS UP LIKE THIS FOR THE PHOTO WITH RIMURU-SAMA, DIDN'T YOU, SHUNA-SAMA?
NO, NO, I CAME HERE FIRST, SO MINE SHOULD TAKE PRIORITY... RIGHT?
GUI (TUG)
GUI
YOU'RE SPLITTING ME APART! I'LL DIVIDE IN HALF!

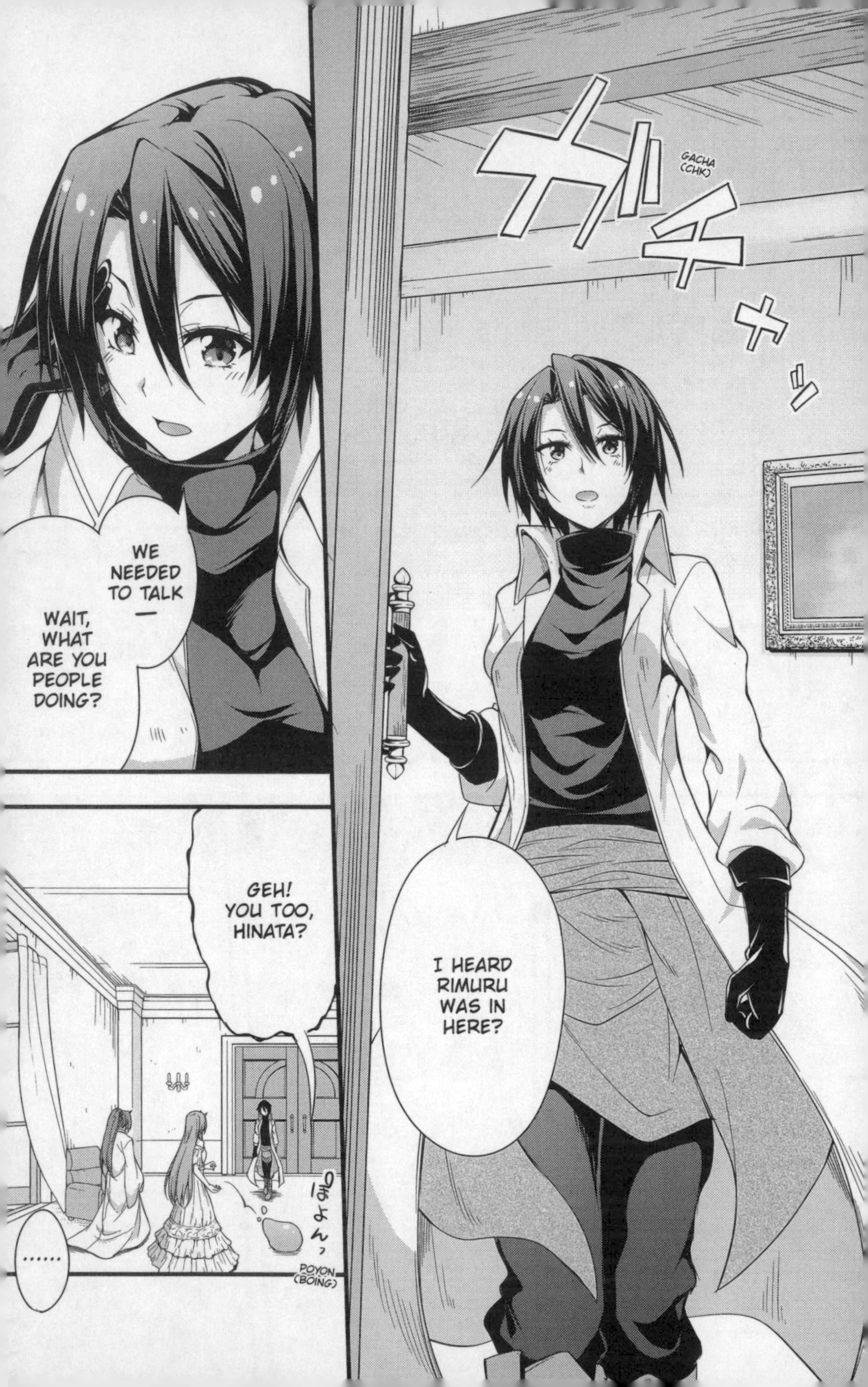
GACHA (CHK)
I HEARD RIMURU WAS IN HERE?
WE NEEDED TO TALK— WAIT, WHAT ARE YOU PEOPLE DOING?
GEH! YOU TOO, HINATA?
POYON (BOING)
......

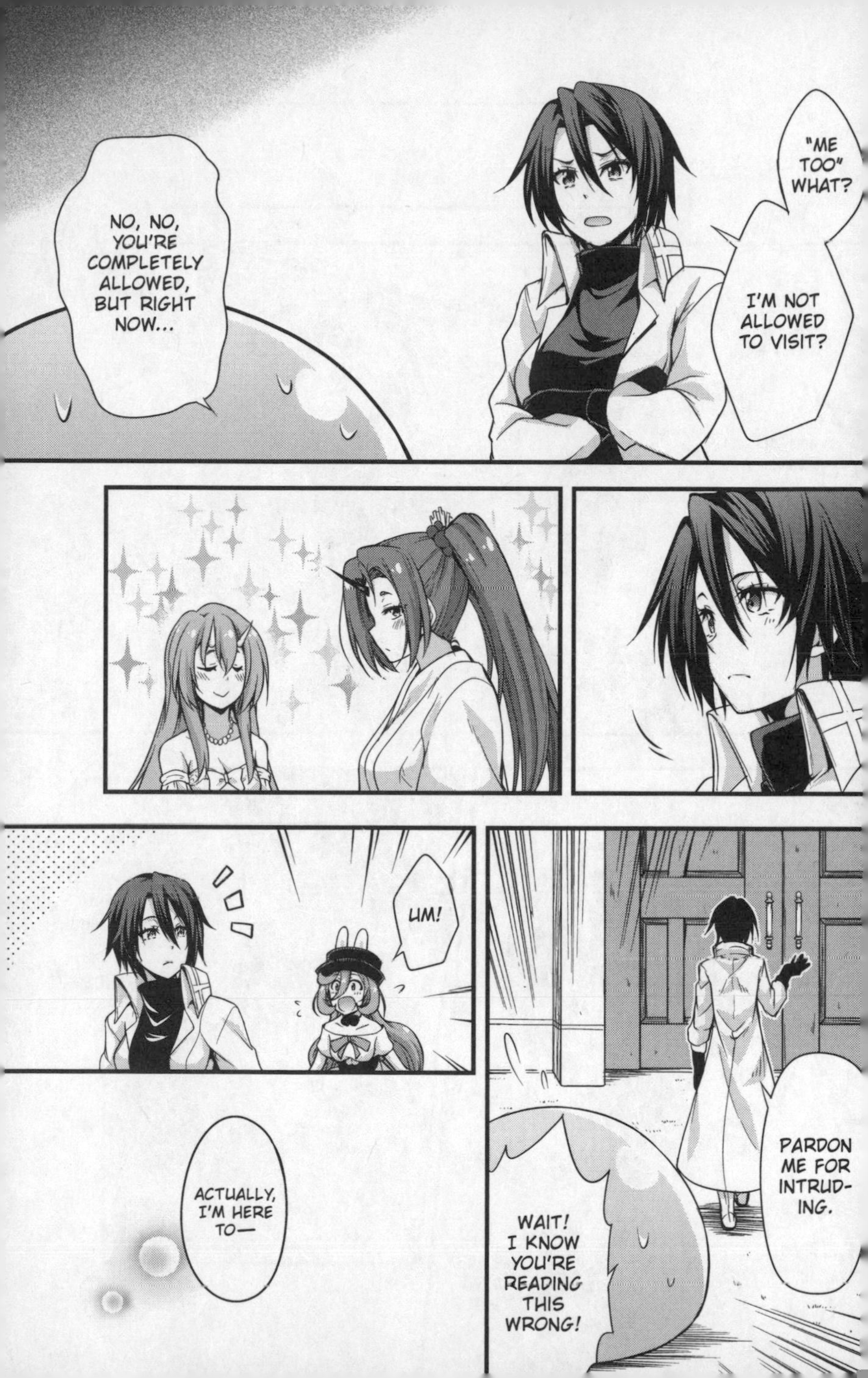
"ME TOO" WHAT?
I'M NOT ALLOWED TO VISIT?
NO, NO, YOU'RE COMPLETELY ALLOWED, BUT RIGHT NOW...
PARDON ME FOR INTRUD-ING.
WAIT! I KNOW YOU'RE READING THIS WRONG!
UM!
ACTUALLY, I'M HERE TO—

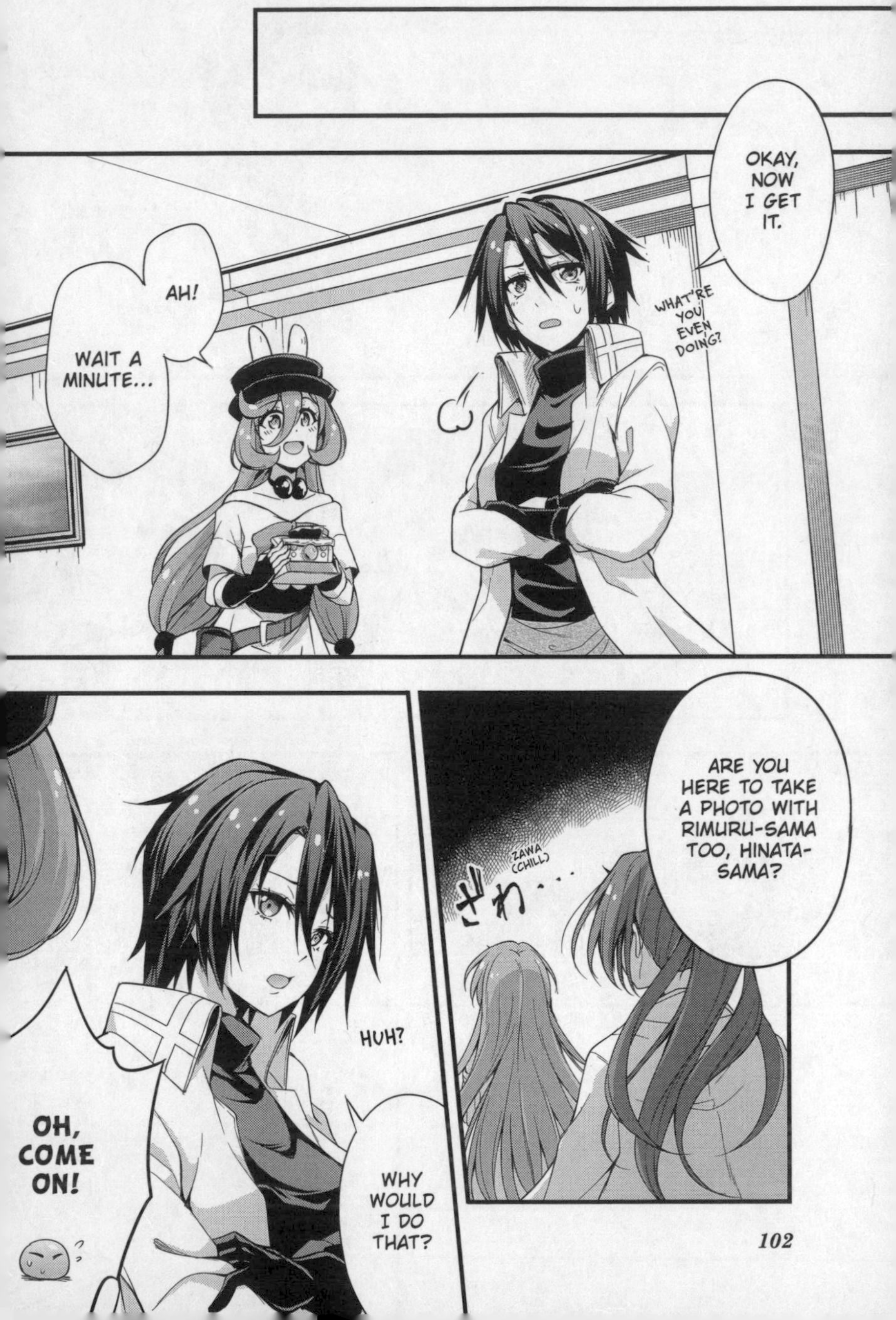
OKAY, NOW I GET IT.
WHAT'RE YOU EVEN DOING?
AH!
WAIT A MINUTE...
ARE YOU HERE TO TAKE A PHOTO WITH RIMURU-SAMA TOO, HINATA-SAMA?
ZAWA (CHILL)
HUH?
WHY WOULD I DO THAT?
OH, COME ON!

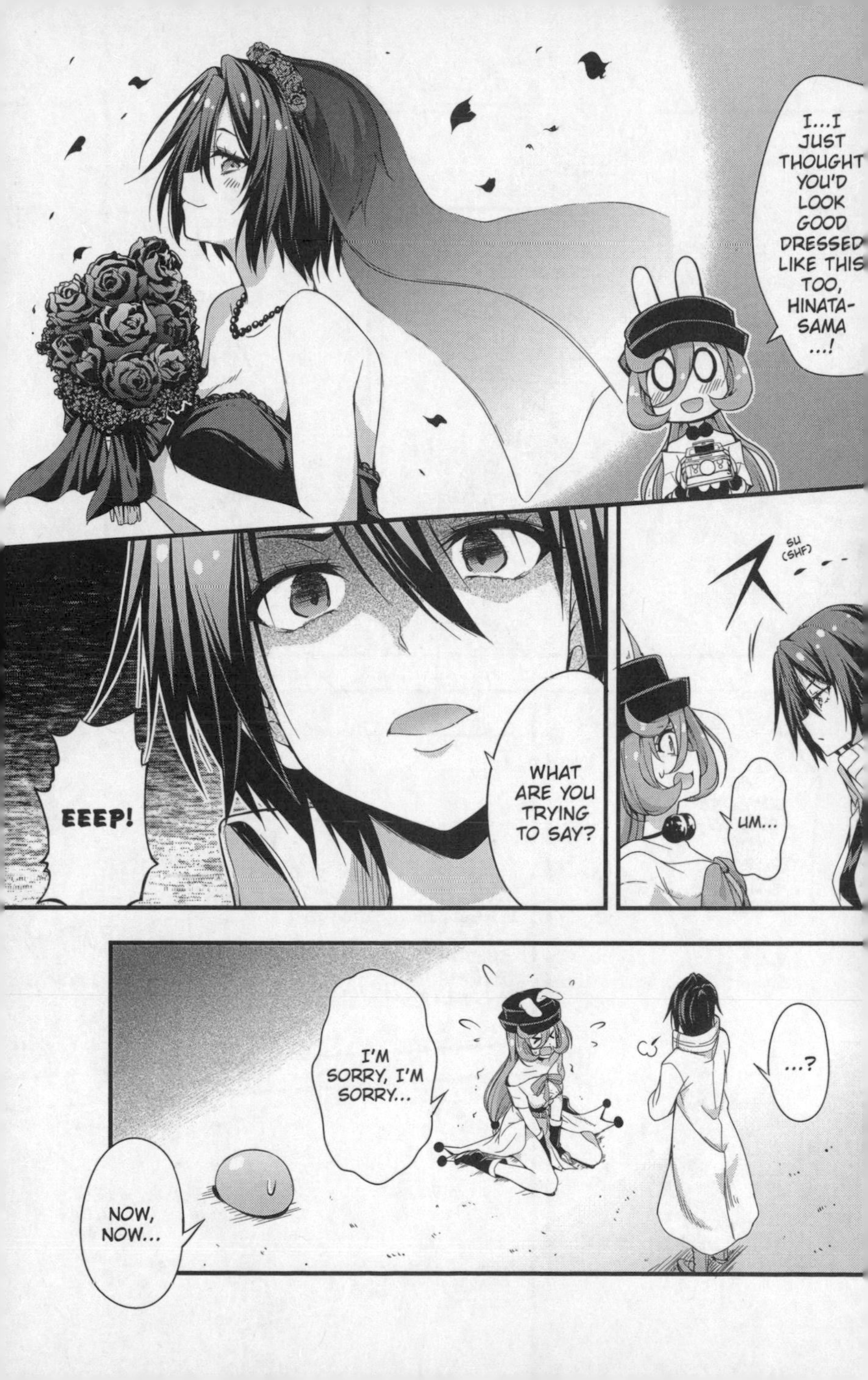
I...I JUST THOUGHT YOU'D LOOK GOOD DRESSED LIKE THIS TOO, HINATA-SAMA ...!
SU (SHF)
UM...
WHAT ARE YOU TRYING TO SAY?
EEEP!
...?
I'M SORRY, I'M SORRY...
NOW, NOW...

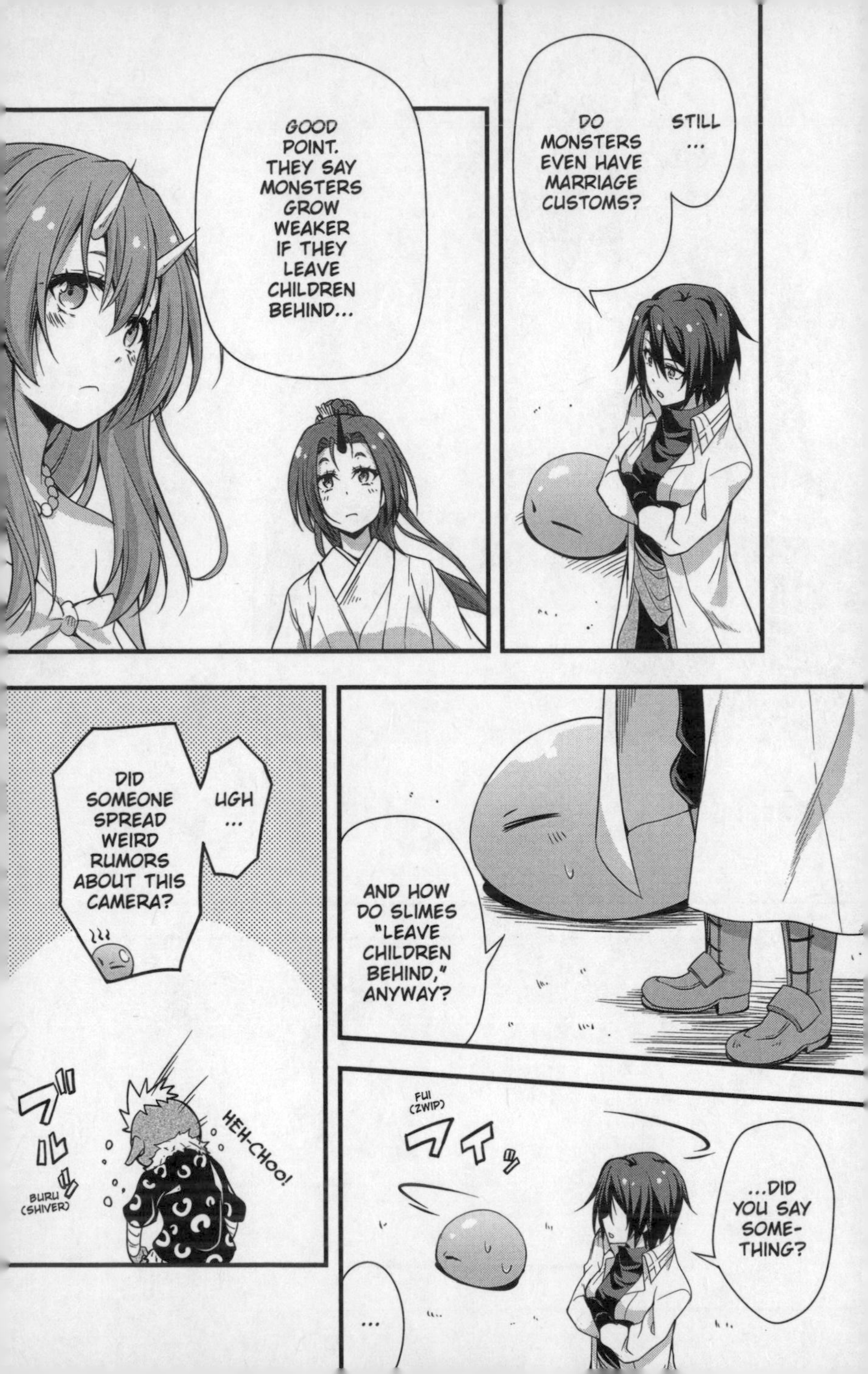
STILL ...
DO MONSTERS EVEN HAVE MARRIAGE CUSTOMS?
GOOD POINT. THEY SAY MONSTERS GROW WEAKER IF THEY LEAVE CHILDREN BEHIND...
AND HOW DO SLIMES "LEAVE CHILDREN BEHIND," ANYWAY?
FUI (ZWIP)
...DID YOU SAY SOME-THING?
...
UGH ...
DID SOMEONE SPREAD WEIRD RUMORS ABOUT THIS CAMERA?
HEH-CHOO!
BURU (SHIVER)

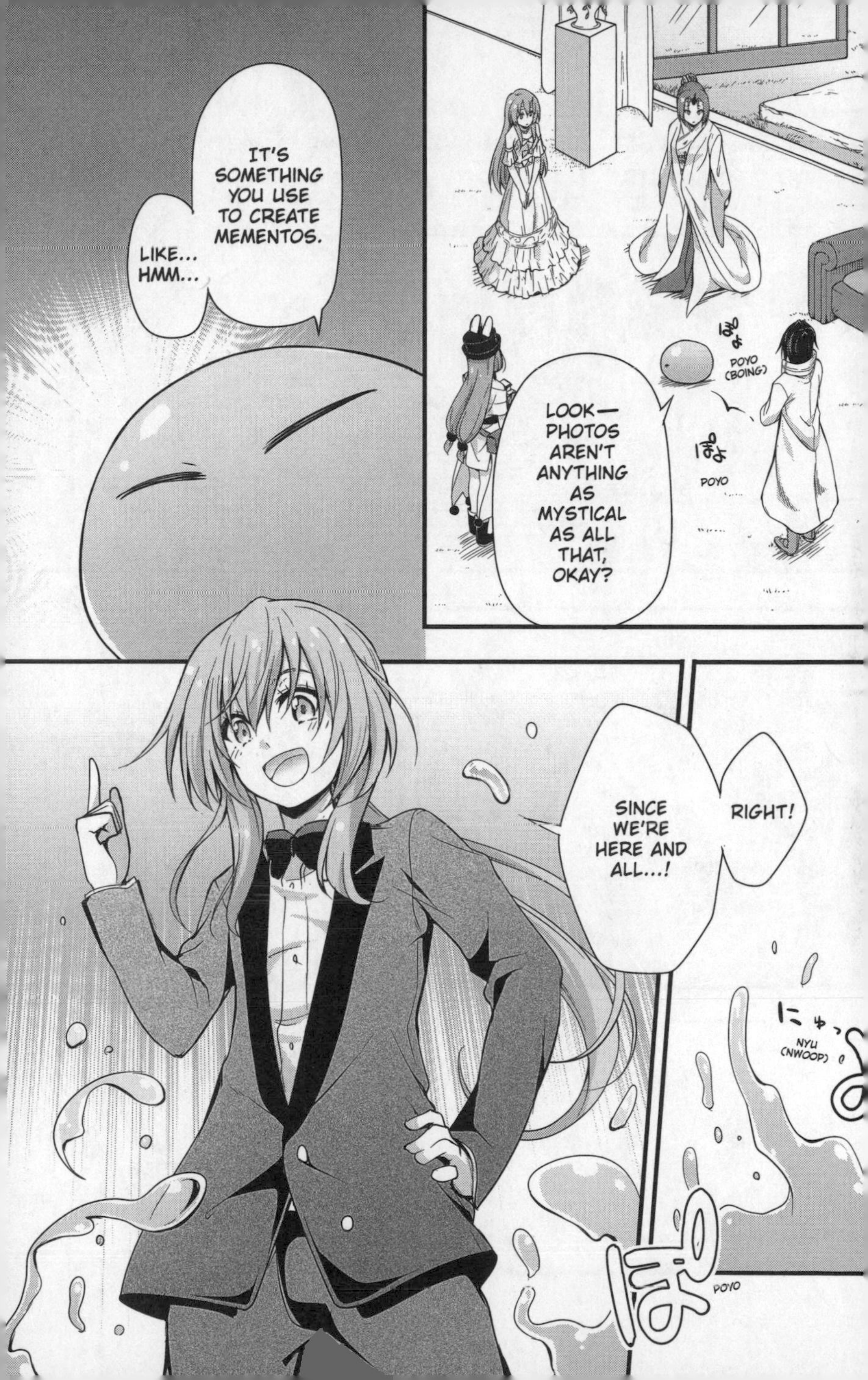
ぽよ
POYO (BOING)
LOOK—PHOTOS AREN'T ANYTHING AS MYSTICAL AS ALL THAT, OKAY?
ぽよ
POYO
IT'S SOMETHING YOU USE TO CREATE MEMENTOS.
LIKE... HMM...
にゅっ
NYU (NWOOP)
RIGHT!
SINCE WE'RE HERE AND ALL...!
ぽ
POYO

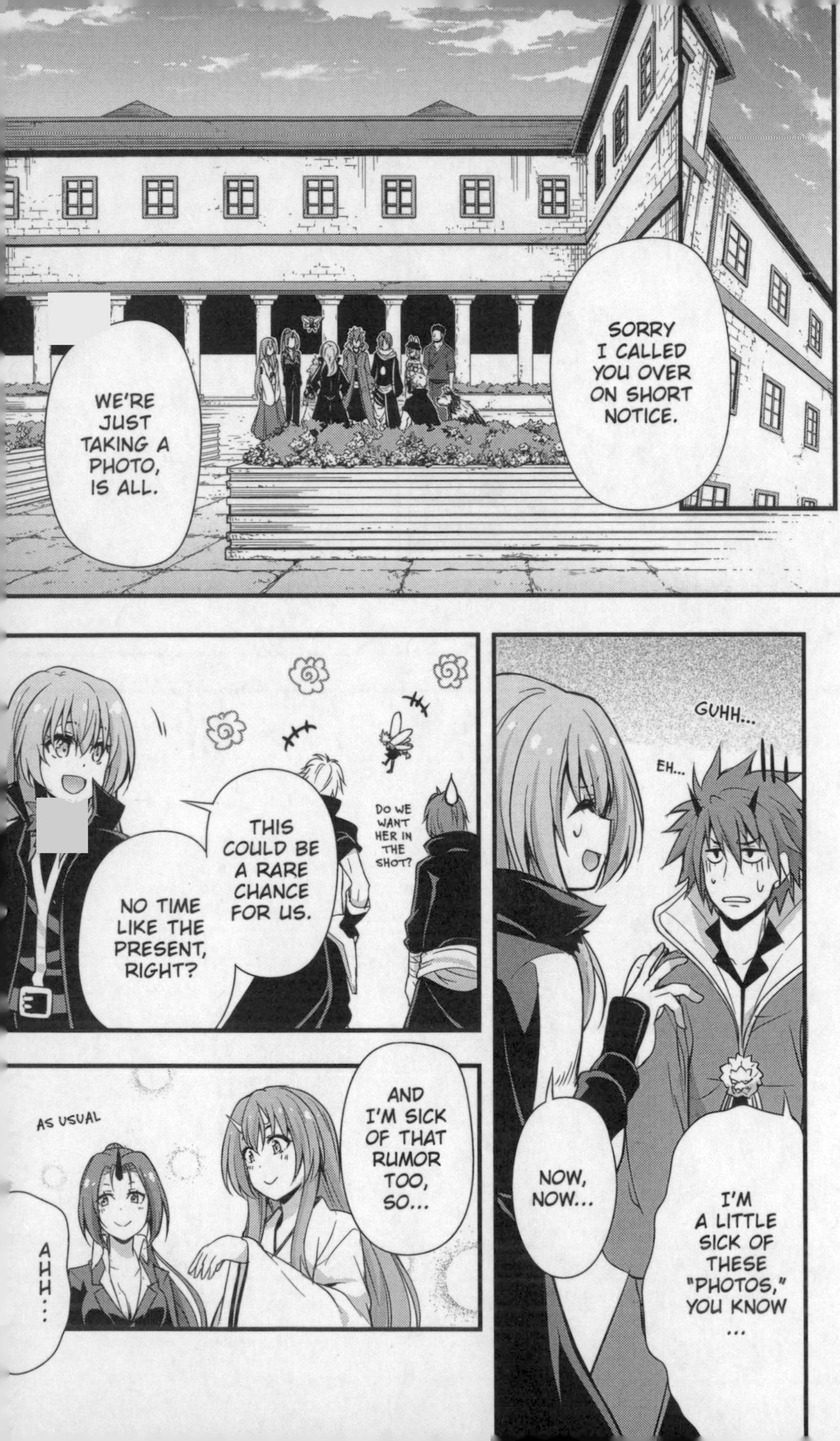
SORRY I CALLED YOU OVER ON SHORT NOTICE.
WE'RE JUST TAKING A PHOTO, IS ALL.
GUHH...
EH...
I'M A LITTLE SICK OF THESE "PHOTOS," YOU KNOW...
NOW, NOW...
DO WE WANT HER IN THE SHOT?
THIS COULD BE A RARE CHANCE FOR US.
NO TIME LIKE THE PRESENT, RIGHT?
AND I'M SICK OF THAT RUMOR TOO, SO...
AS USUAL
AHH...

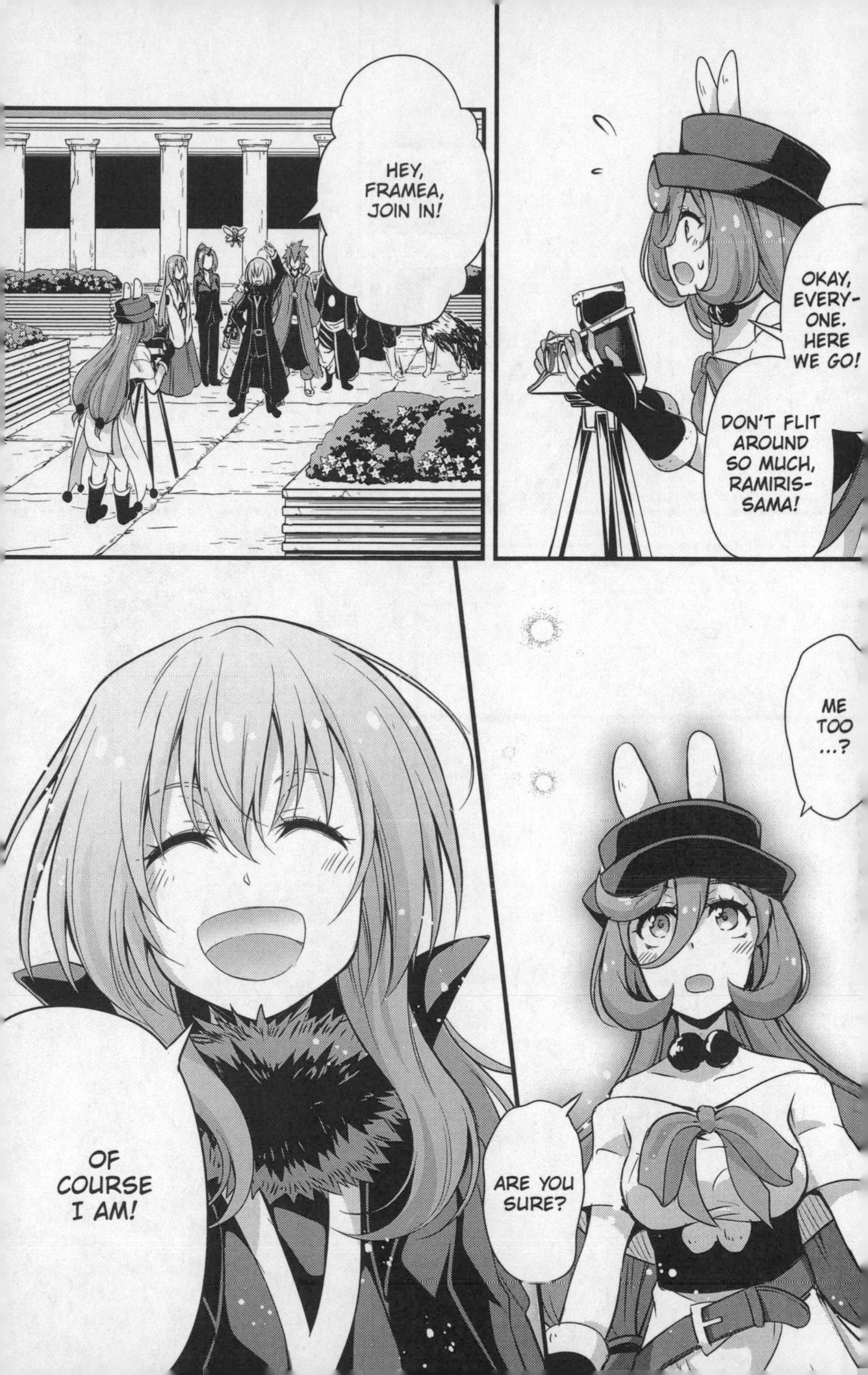
OKAY, EVERYONE. HERE WE GO!
DON'T FLIT AROUND SO MUCH, RAMIRIS-SAMA!
HEY, FRAMEA, JOIN IN!
ME TOO ...?
ARE YOU SURE?
OF COURSE I AM!

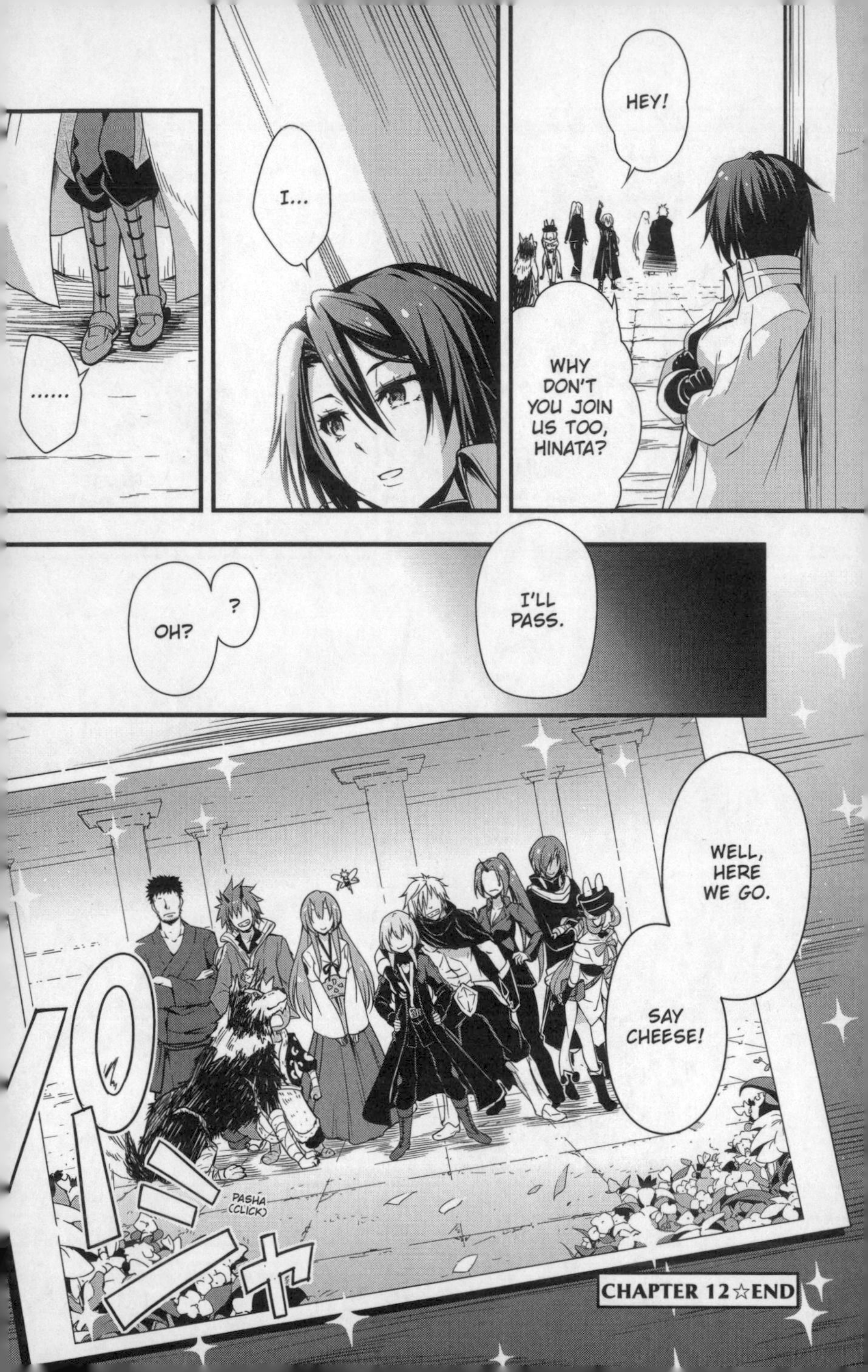
HEY!
WHY DON'T YOU JOIN US TOO, HINATA?
I...
......
I'LL PASS.
?
OH?
WELL, HERE WE GO.
SAY CHEESE!
PASHA (CLICK)
CHAPTER 12☆END

That Time I Got Reincarnated as a SLIME
The Ways of the Monster Nation

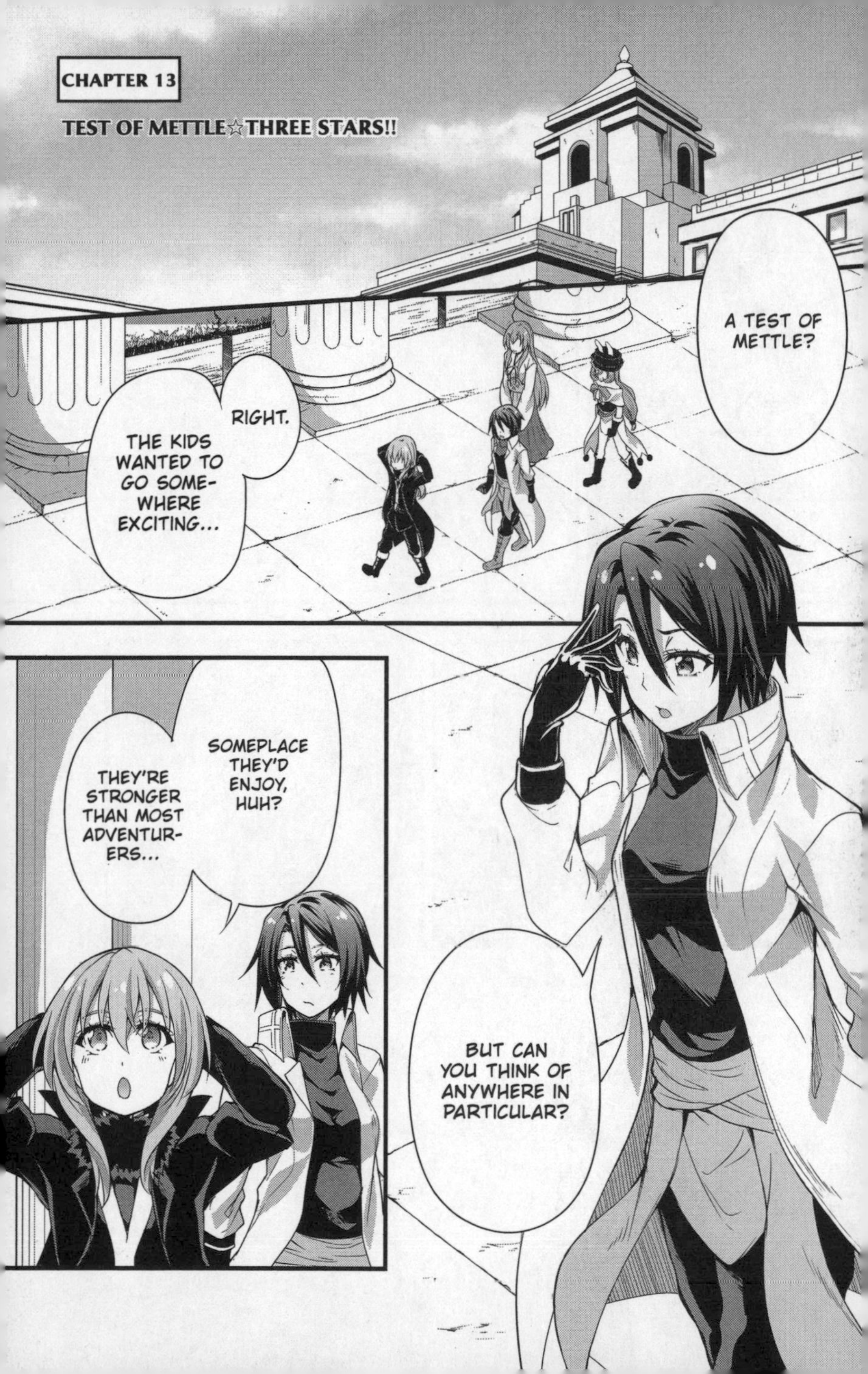
CHAPTER 13
TEST OF METTLE☆THREE STARS!!
A TEST OF METTLE?
RIGHT.
THE KIDS WANTED TO GO SOMEWHERE EXCITING...
SOMEPLACE THEY'D ENJOY, HUH?
THEY'RE STRONGER THAN MOST ADVENTURERS...
BUT CAN YOU THINK OF ANYWHERE IN PARTICULAR?

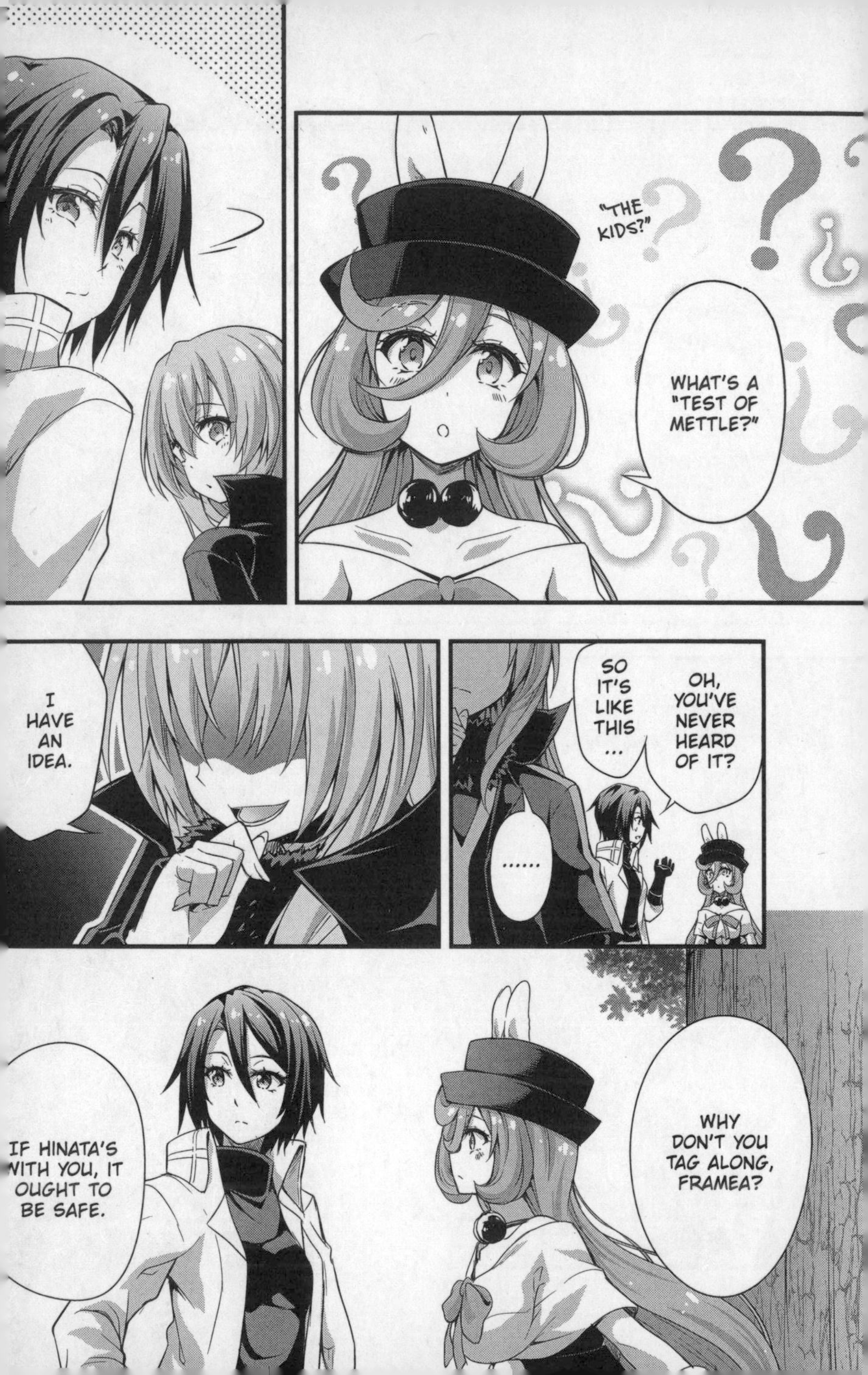
"THE KIDS?"
WHAT'S A "TEST OF METTLE?"
OH, YOU'VE NEVER HEARD OF IT?
SO IT'S LIKE THIS...
......
I HAVE AN IDEA.
WHY DON'T YOU TAG ALONG, FRAMEA?
IF HINATA'S WITH YOU, IT OUGHT TO BE SAFE.

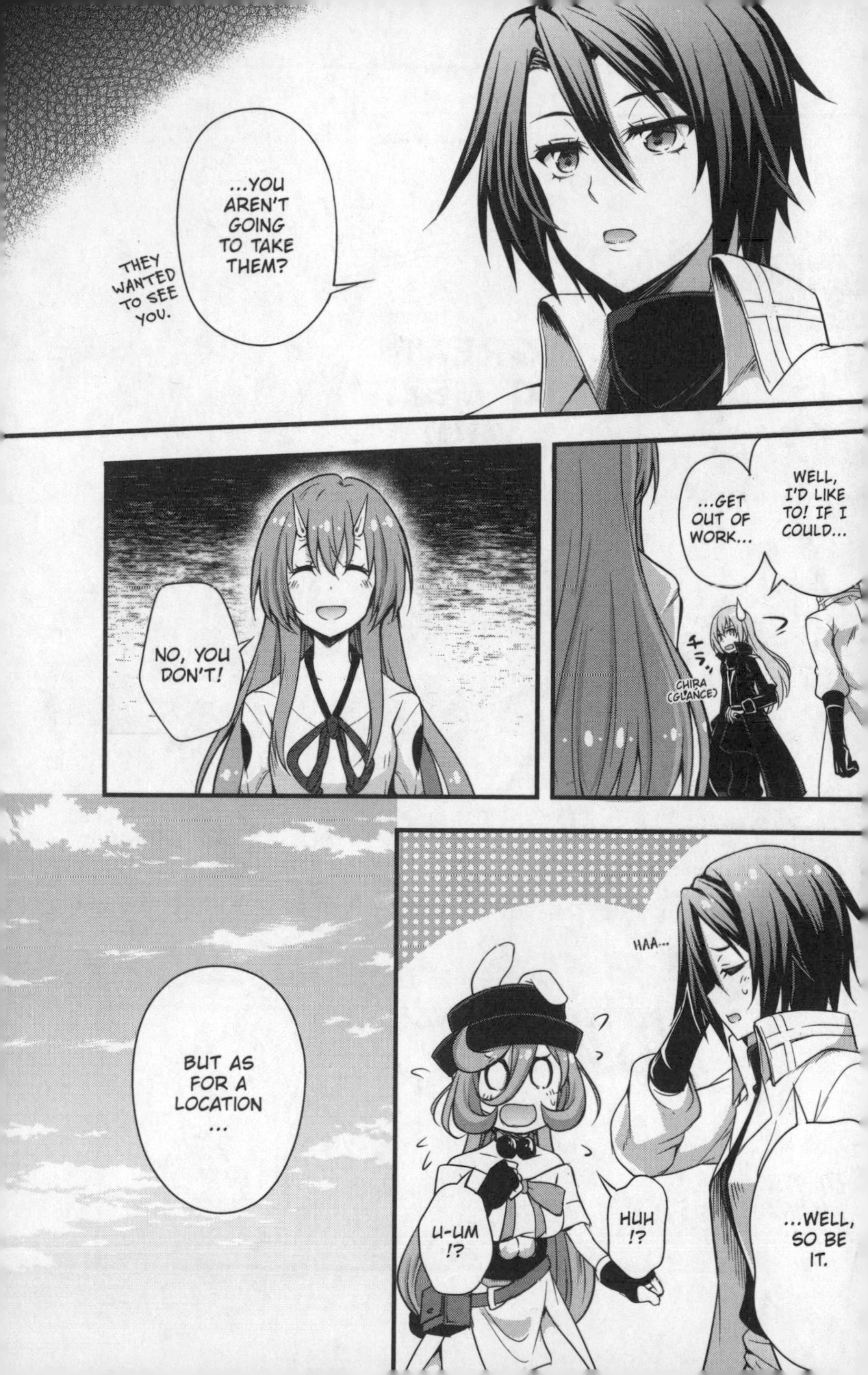
...YOU AREN'T GOING TO TAKE THEM?
THEY WANTED TO SEE YOU.
WELL, I'D LIKE TO! IF I COULD...
...GET OUT OF WORK...
チラッ
CHIRA (GLANCE)
NO, YOU DON'T!
HAA...
...WELL, SO BE IT.
HUH !?
U-UM !?
BUT AS FOR A LOCATION ...

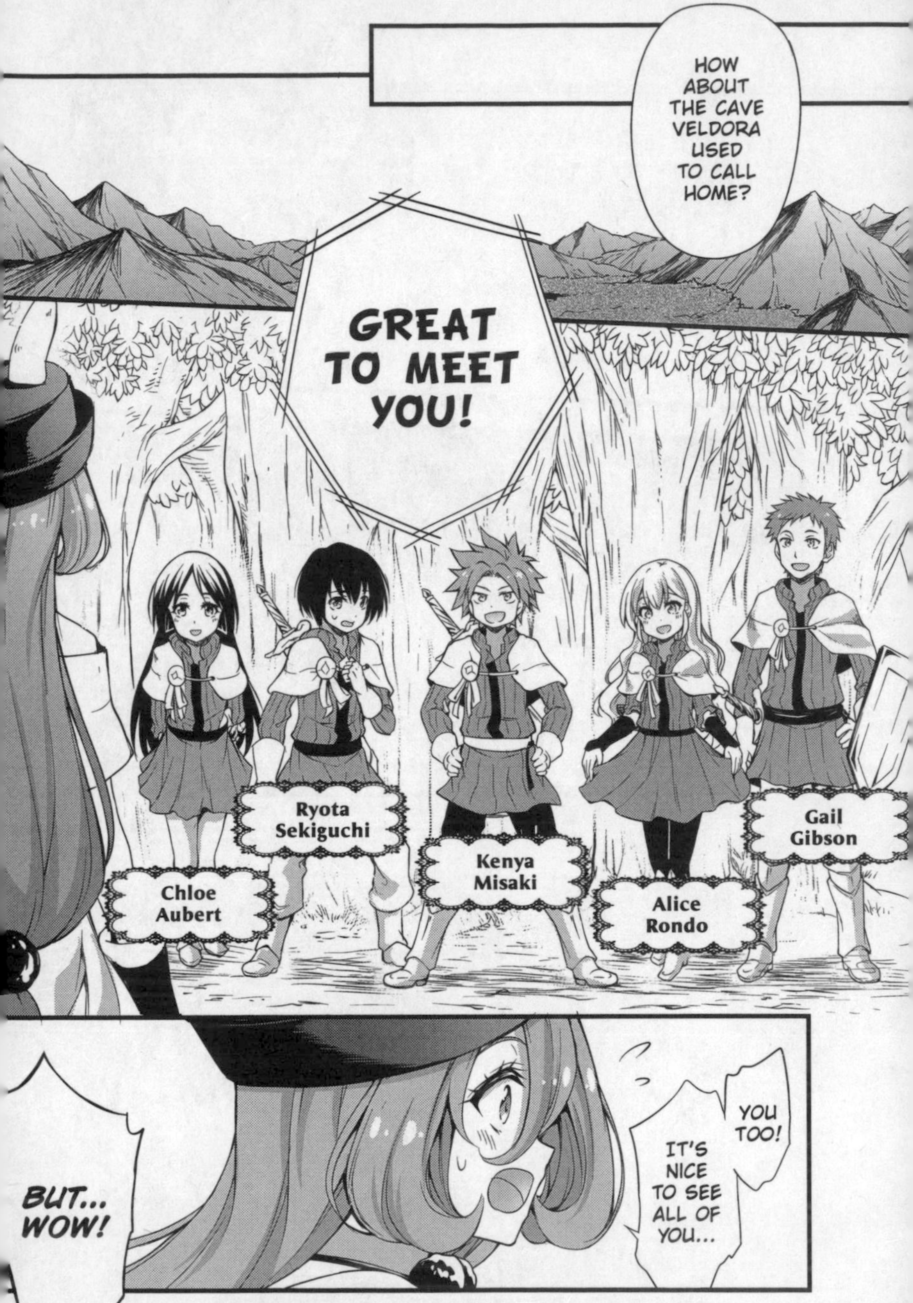
HOW ABOUT THE CAVE VELDORA USED TO CALL HOME?
GREAT TO MEET YOU!
Gail Gibson
Alice Rondo
Kenya Misaki
Ryota Sekiguchi
Chloe Aubert
YOU TOO!
IT'S NICE TO SEE ALL OF YOU...
BUT... WOW!

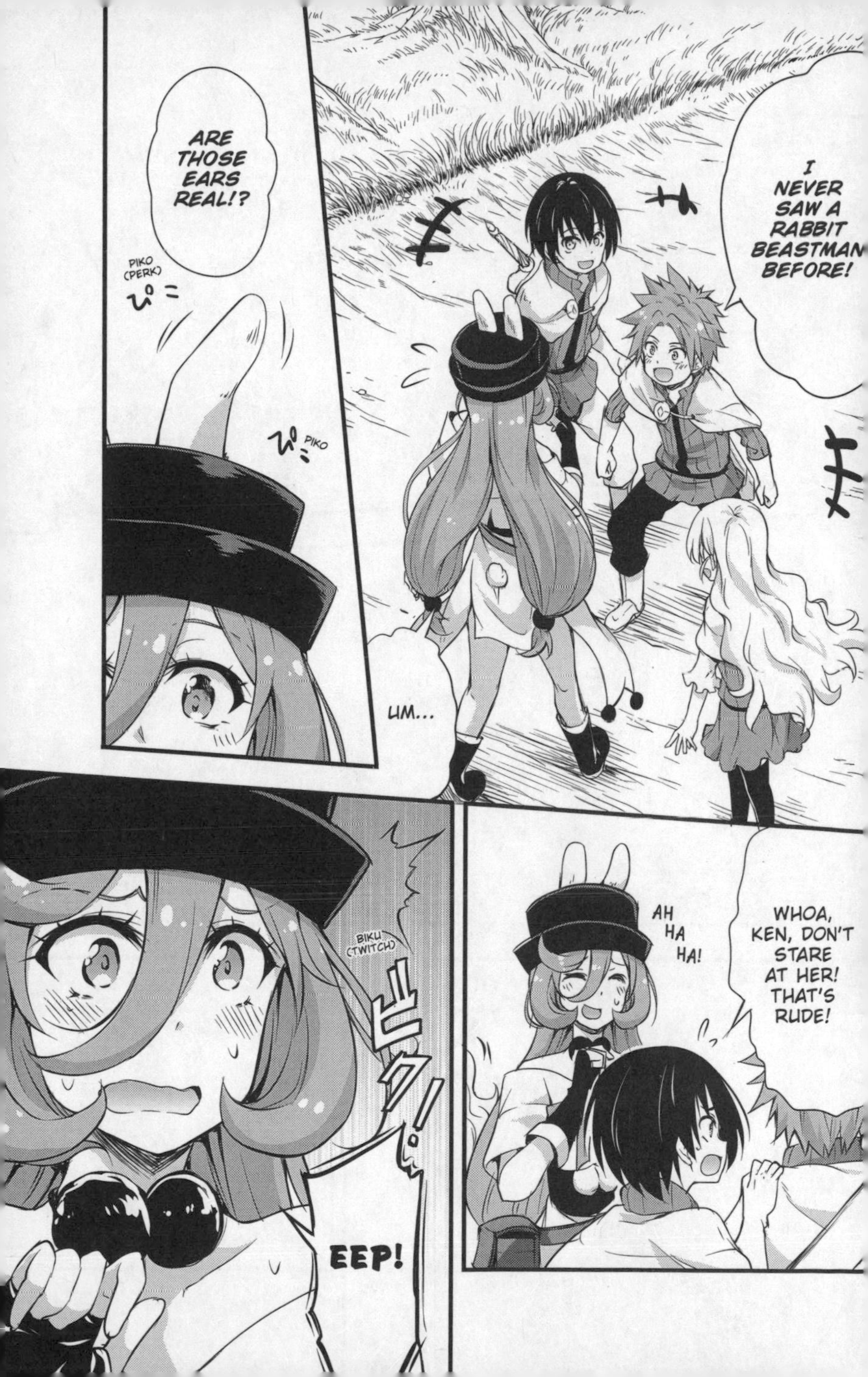
I NEVER SAW A RABBIT BEASTMAN BEFORE!
UM...
ARE THOSE EARS REAL!?
PIKO (PERK)
ぴ=
ぴ=
PIKO
WHOA, KEN, DON'T STARE AT HER! THAT'S RUDE!
AH HA HA!
BIKU (TWITCH)
ビクッ!
EEP!

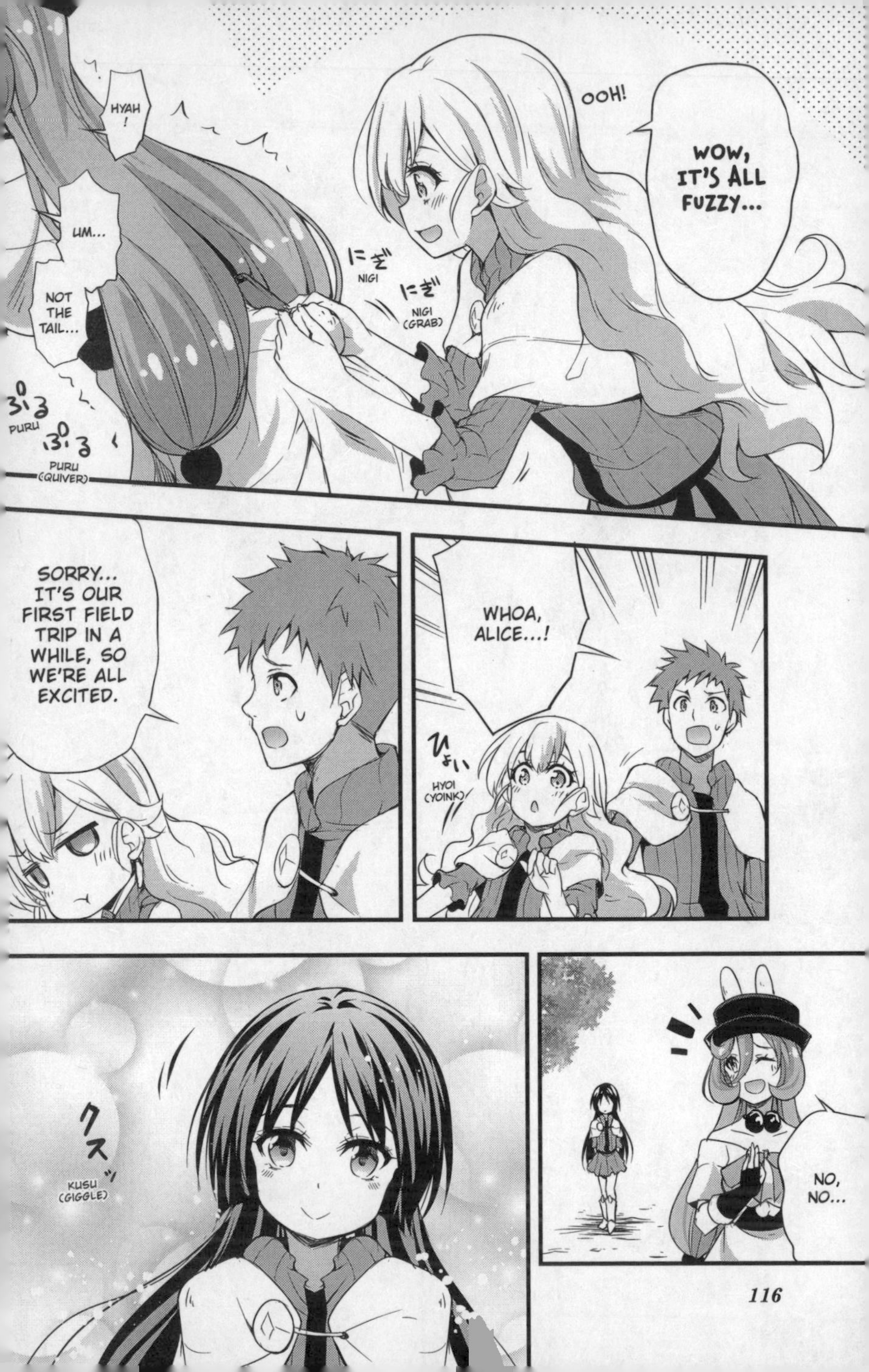
OOH!
WOW, IT'S ALL FUZZY...
にぎ
NIGI
にぎ
NIGI (GRAB)
HYAH!
UM...
NOT THE TAIL...
ぷる
PURU
ぷる
PURU (QUIVER)
WHOA, ALICE...!
ひょい
HYOI (YOINK)
SORRY... IT'S OUR FIRST FIELD TRIP IN A WHILE, SO WE'RE ALL EXCITED.
NO, NO...
クスッ
KUSU (GIGGLE)

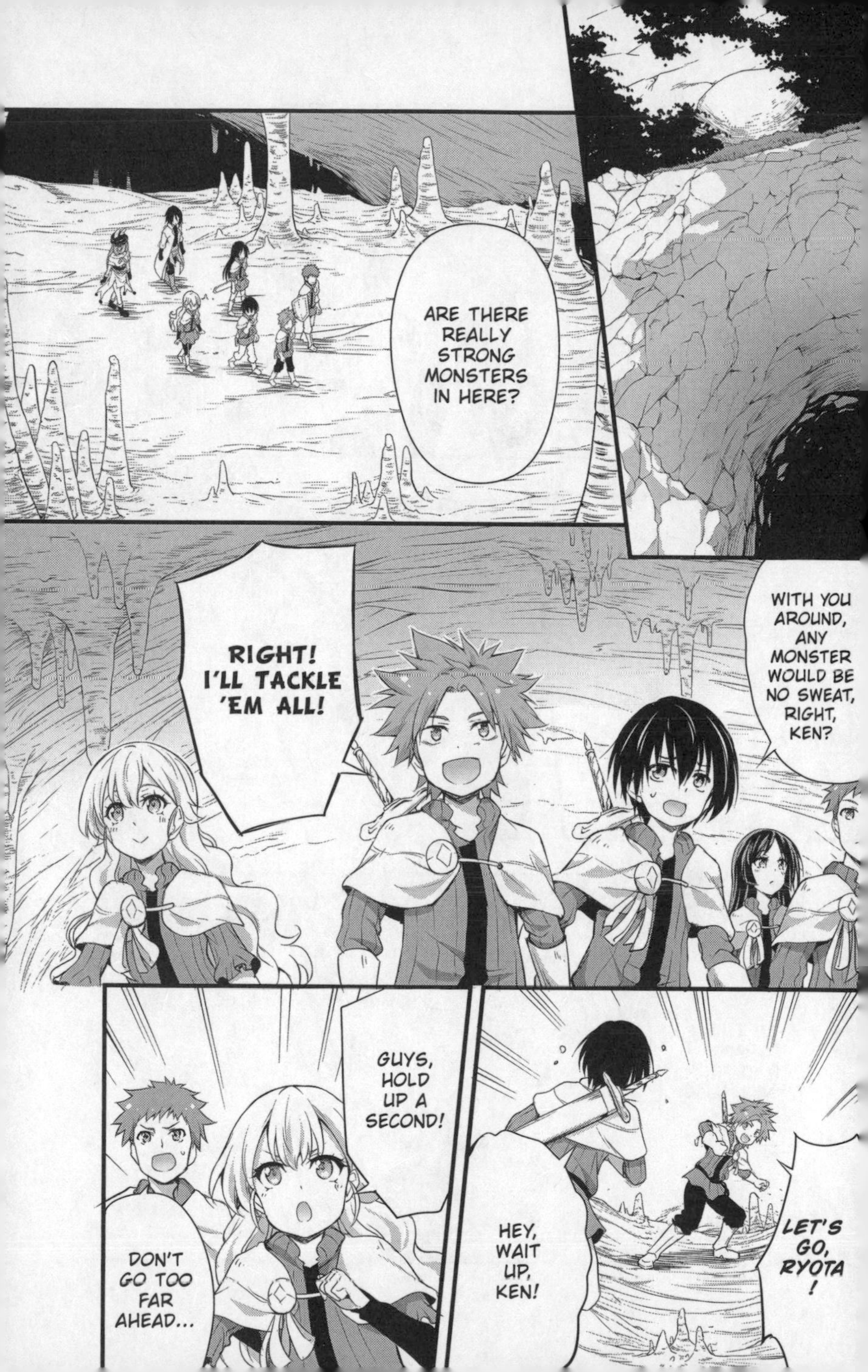
ARE THERE REALLY STRONG MONSTERS IN HERE?
WITH YOU AROUND, ANY MONSTER WOULD BE NO SWEAT, RIGHT, KEN?
RIGHT! I'LL TACKLE 'EM ALL!
LET'S GO, RYOTA!
HEY, WAIT UP, KEN!
GUYS, HOLD UP A SECOND!
DON'T GO TOO FAR AHEAD...

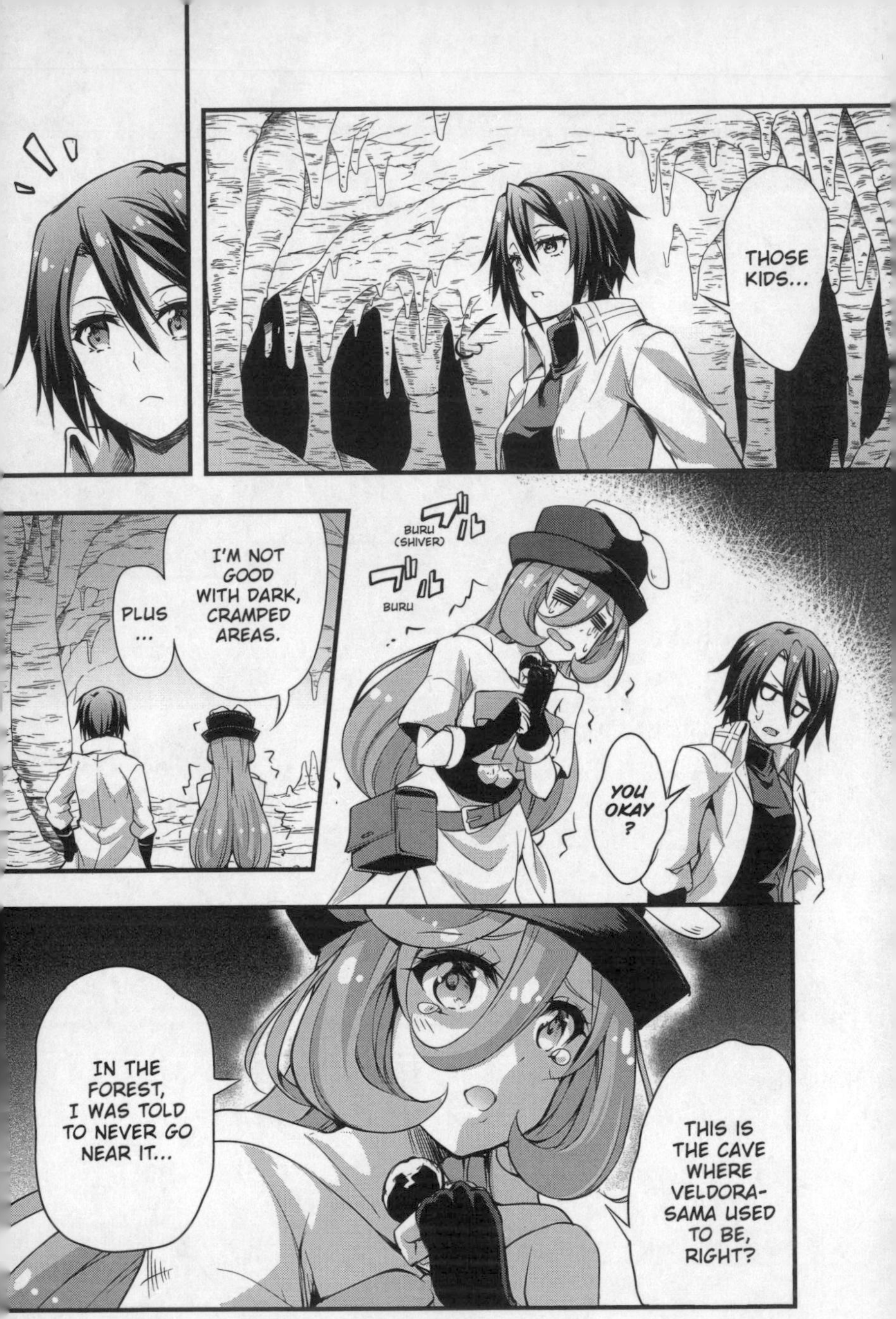
THOSE KIDS...
ブル
BURU (SHIVER)
ブル
BURU
YOU OKAY?
I'M NOT GOOD WITH DARK, CRAMPED AREAS.
PLUS ...
THIS IS THE CAVE WHERE VELDORA-SAMA USED TO BE, RIGHT?
IN THE FOREST, I WAS TOLD TO NEVER GO NEAR IT...

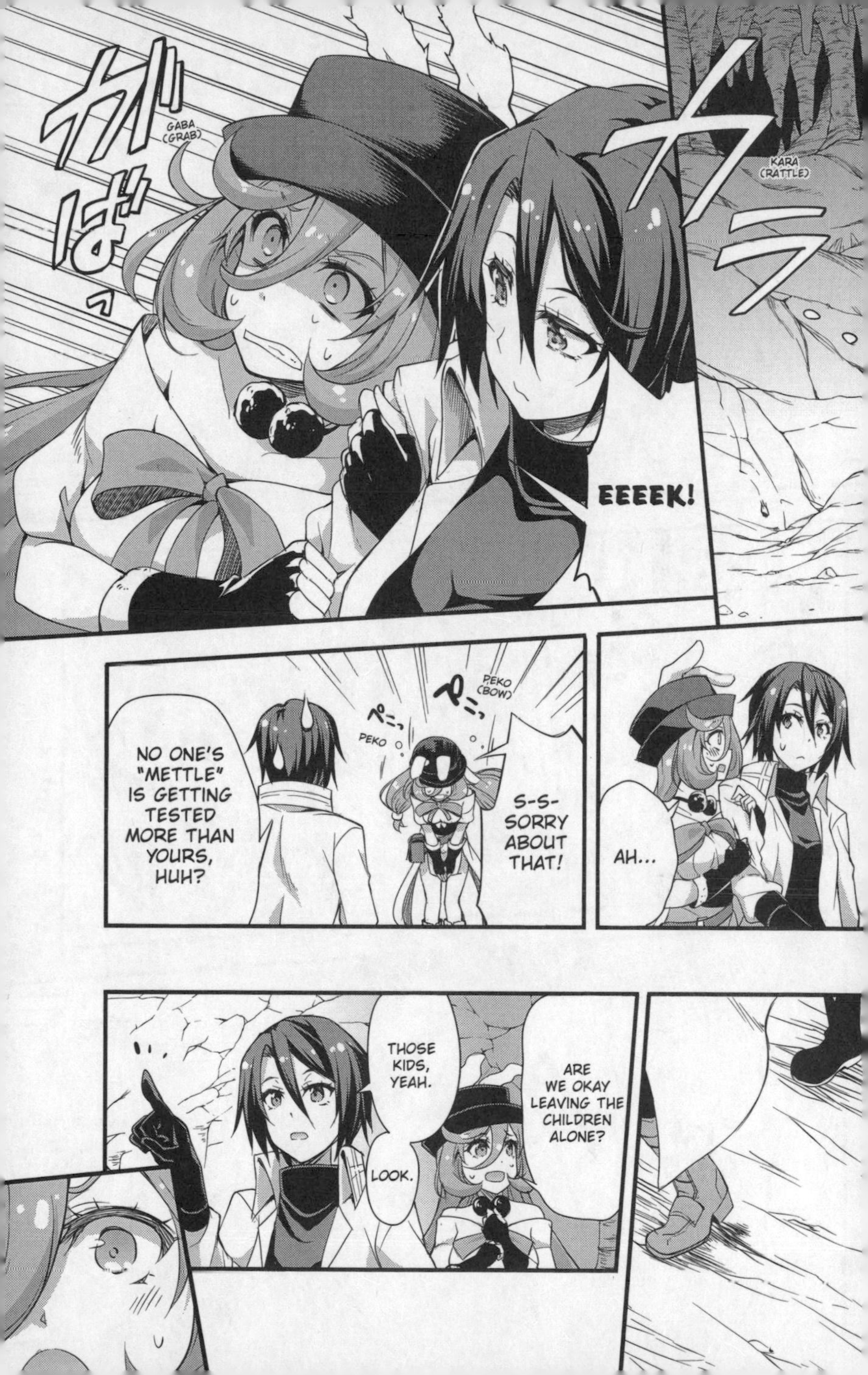
KARA (RATTLE)
GABA (GRAB)
EEEEK!
AH...
P,EKO (BOW)
S-S-SORRY ABOUT THAT!
PEKO
NO ONE'S "METTLE" IS GETTING TESTED MORE THAN YOURS, HUH?
ARE WE OKAY LEAVING THE CHILDREN ALONE?
THOSE KIDS, YEAH.
LOOK.

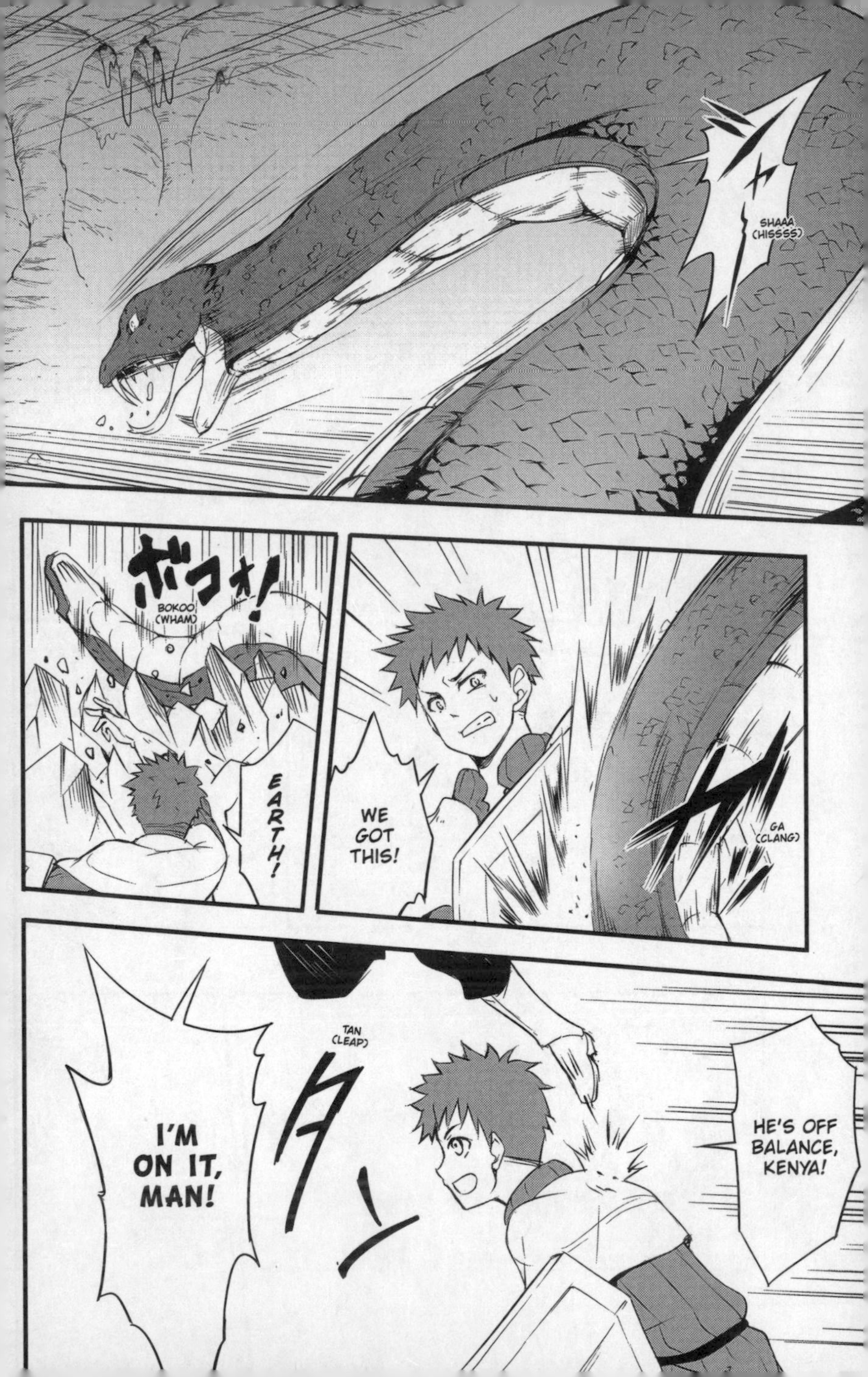

SHAAA (HISSSS)
GA (CLANG)
WE GOT THIS!
ボコォ!
BOKOO (WHAM)
EARTH!
HE'S OFF BALANCE, KENYA!
TAN (LEAP)
タン
I'M ON IT, MAN!

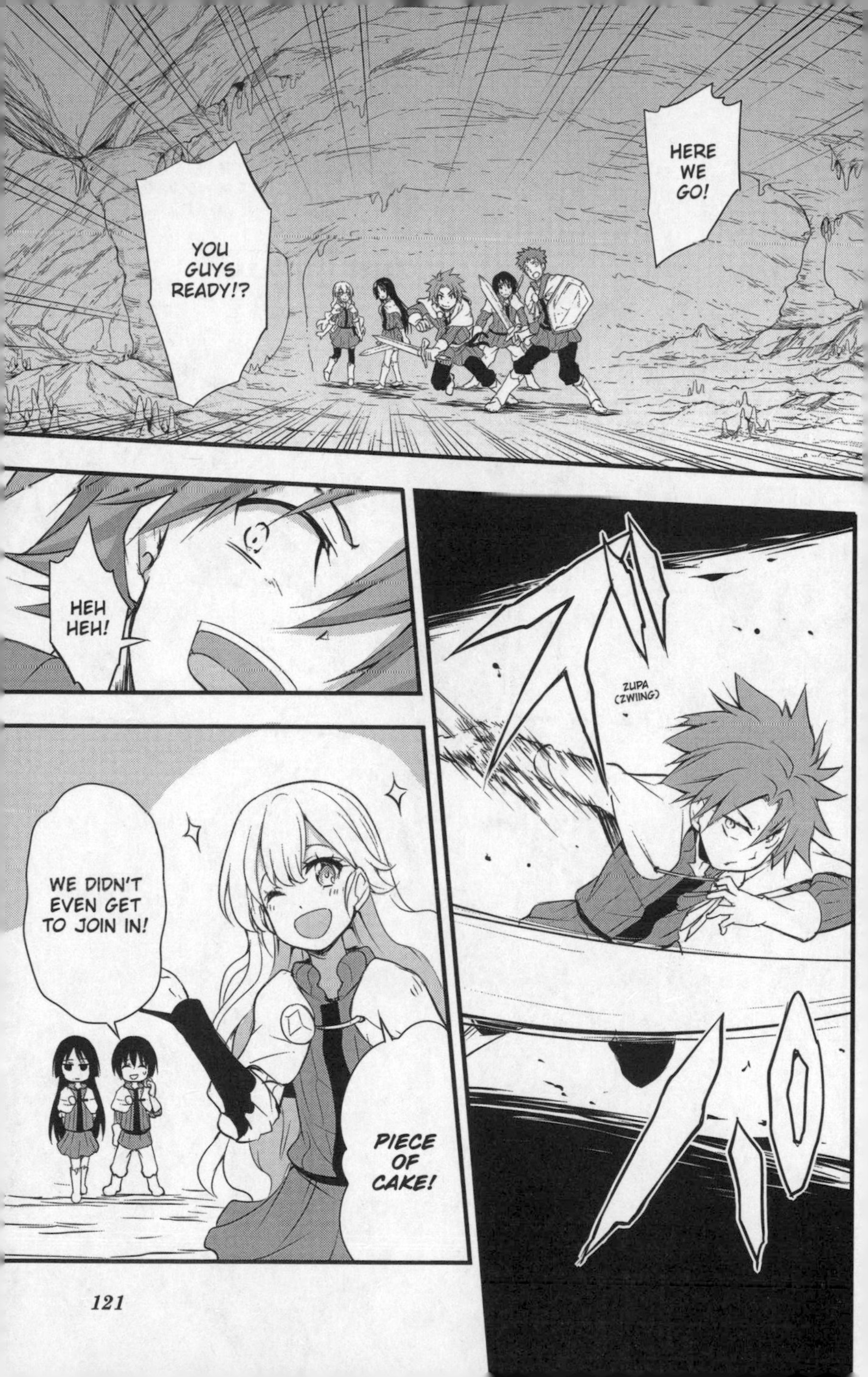
HERE WE GO!
YOU GUYS READY!?
ZUPA (ZWIING)
HEH HEH!
PIECE OF CAKE!
WE DIDN'T EVEN GET TO JOIN IN!

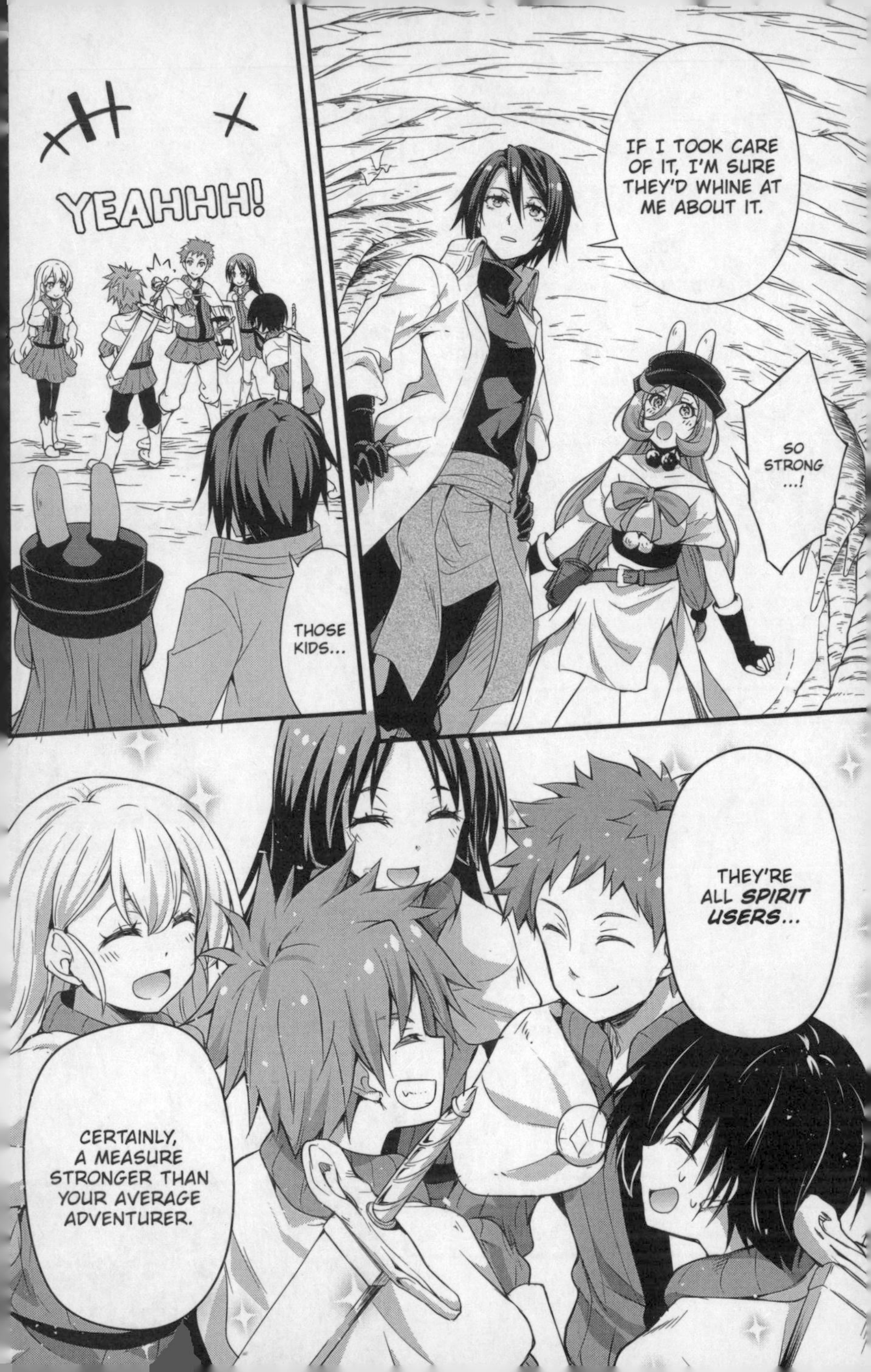
IF I TOOK CARE OF IT, I'M SURE THEY'D WHINE AT ME ABOUT IT.
SO STRONG ...!
YEAHHH!
THOSE KIDS...
THEY'RE ALL *SPIRIT USERS*...
CERTAINLY, A MEASURE STRONGER THAN YOUR AVERAGE ADVENTURER.

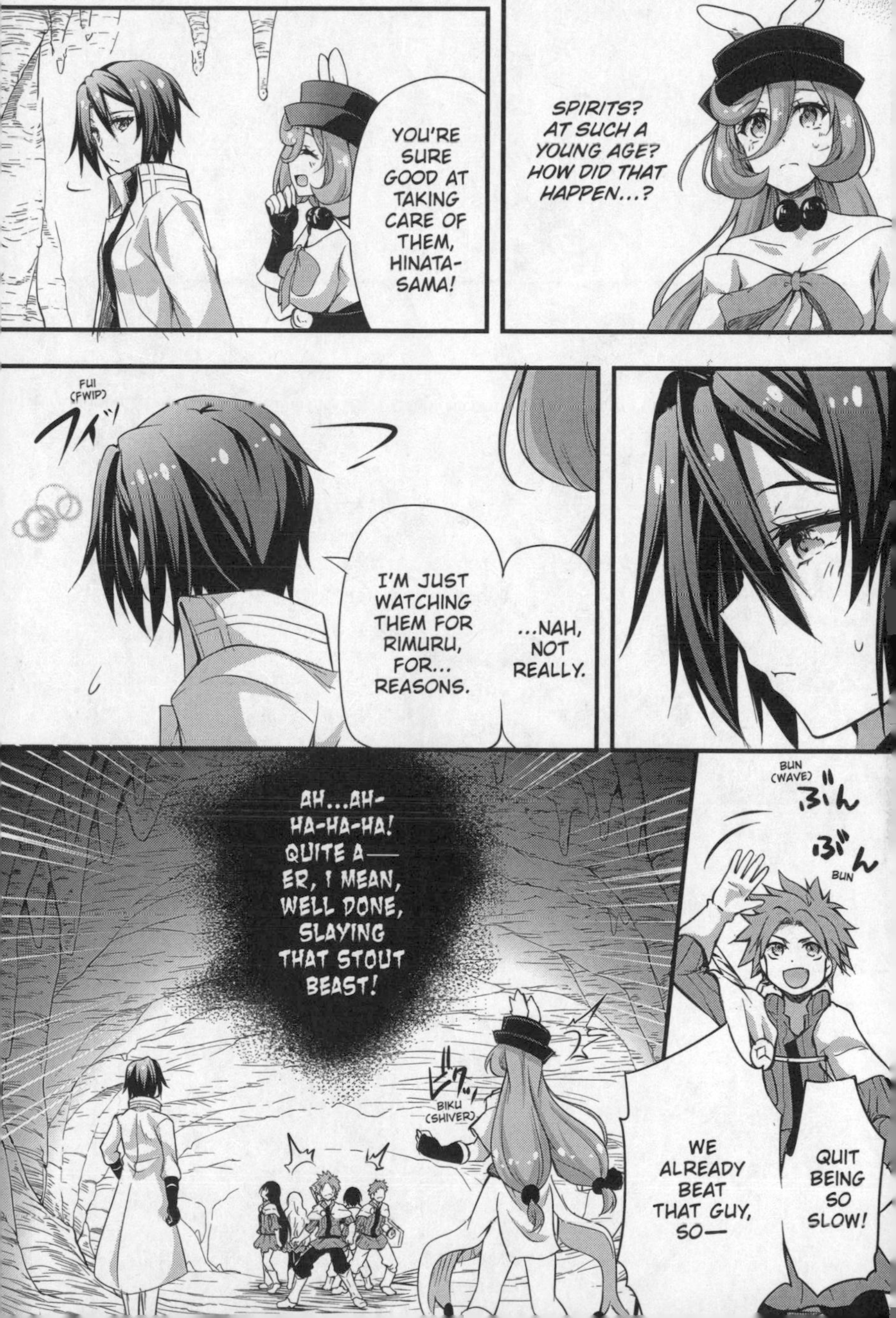
SPIRITS? AT SUCH A YOUNG AGE? HOW DID THAT HAPPEN...?
YOU'RE SURE GOOD AT TAKING CARE OF THEM, HINATA-SAMA!
...NAH, NOT REALLY.
I'M JUST WATCHING THEM FOR RIMURU, FOR... REASONS.
FUI (FWIP)
BUN (WAVE)
BUN
QUIT BEING SO SLOW!
WE ALREADY BEAT THAT GUY, SO—
AH...AH-HA-HA-HA! QUITE A— ER, I MEAN, WELL DONE, SLAYING THAT STOUT BEAST!
BIKU (SHIVER)

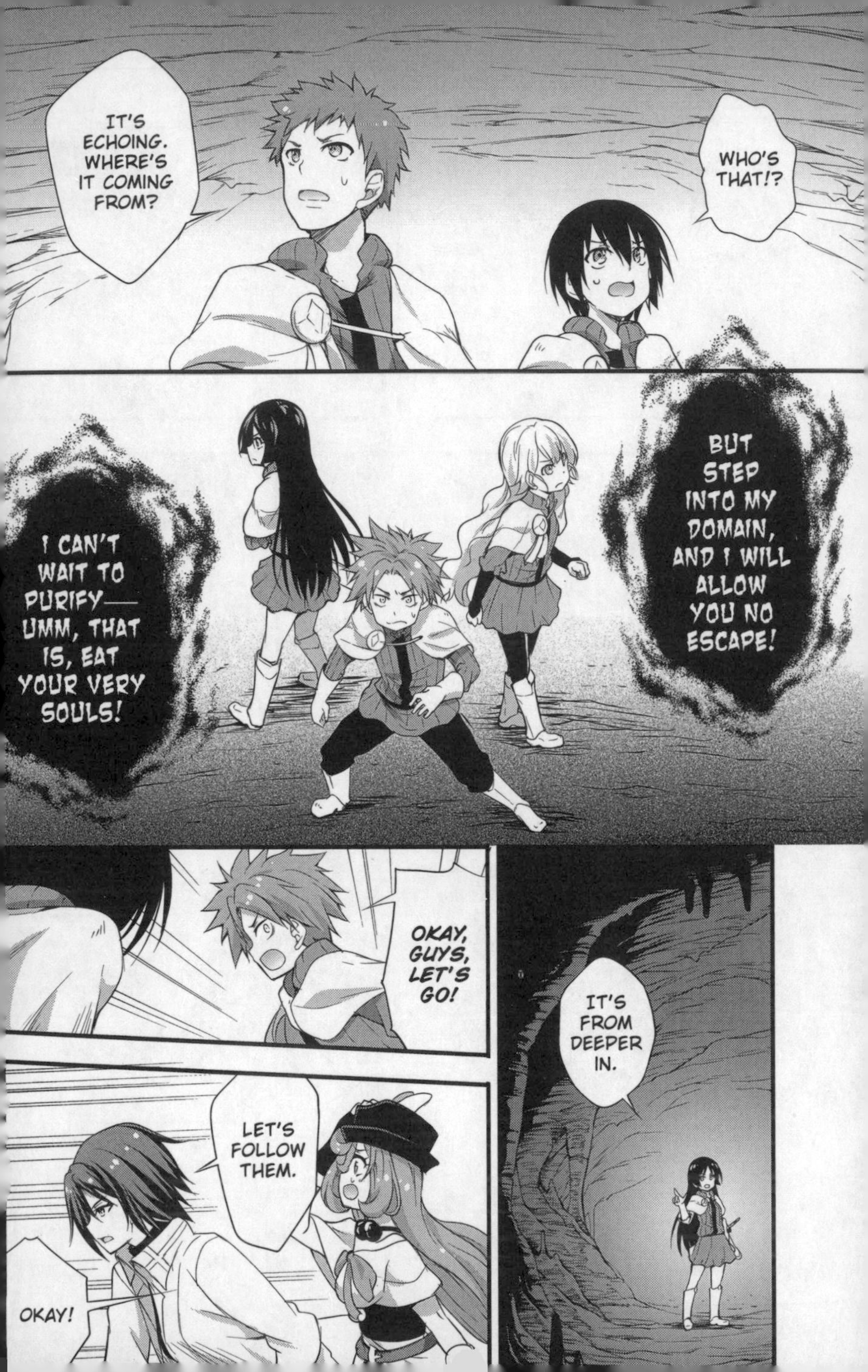
WHO'S THAT!?
IT'S ECHOING. WHERE'S IT COMING FROM?
BUT STEP INTO MY DOMAIN, AND I WILL ALLOW YOU NO ESCAPE!
I CAN'T WAIT TO PURIFY—UMM, THAT IS, EAT YOUR VERY SOULS!
IT'S FROM DEEPER IN.
OKAY, GUYS, LET'S GO!
LET'S FOLLOW THEM.
OKAY!

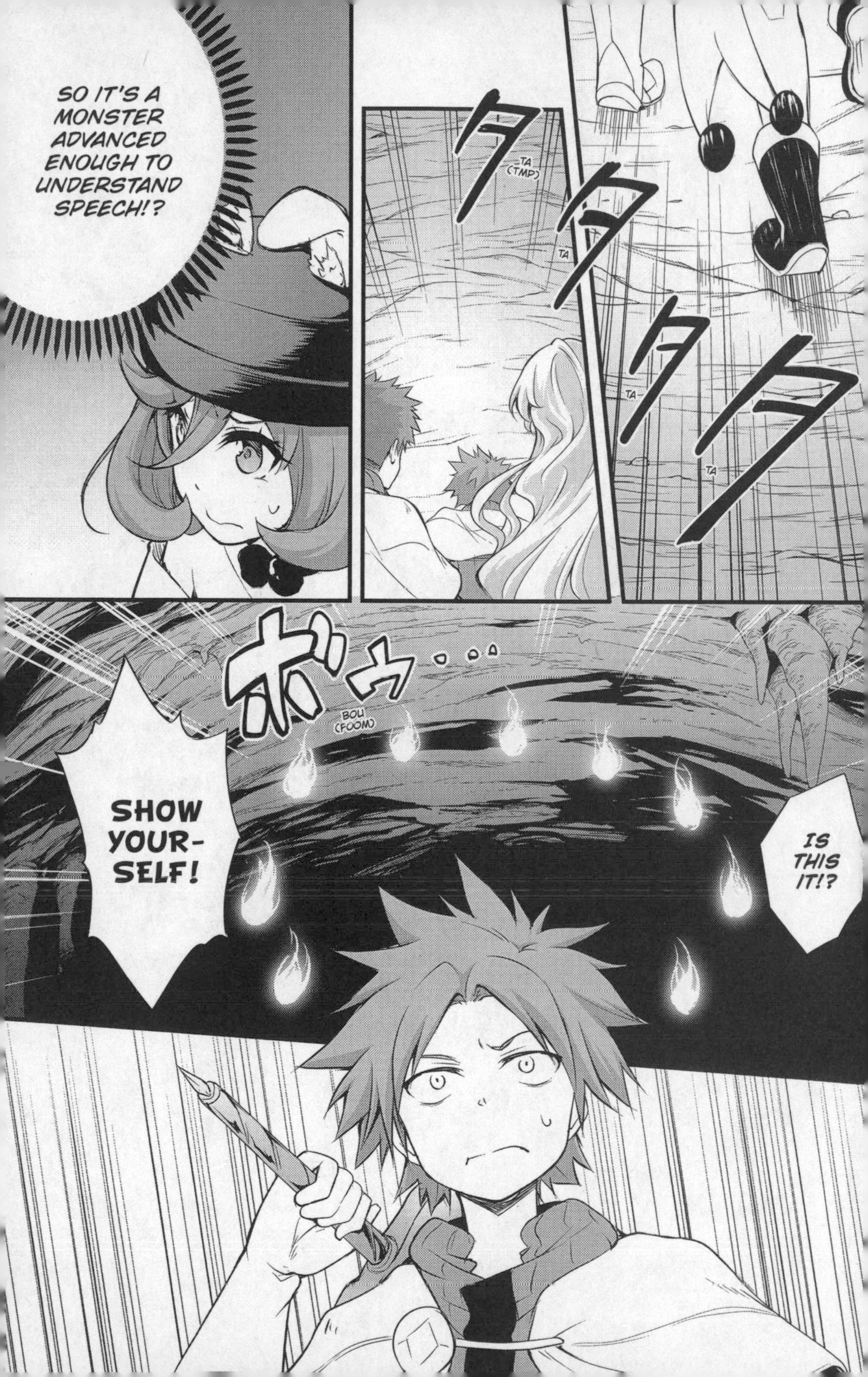

タタタタ
TA (TMP)
TA
TA
TA
SO IT'S A MONSTER ADVANCED ENOUGH TO UNDERSTAND SPEECH!?
IS THIS IT!?
ボゥ…
BOU (FOOM)
SHOW YOUR-SELF!

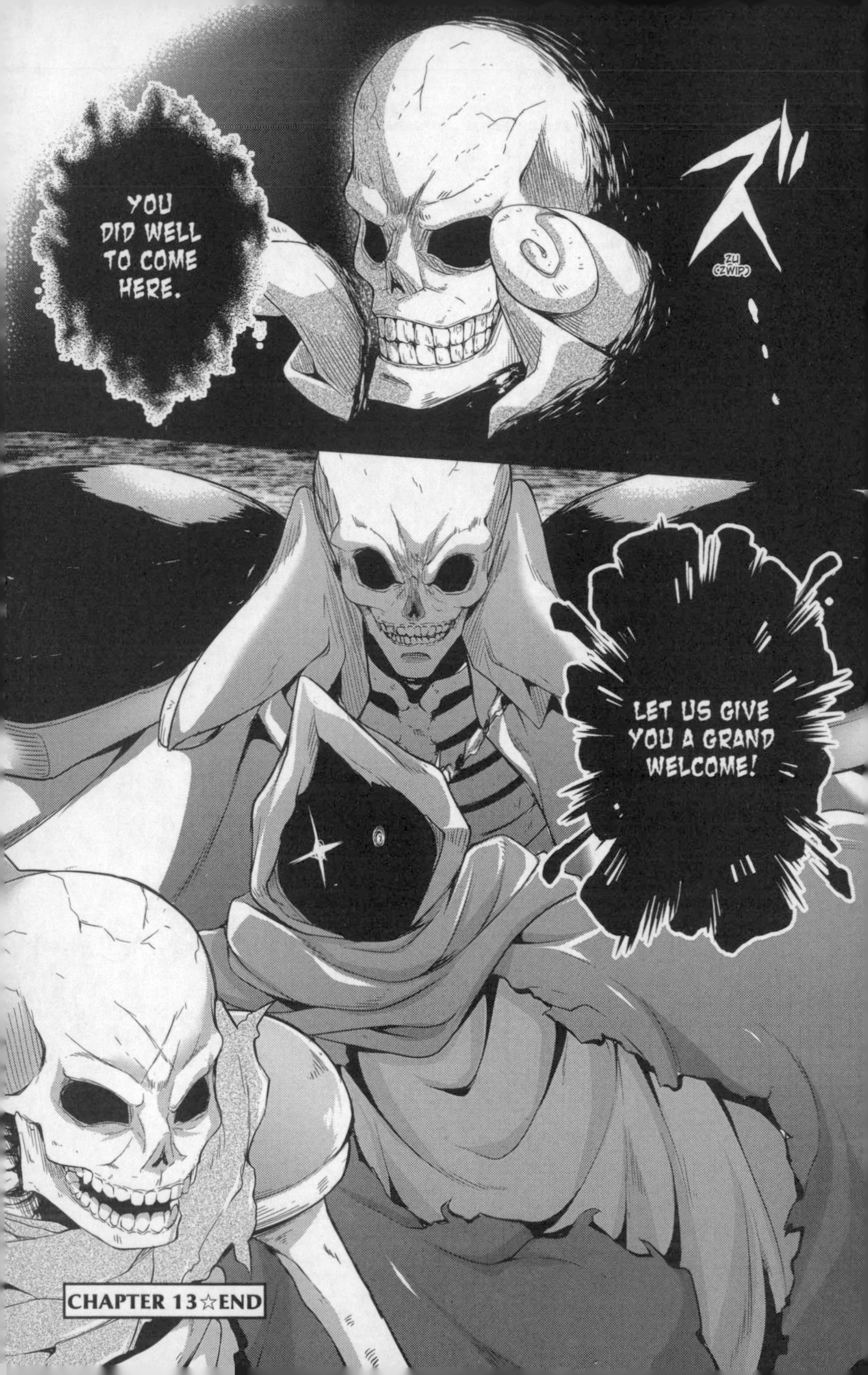
ズ
ZU (ZWIP)
YOU DID WELL TO COME HERE.
LET US GIVE YOU A GRAND WELCOME!
CHAPTER 13☆END

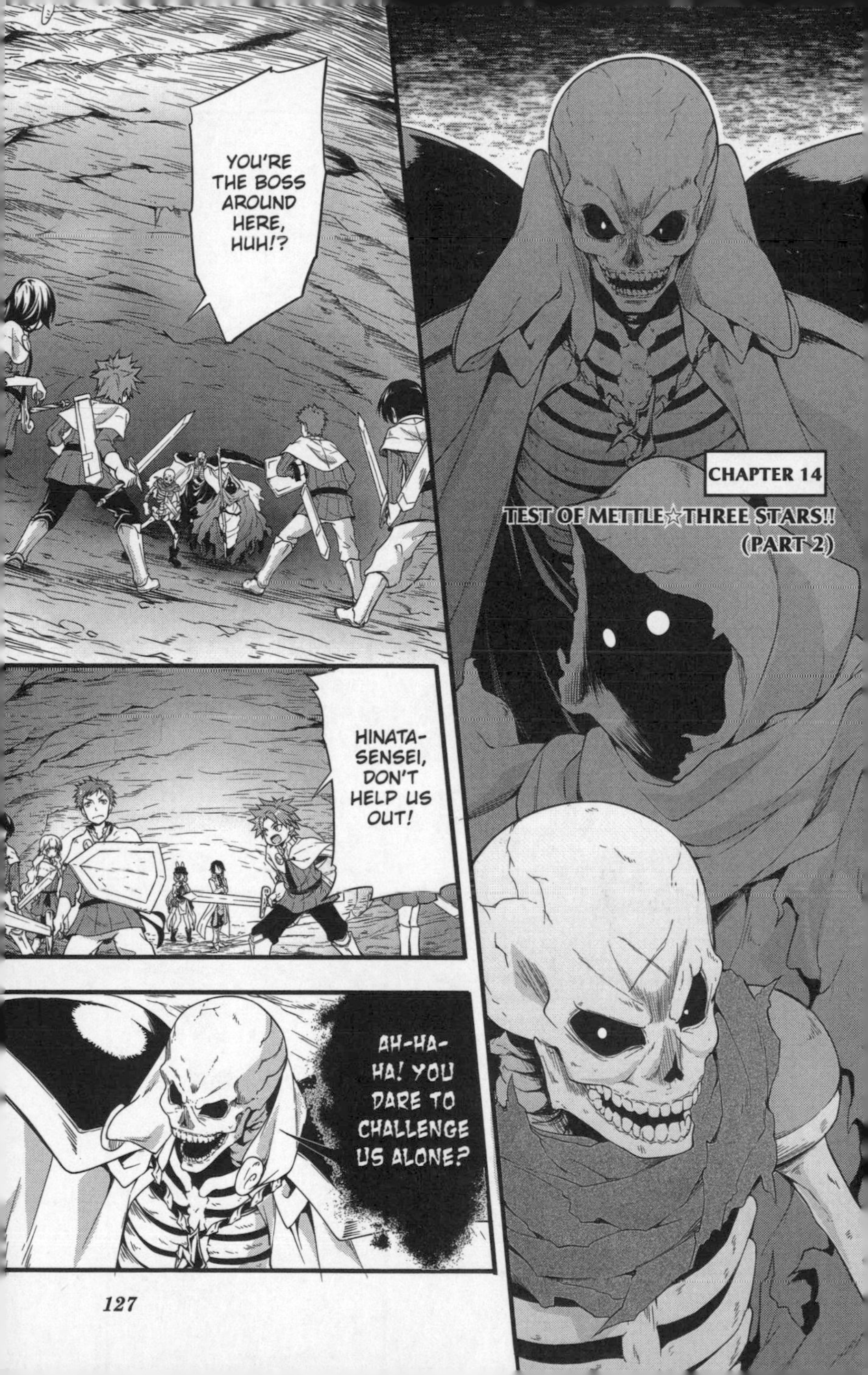
CHAPTER 14
TEST OF METTLE☆THREE STARS!! (PART 2)
YOU'RE THE BOSS AROUND HERE, HUH!?
HINATA-SENSEI, DON'T HELP US OUT!
AH-HA-HA! YOU DARE TO CHALLENGE US ALONE?

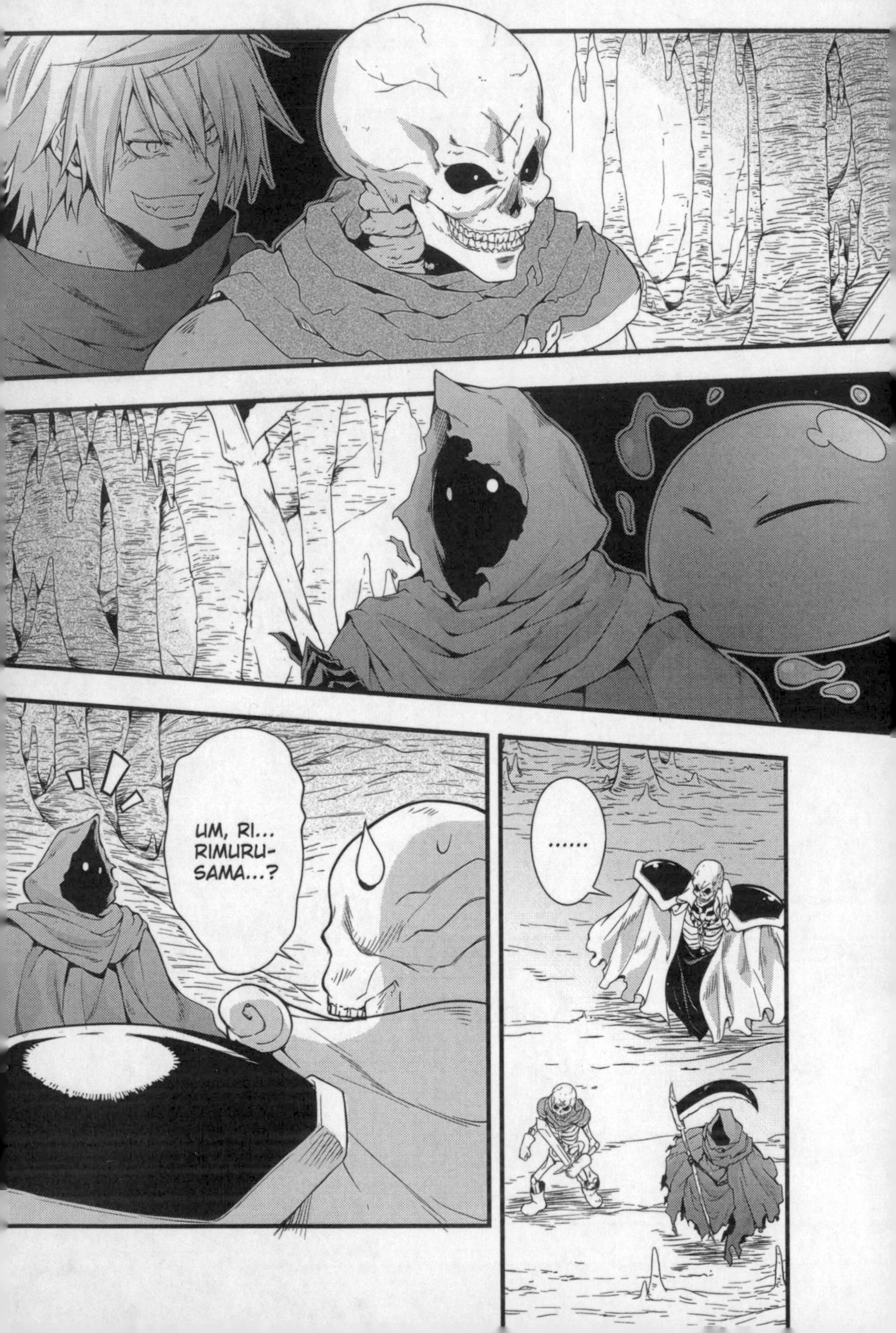
......
UM, RI... RIMURU-SAMA...?

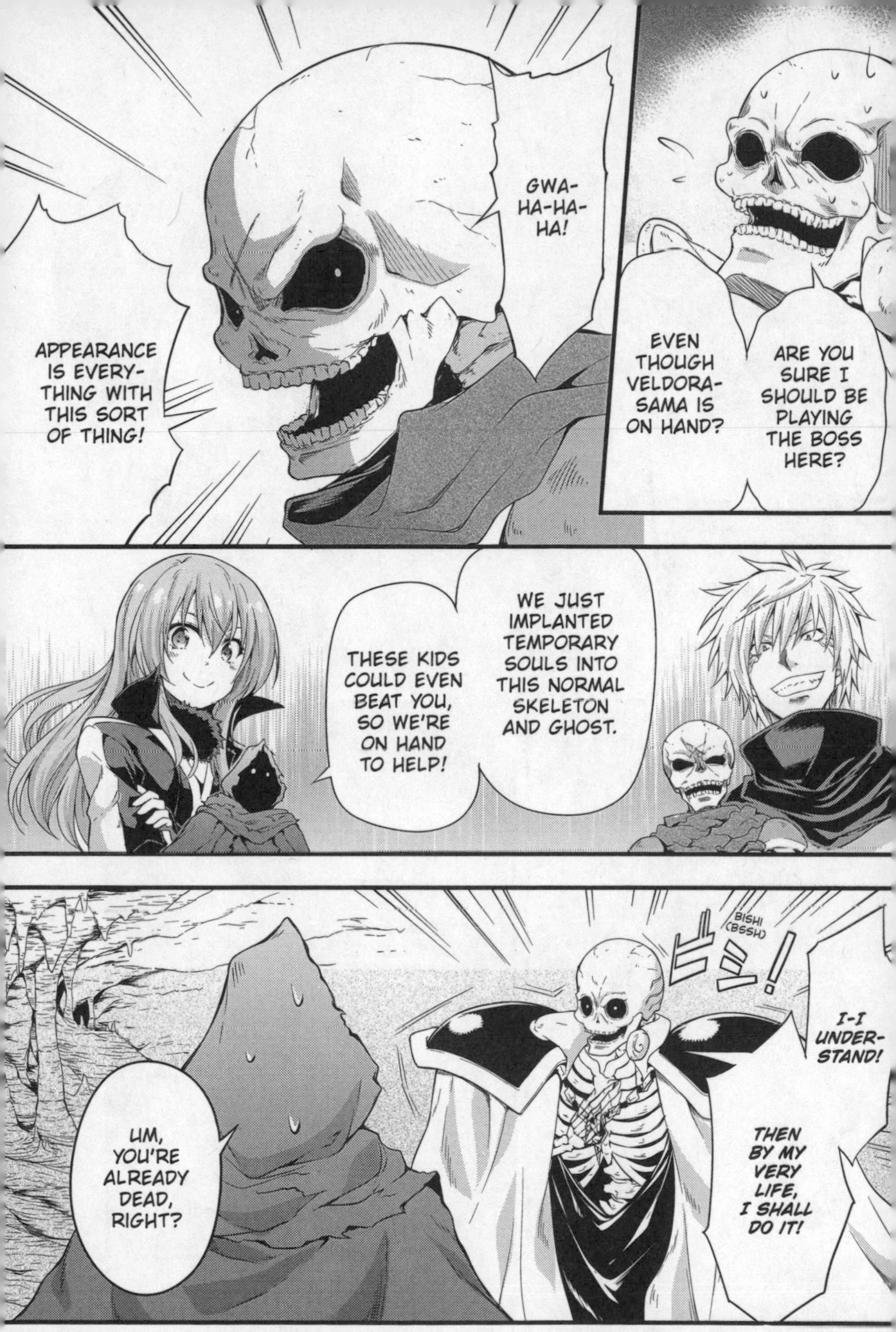
ARE YOU SURE I SHOULD BE PLAYING THE BOSS HERE?
EVEN THOUGH VELDORA-SAMA IS ON HAND?
GWA-HA-HA-HA!
APPEARANCE IS EVERY-THING WITH THIS SORT OF THING!
WE JUST IMPLANTED TEMPORARY SOULS INTO THIS NORMAL SKELETON AND GHOST.
THESE KIDS COULD EVEN BEAT YOU, SO WE'RE ON HAND TO HELP!
BISHI (BSSH)
I-I UNDER-STAND!
THEN BY MY VERY LIFE, I SHALL DO IT!
UM, YOU'RE ALREADY DEAD, RIGHT?

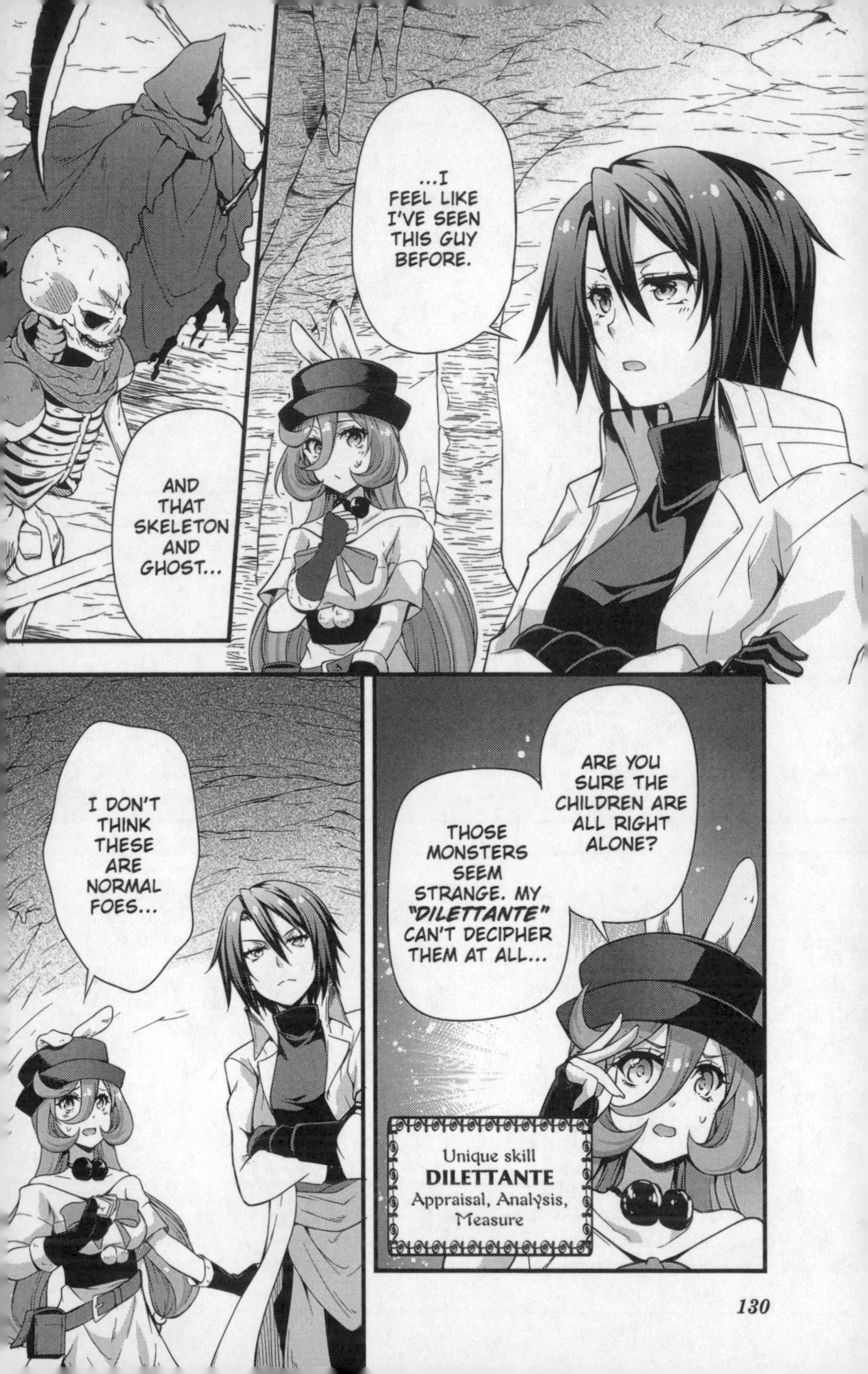
...I FEEL LIKE I'VE SEEN THIS GUY BEFORE.
AND THAT SKELETON AND GHOST...
ARE YOU SURE THE CHILDREN ARE ALL RIGHT ALONE?
THOSE MONSTERS SEEM STRANGE. MY "DILETTANTE" CAN'T DECIPHER THEM AT ALL...
Unique skill
DILETTANTE
Appraisal, Analysis, Measure
I DON'T THINK THESE ARE NORMAL FOES...

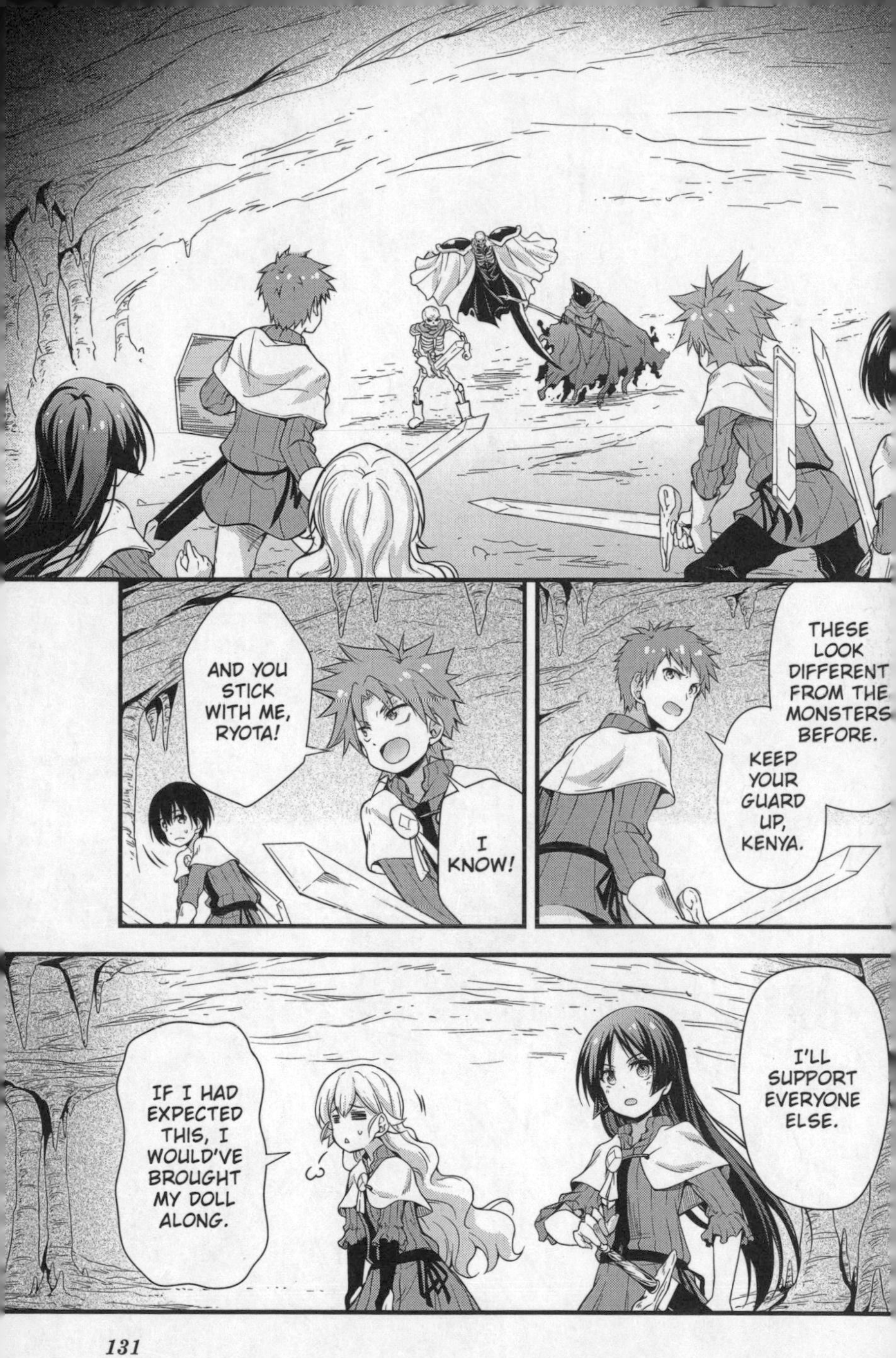
THESE LOOK DIFFERENT FROM THE MONSTERS BEFORE.
KEEP YOUR GUARD UP, KENYA.
I KNOW!
AND YOU STICK WITH ME, RYOTA!
I'LL SUPPORT EVERYONE ELSE.
IF I HAD EXPECTED THIS, I WOULD'VE BROUGHT MY DOLL ALONG.

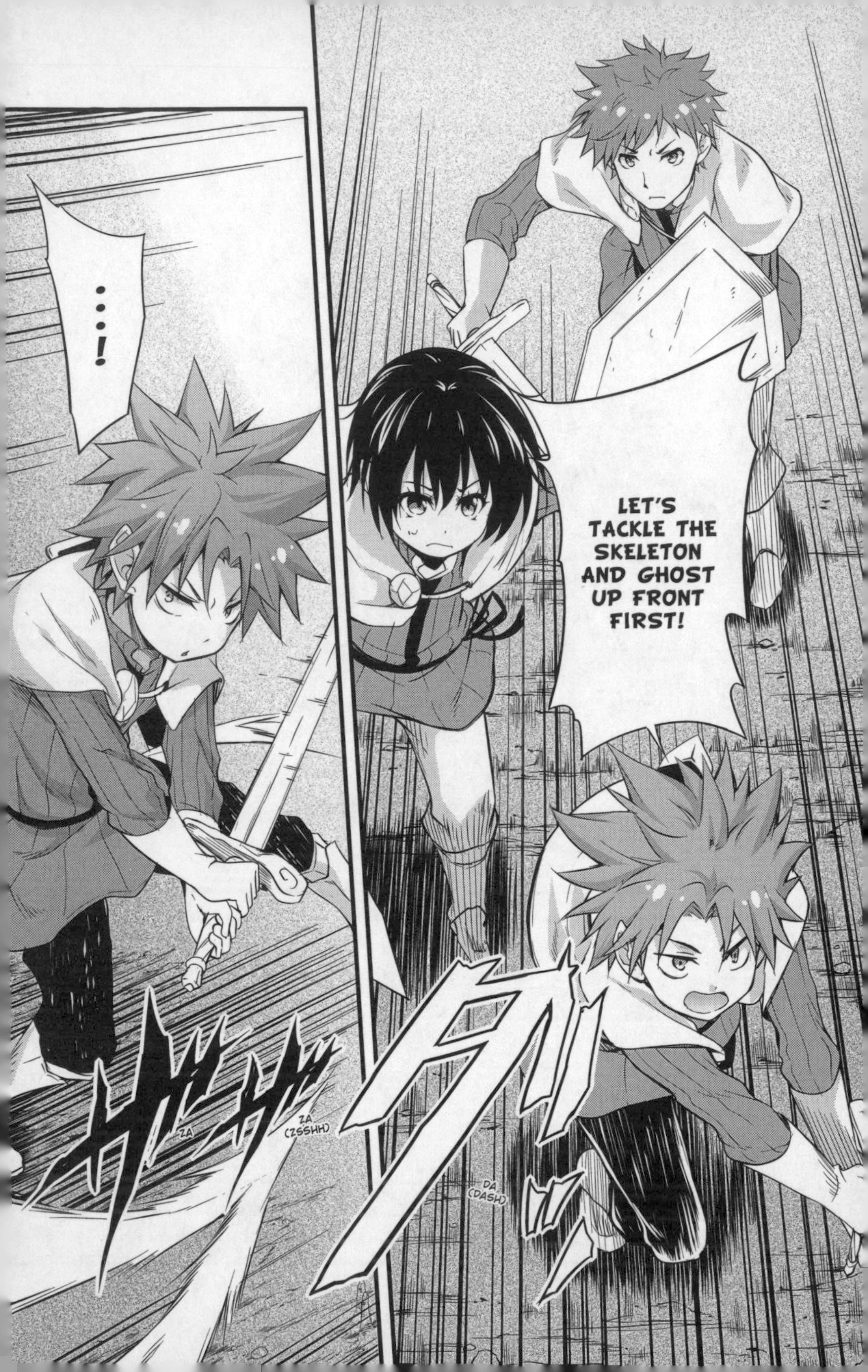
LET'S TACKLE THE SKELETON AND GHOST UP FRONT FIRST!
DA (DASH)
...!
ZA
ZA (ZSSHH)

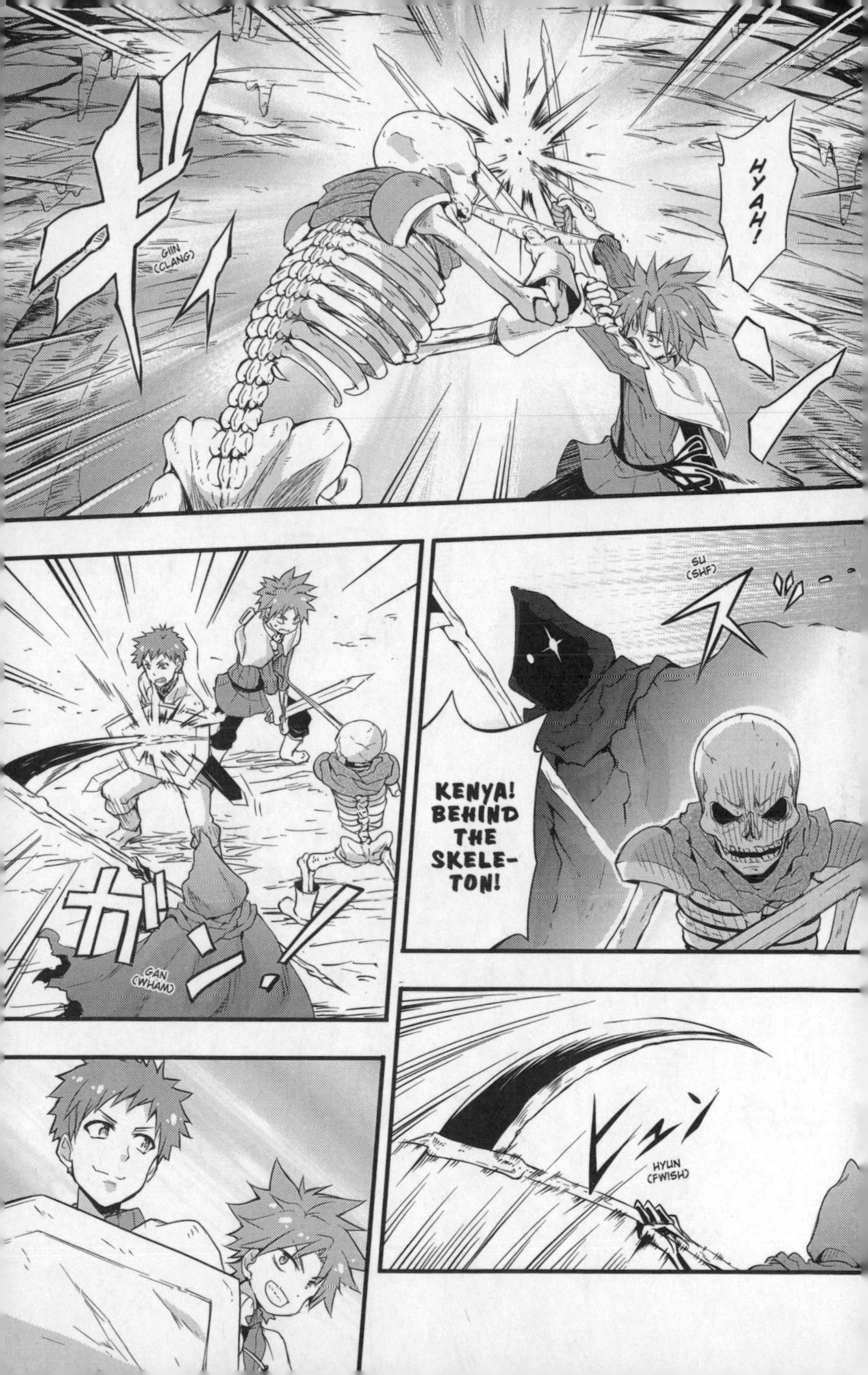
HYAH!
GIIN (CLANG)
SU (SHF)
KENYA! BEHIND THE SKELE-TON!
GAN (WHAM)
HYUN (FWISH)

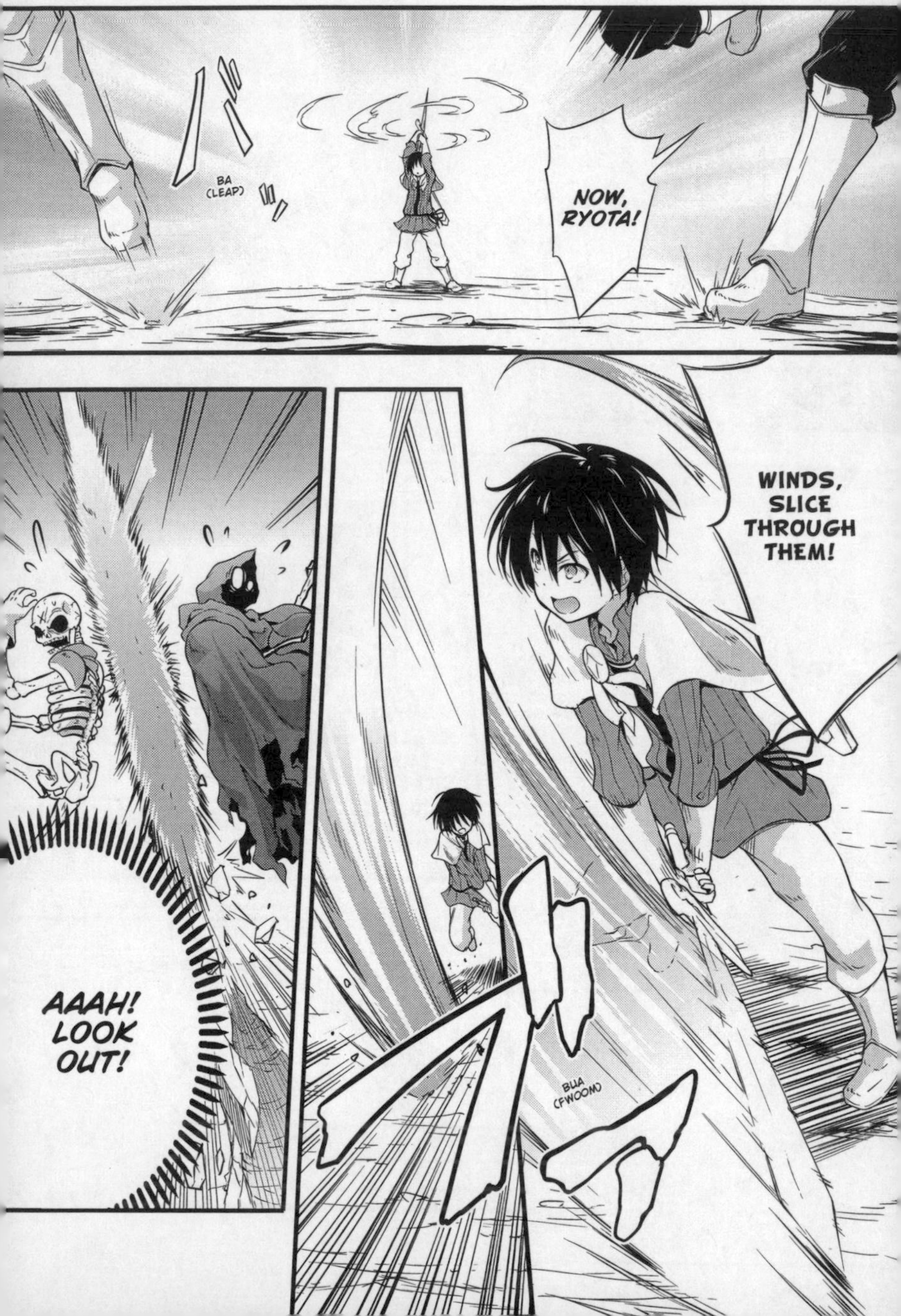
NOW, RYOTA!
BA (LEAP)
WINDS, SLICE THROUGH THEM!
BUA (FWOOM)
AAAH! LOOK OUT!

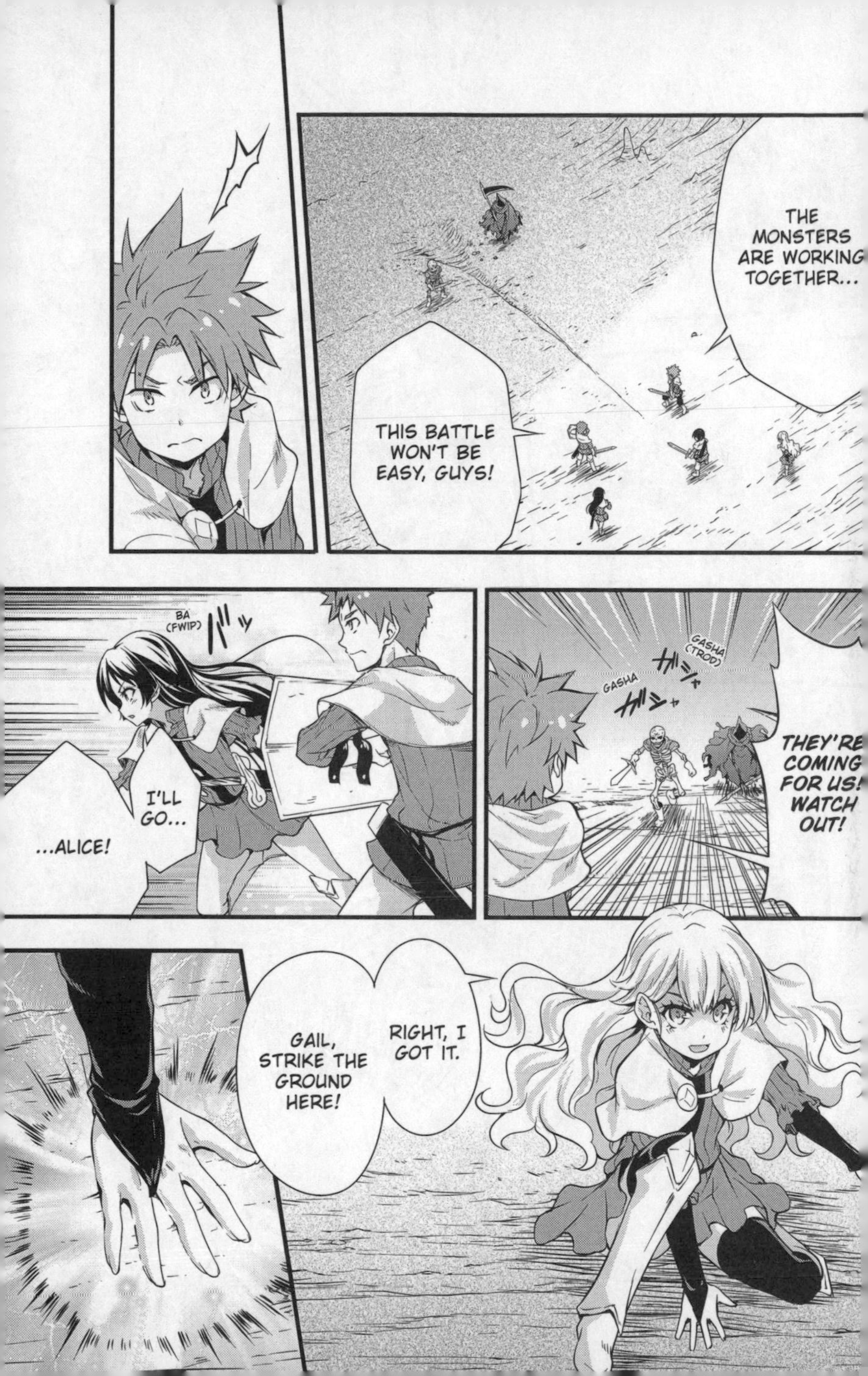
THE MONSTERS ARE WORKING TOGETHER...
THIS BATTLE WON'T BE EASY, GUYS!
GASHA (TROD)
GASHA
THEY'RE COMING FOR US! WATCH OUT!
BA (FWIP)
I'LL GO...
...ALICE!
RIGHT, I GOT IT.
GAIL, STRIKE THE GROUND HERE!

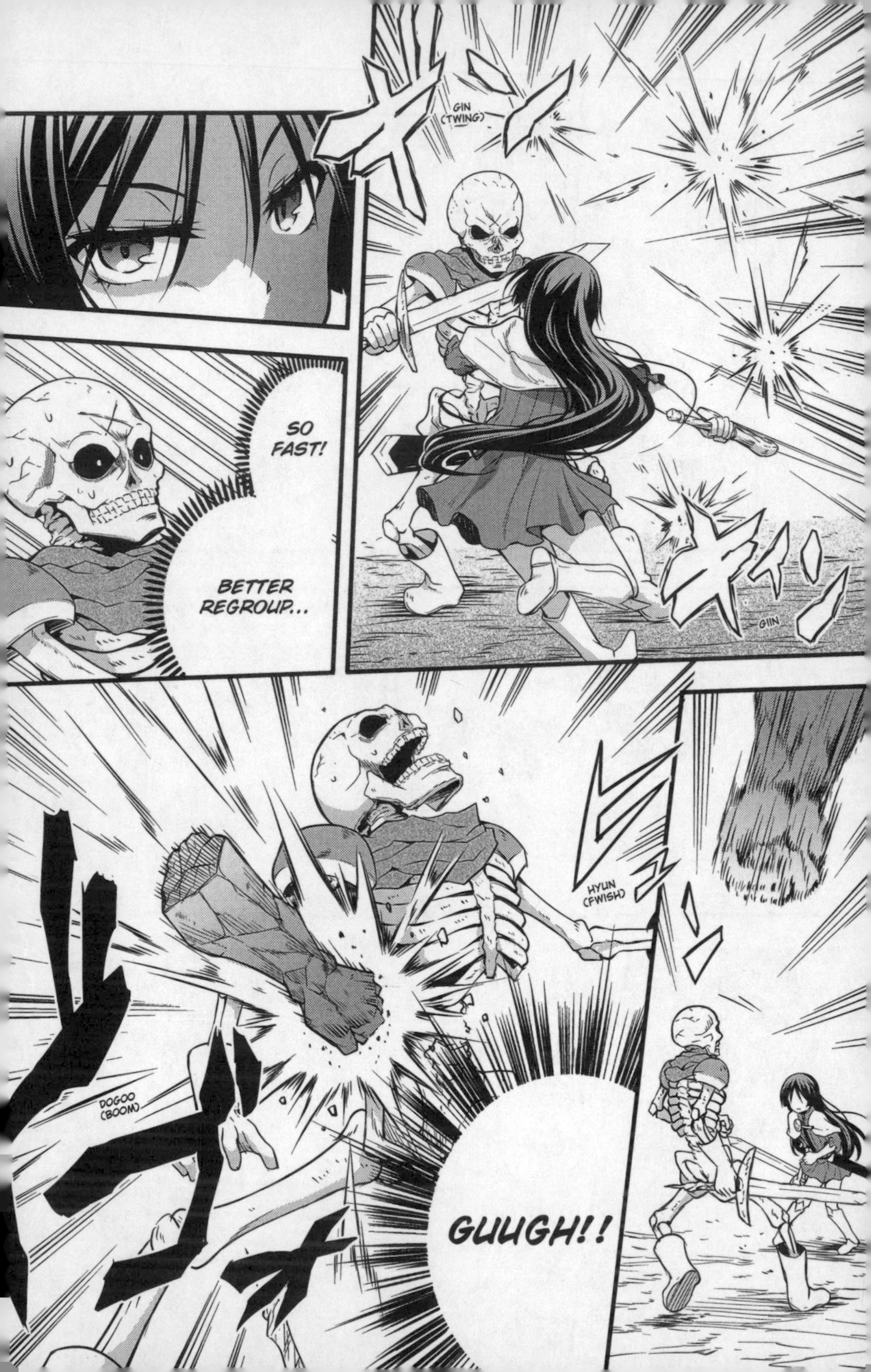
GIN
(TWING)
GIIN
SO FAST!
BETTER REGROUP...
HYUN
(FWISH)
GUUGH!!
DOGOO
(BOOM)

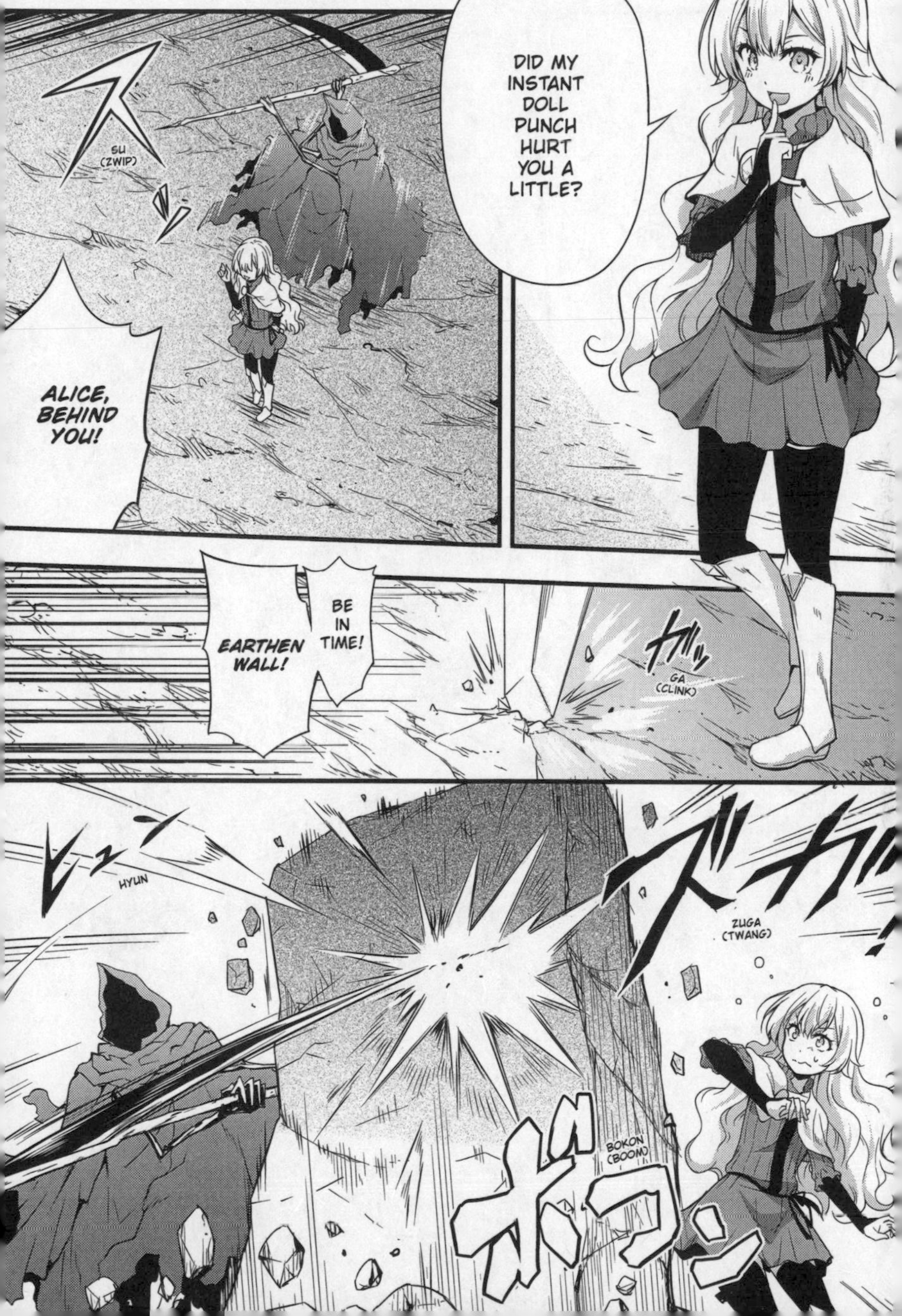
DID MY INSTANT DOLL PUNCH HURT YOU A LITTLE?
SU (ZWIP)
ALICE, BEHIND YOU!
GA (CLINK)
BE IN TIME!
EARTHEN WALL!
ZUGA (TWANG)
HYUN
BOKON (BOOM)

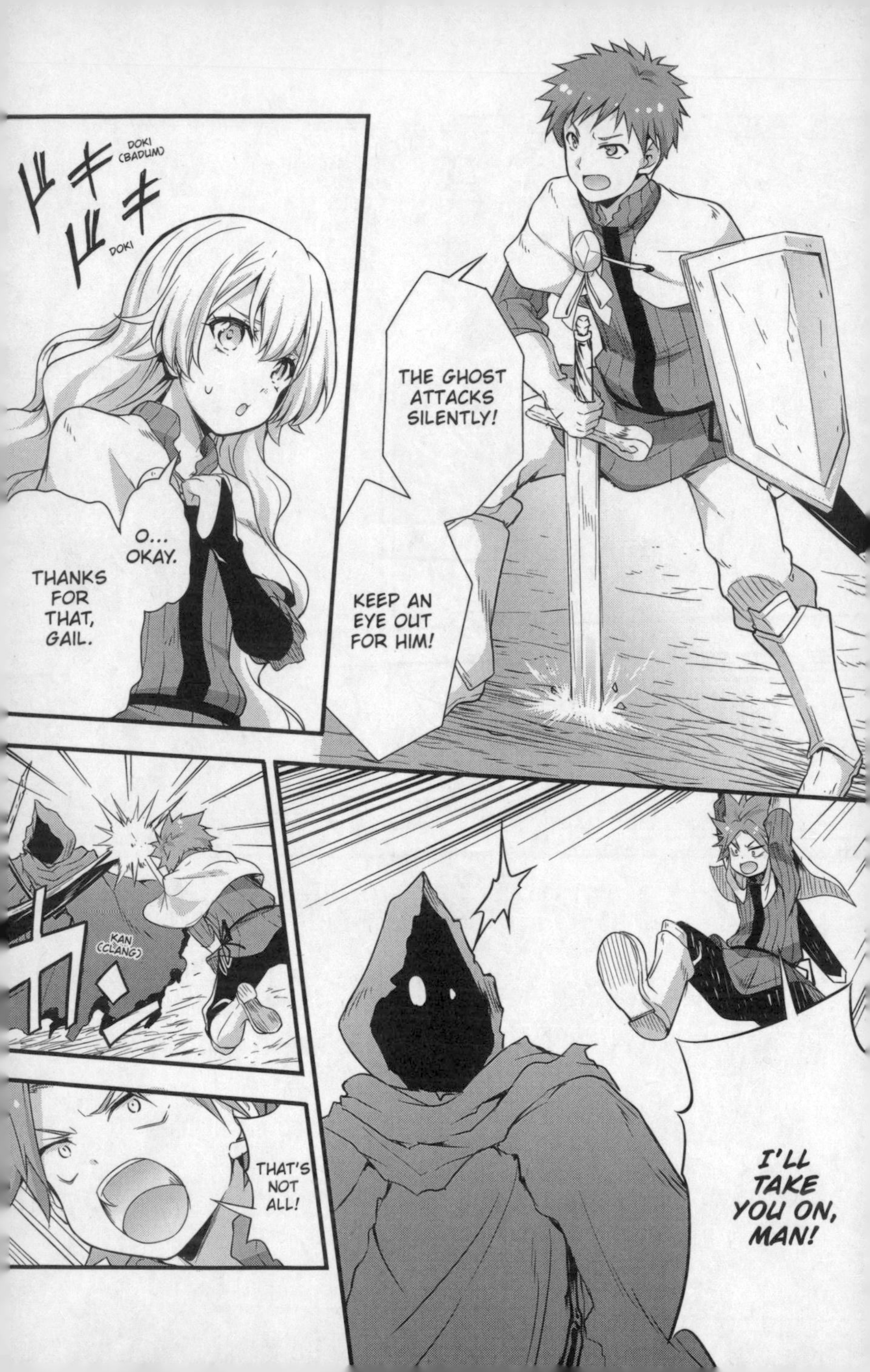
THE GHOST ATTACKS SILENTLY!
KEEP AN EYE OUT FOR HIM!
DOKI (BADUM)
DOKI
O... OKAY.
THANKS FOR THAT, GAIL.
I'LL TAKE YOU ON, MAN!
KAN (CLANG)
THAT'S NOT ALL!

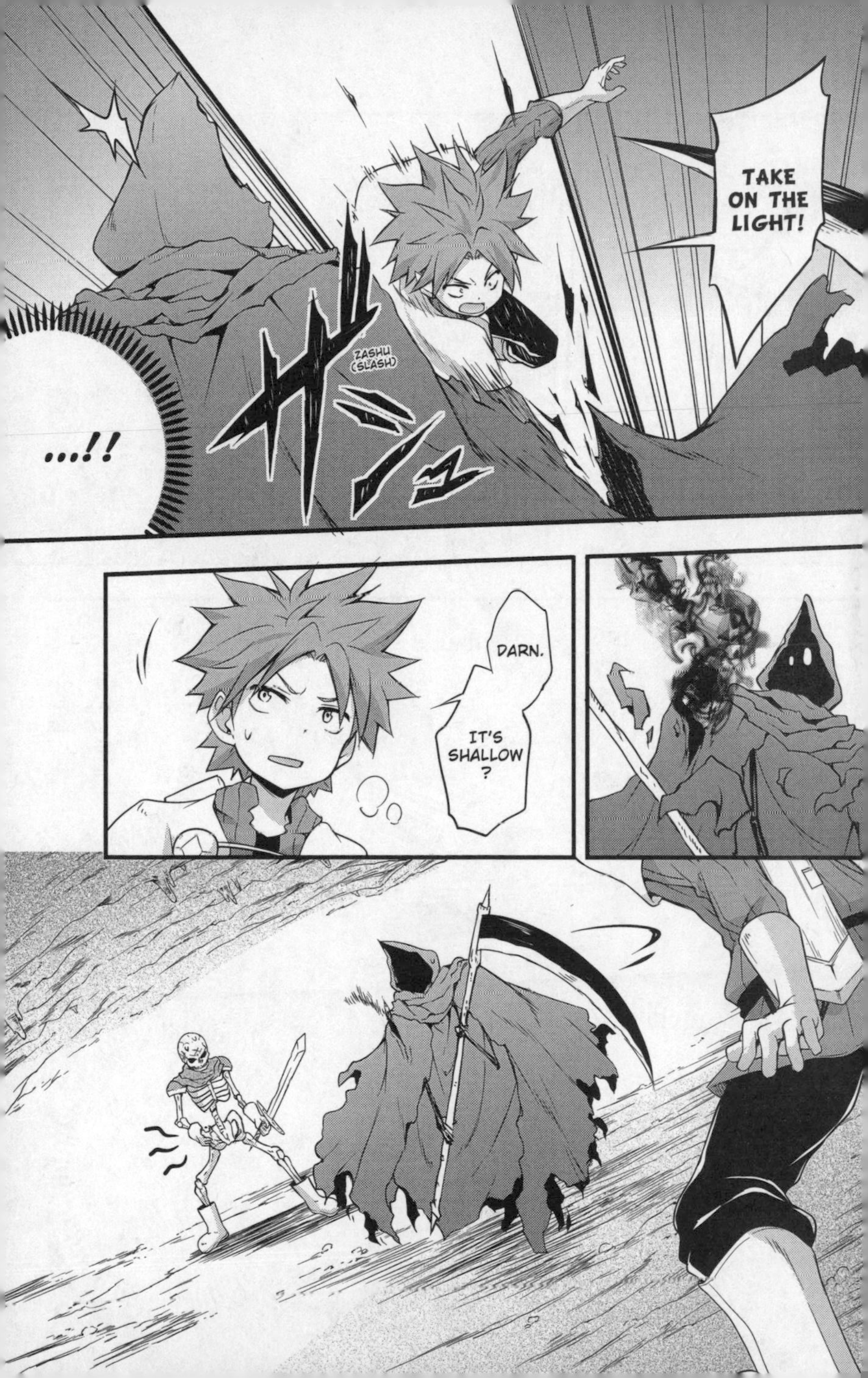
TAKE ON THE LIGHT!
ZASHU (SLASH)
...!!
DARN.
IT'S SHALLOW ?

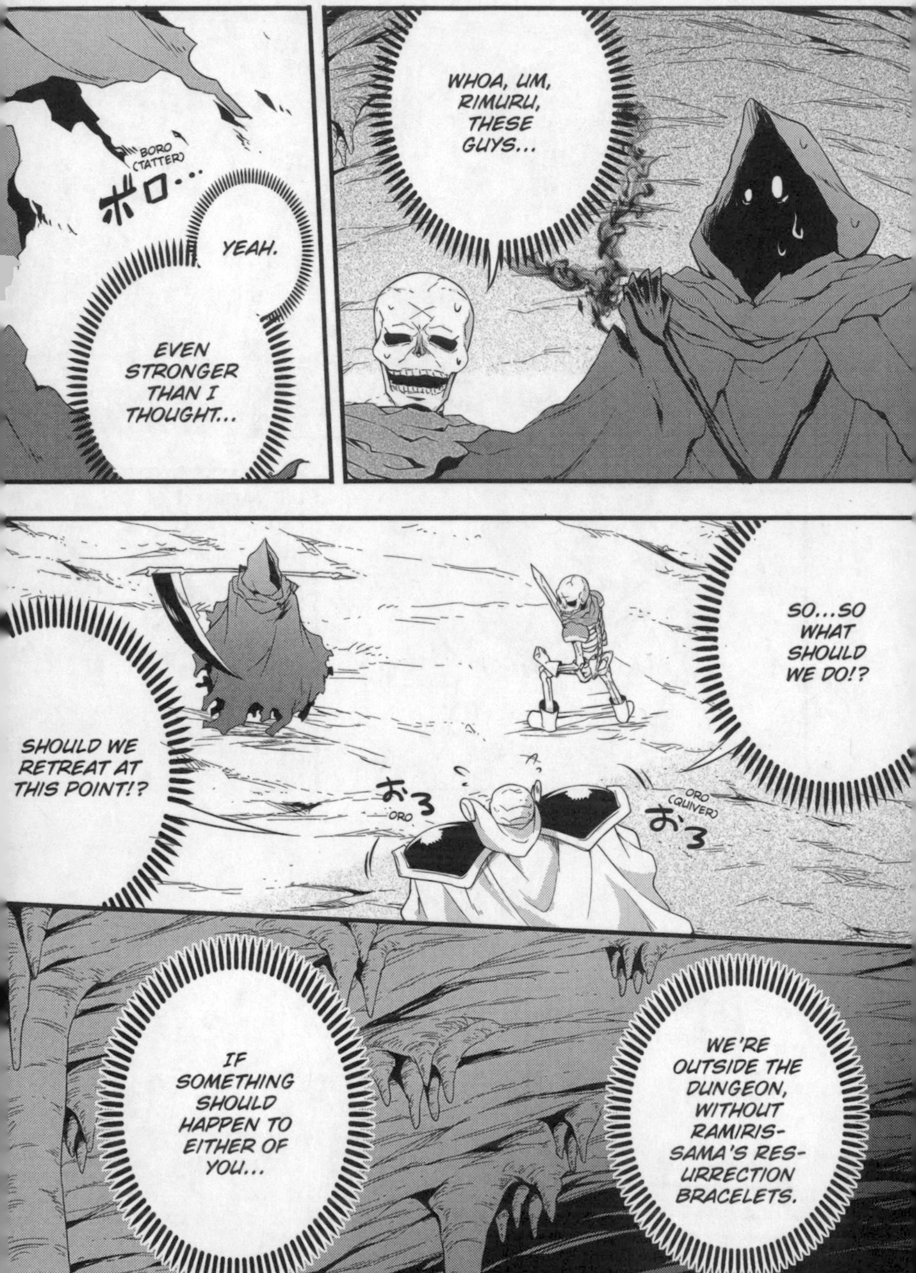
WHOA, UM, RIMURU, THESE GUYS...
BORO (TATTER)
ボロ…
YEAH.
EVEN STRONGER THAN I THOUGHT...
SO...SO WHAT SHOULD WE DO!?
SHOULD WE RETREAT AT THIS POINT!?
ORO (QUIVER)
おろ
おろ
ORO
WE'RE OUTSIDE THE DUNGEON, WITHOUT RAMIRIS-SAMA'S RES-URRECTION BRACELETS.
IF SOMETHING SHOULD HAPPEN TO EITHER OF YOU...

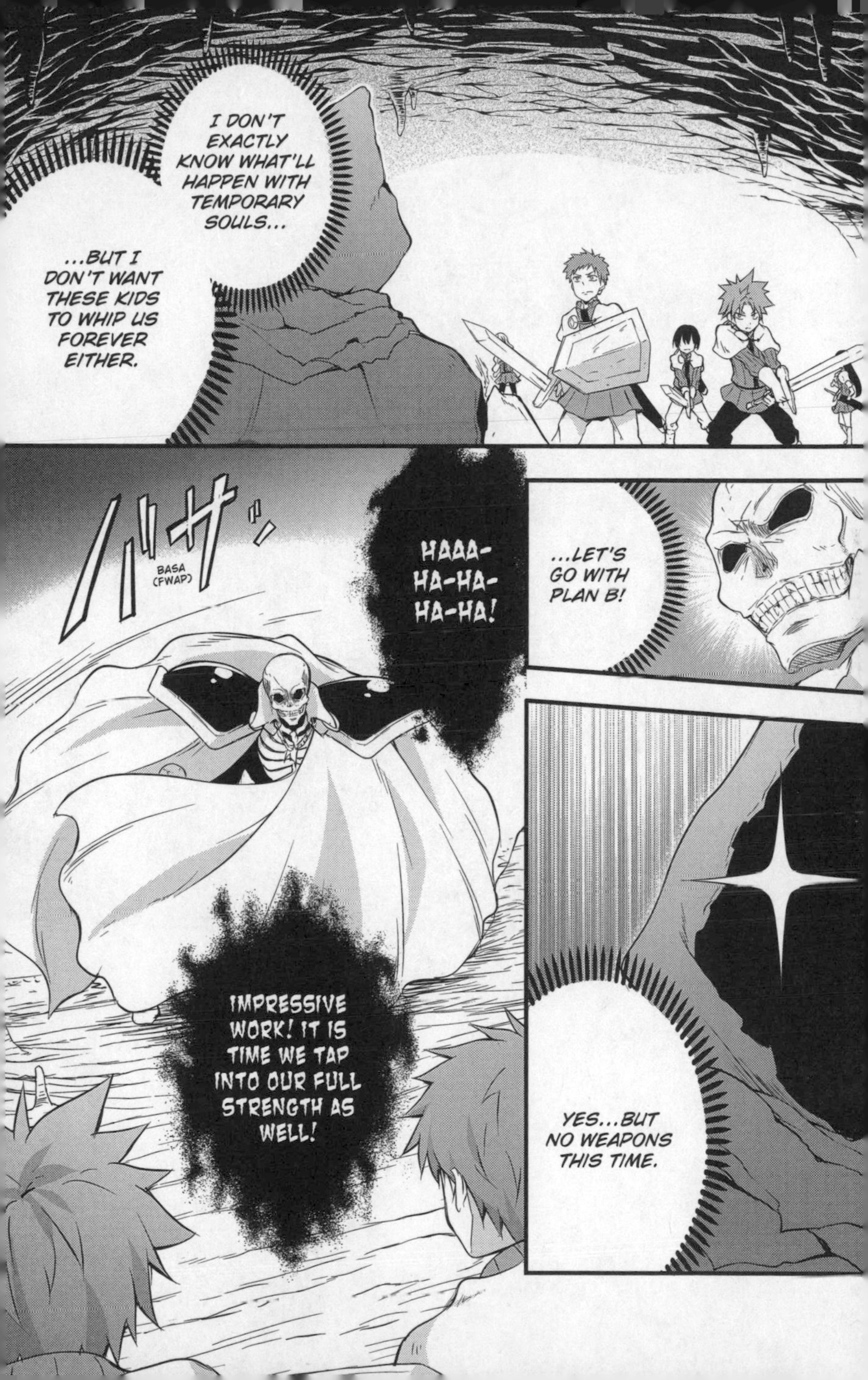
I DON'T EXACTLY KNOW WHAT'LL HAPPEN WITH TEMPORARY SOULS...
...BUT I DON'T WANT THESE KIDS TO WHIP US FOREVER EITHER.
...LET'S GO WITH PLAN B!
YES...BUT NO WEAPONS THIS TIME.
バサッ
BASA (FWAP)
HAAA-HA-HA-HA-HA!
IMPRESSIVE WORK! IT IS TIME WE TAP INTO OUR FULL STRENGTH AS WELL!

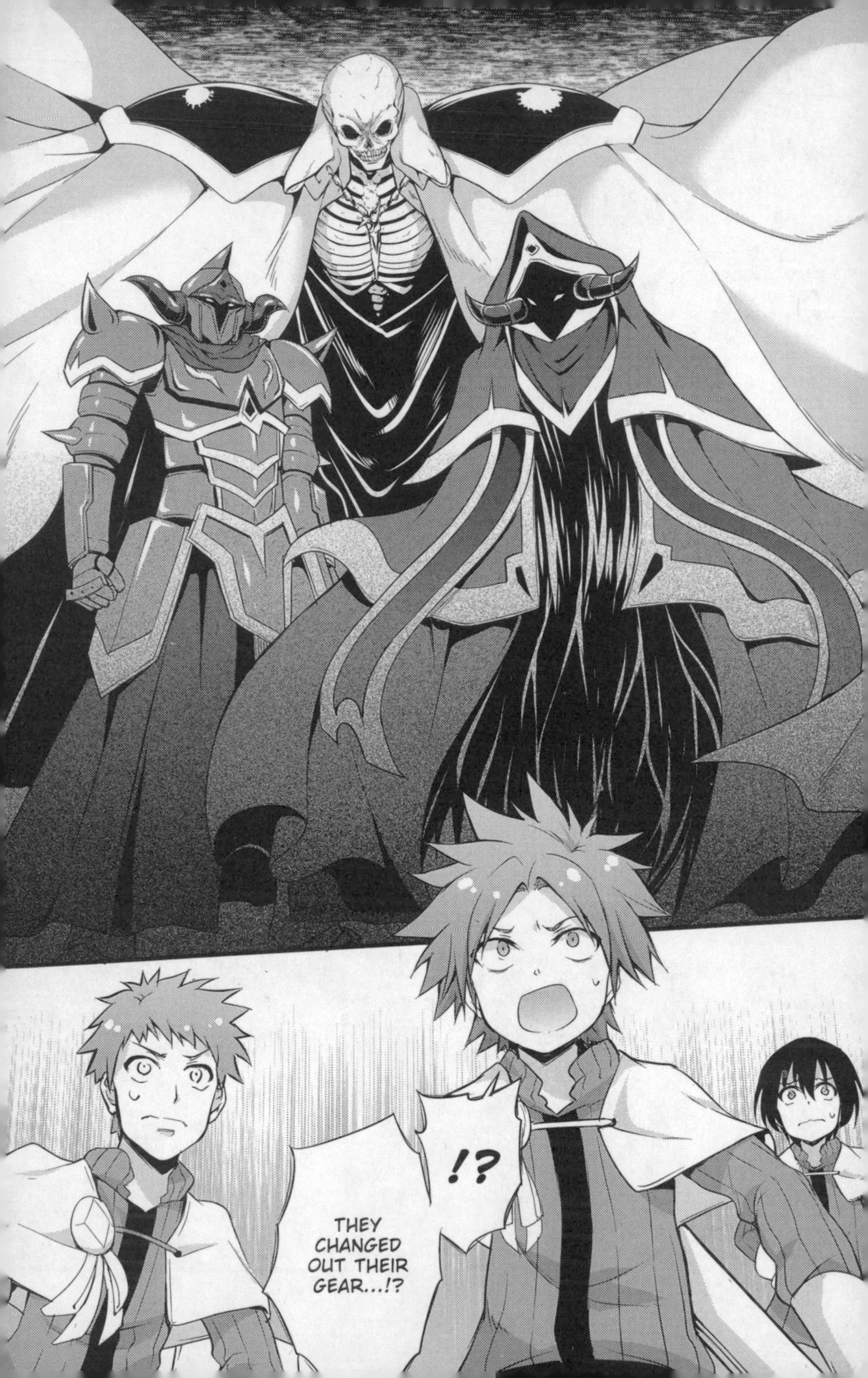
!?
THEY CHANGED OUT THEIR GEAR...!?

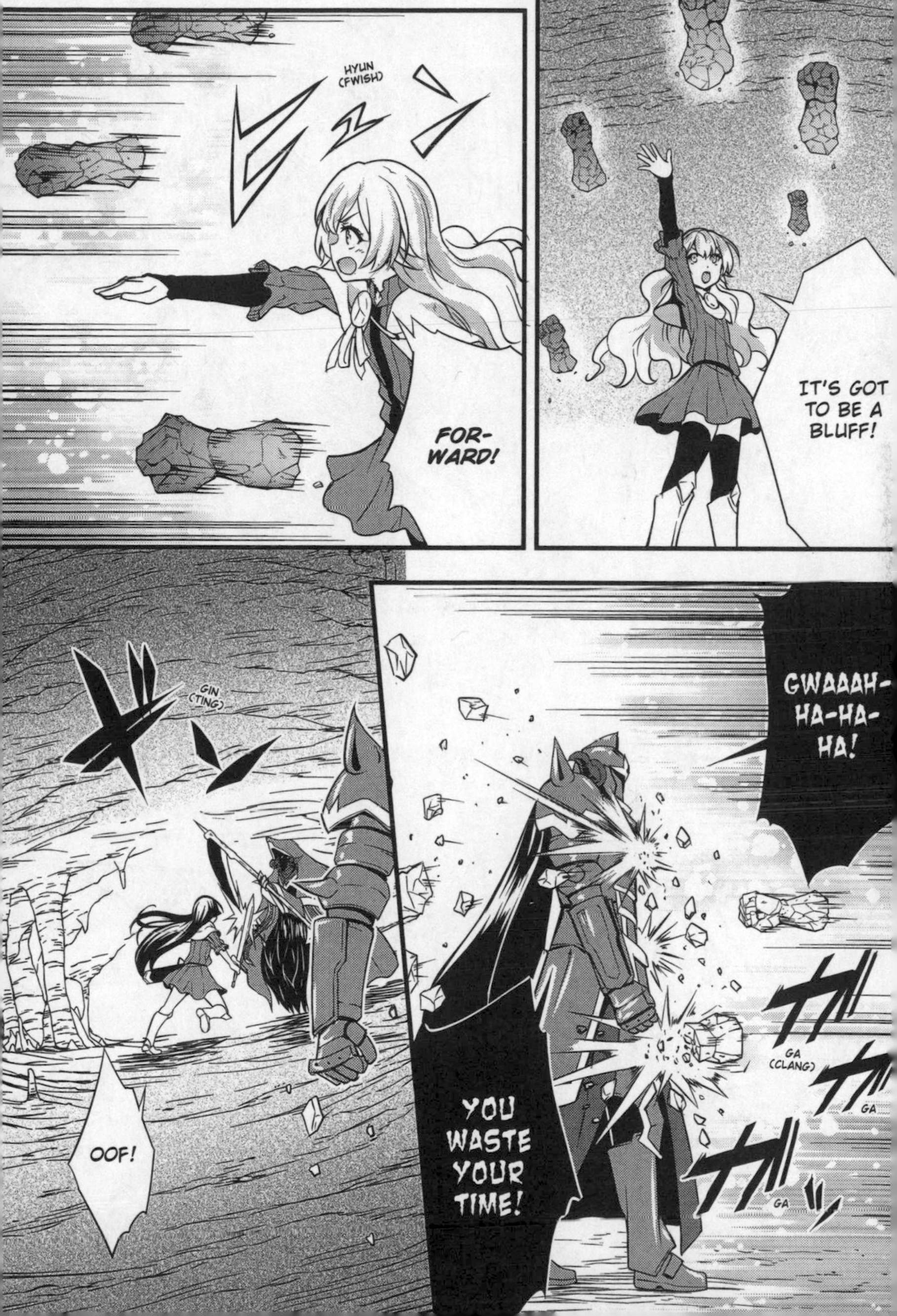
IT'S GOT TO BE A BLUFF!
HYUN (FWISH)
FOR-WARD!
GWAAAH-HA-HA-HA!
GA (CLANG)
GA
GA
YOU WASTE YOUR TIME!
GIN (TING)
OOF!

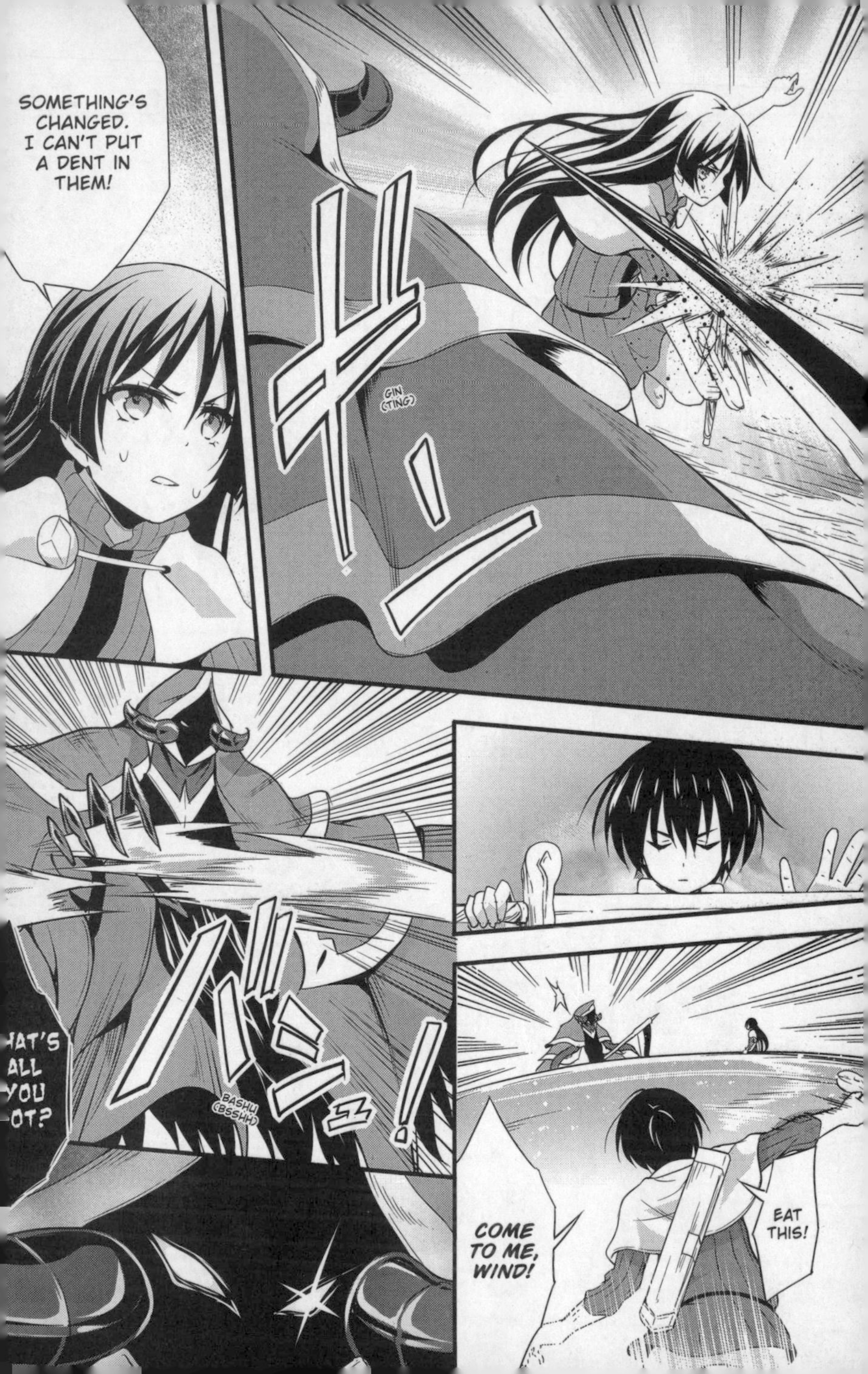
GIN (TING)
SOMETHING'S CHANGED. I CAN'T PUT A DENT IN THEM!
EAT THIS!
COME TO ME, WIND!
BASHU (BSSHH)
HAT'S ALL YOU OT?

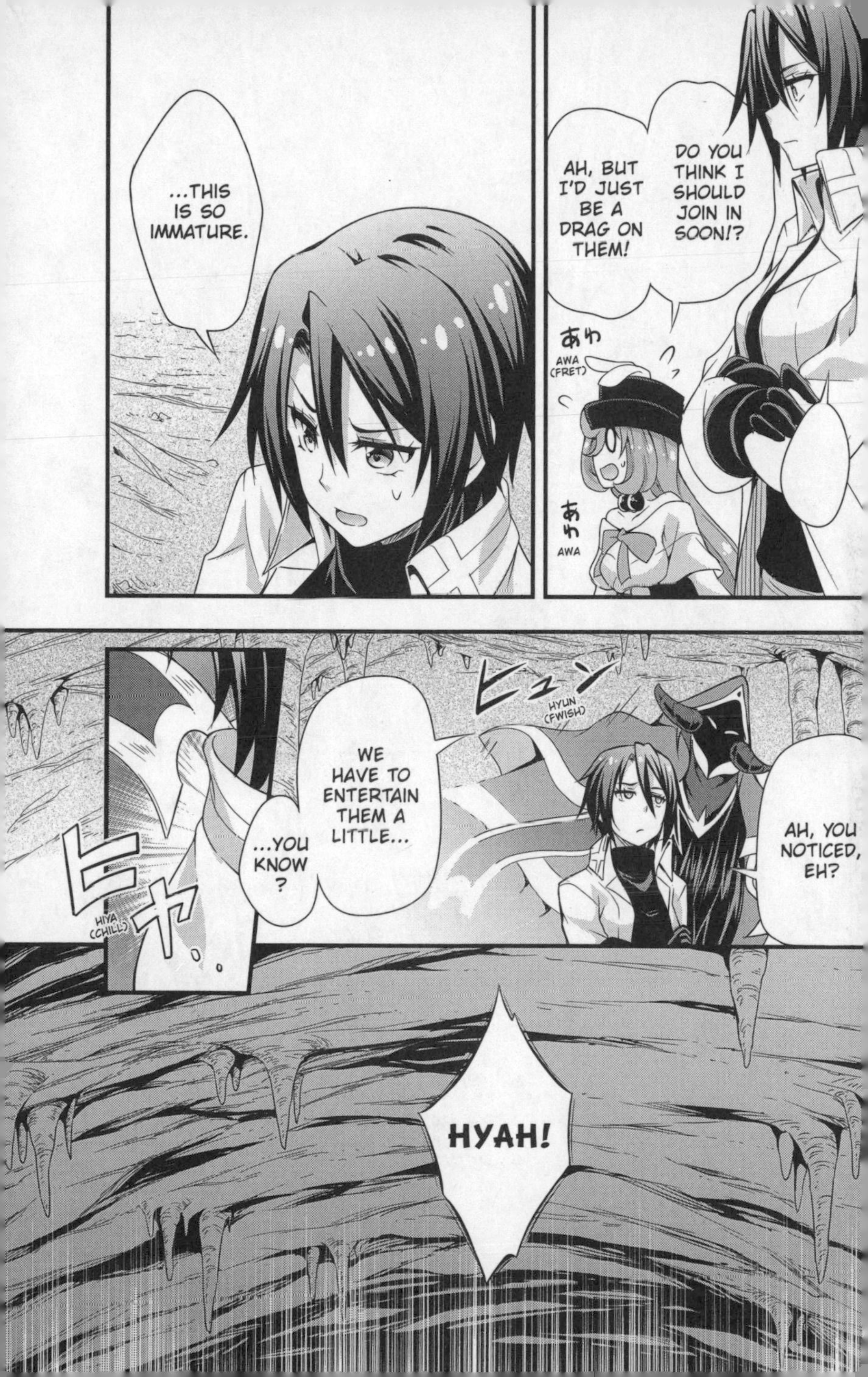
DO YOU THINK I SHOULD JOIN IN SOON!?
AH, BUT I'D JUST BE A DRAG ON THEM!
あわ
AWA (FRET)
あわ
AWA
...THIS IS SO IMMATURE.
AH, YOU NOTICED, EH?
ヒュン
HYUN (FWISH)
WE HAVE TO ENTERTAIN THEM A LITTLE...
...YOU KNOW?
ヒャ
HIYA (CHILL)
HYAH!

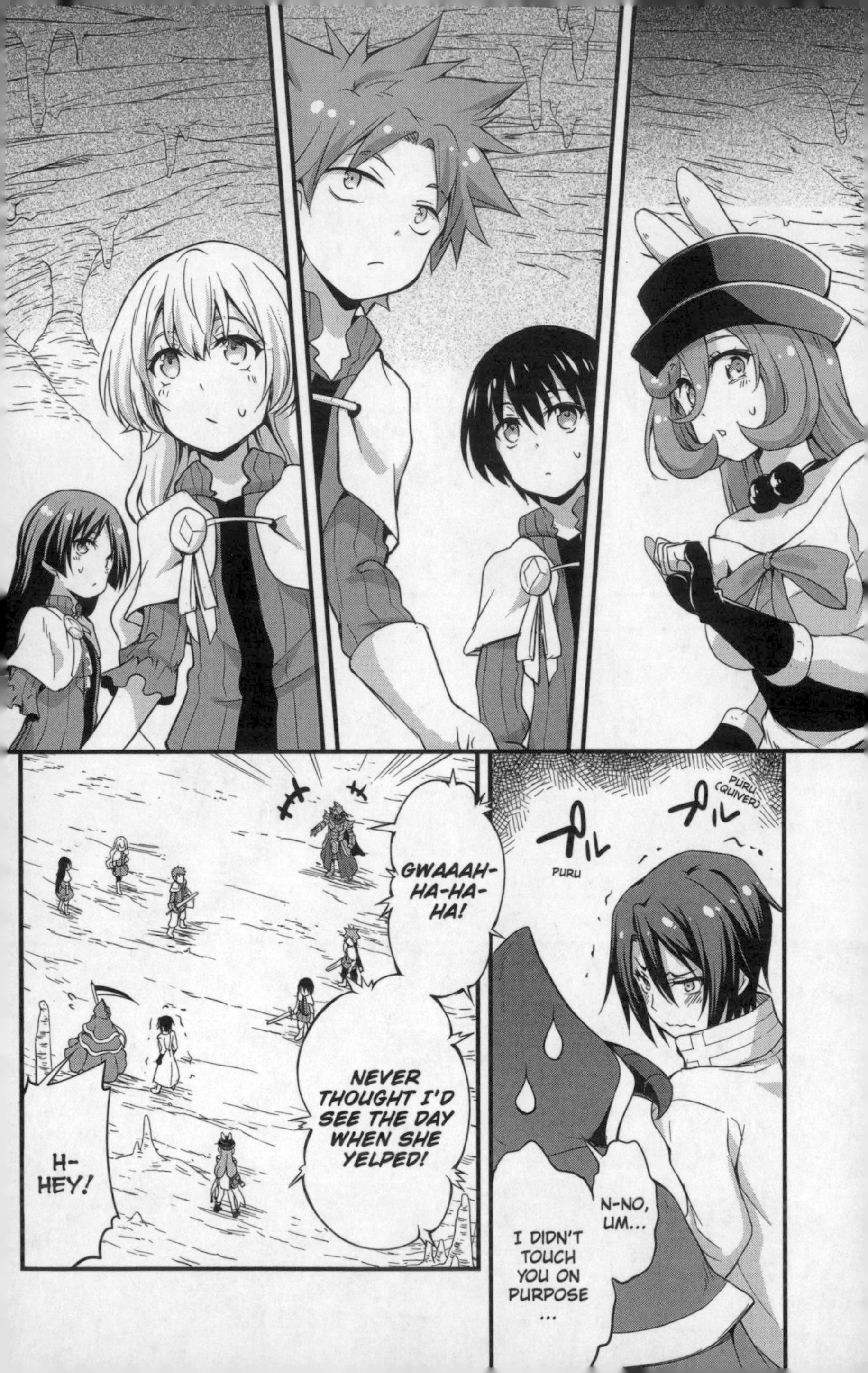
プル
PURU (QUIVER)
プル
PURU
N-NO, UM...
I DIDN'T TOUCH YOU ON PURPOSE ...
GWAAAH-HA-HA-HA!
NEVER THOUGHT I'D SEE THE DAY WHEN SHE YELPED!
H-HEY!

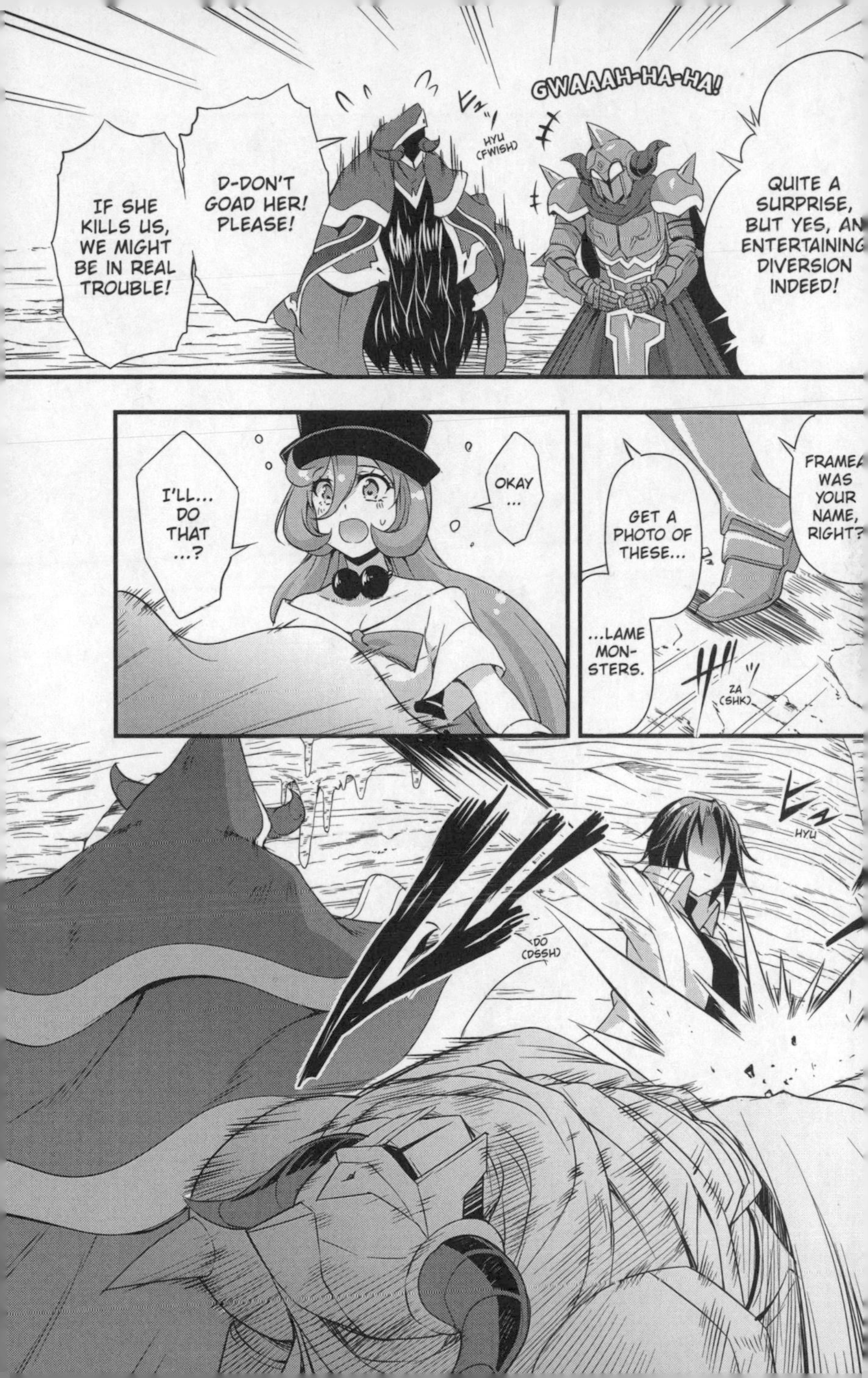
QUITE A SURPRISE, BUT YES, AN ENTERTAINING DIVERSION INDEED!
GWAAAH-HA-HA!
HYU (FWISH)
D-DON'T GOAD HER! PLEASE!
IF SHE KILLS US, WE MIGHT BE IN REAL TROUBLE!
FRAMEA WAS YOUR NAME, RIGHT?
GET A PHOTO OF THESE...
...LAME MON-STERS.
ZA (SHK)
OKAY ...
I'LL... DO THAT ...?
HYU
DO (DSSH)

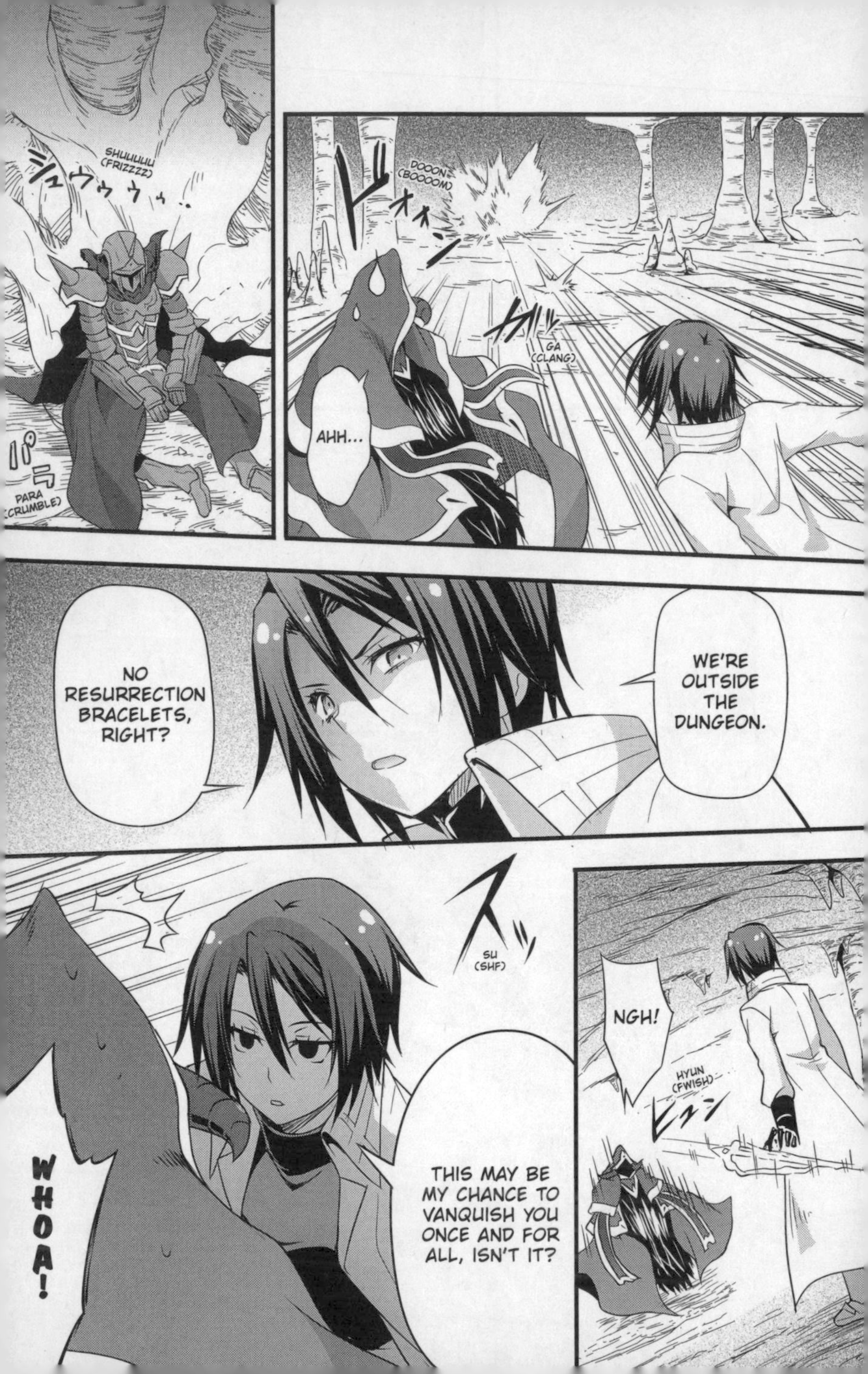
DOOON (BOOOOM)
GA (CLANG)
AHH...
SHUUUUU (FRIZZZZ)
PARA (CRUMBLE)
WE'RE OUTSIDE THE DUNGEON.
NO RESURRECTION BRACELETS, RIGHT?
NGH!
HYUN (FWISH)
SU (SHF)
THIS MAY BE MY CHANCE TO VANQUISH YOU ONCE AND FOR ALL, ISN'T IT?
WHOA!

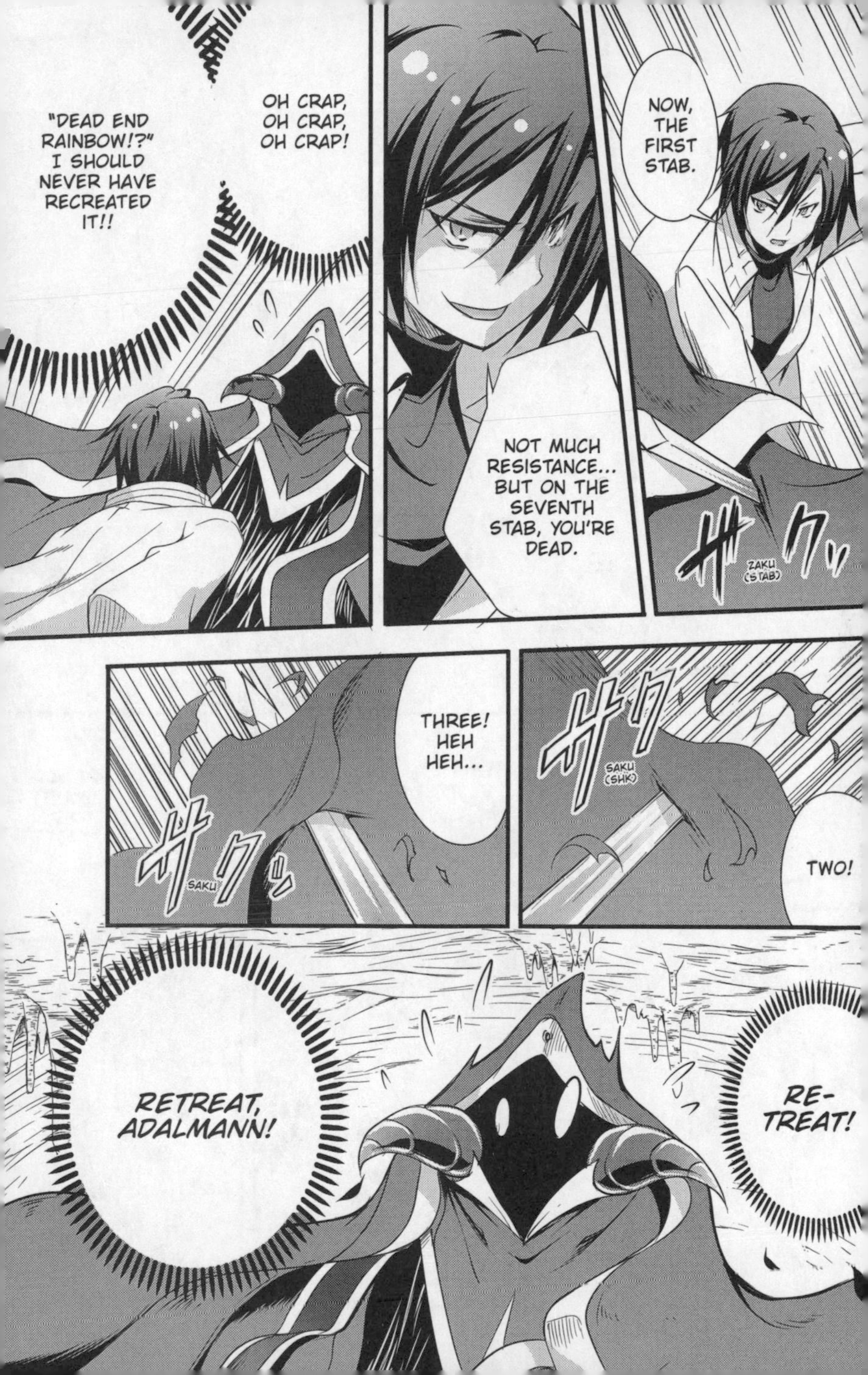
NOW, THE FIRST STAB.
ZAKU (STAB)
NOT MUCH RESISTANCE... BUT ON THE SEVENTH STAB, YOU'RE DEAD.
OH CRAP, OH CRAP, OH CRAP!
"DEAD END RAINBOW!?" I SHOULD NEVER HAVE RECREATED IT!!
SAKU (SHK)
TWO!
THREE! HEH HEH...
SAKU
RE-TREAT!
RETREAT, ADALMANN!

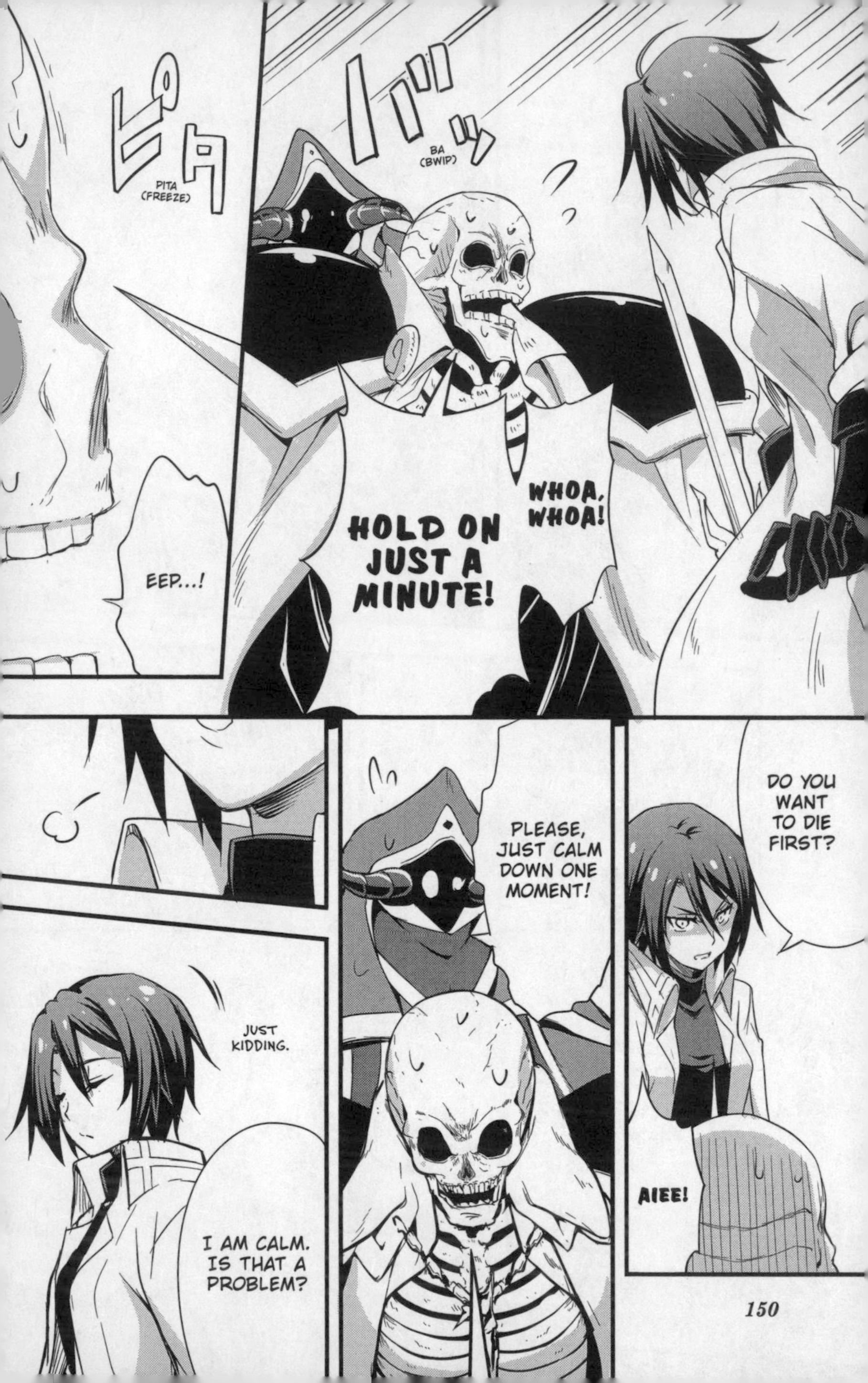
BA (BWIP)
WHOA, WHOA!
HOLD ON JUST A MINUTE!
PITA (FREEZE)
EEP...!
DO YOU WANT TO DIE FIRST?
AIEE!
PLEASE, JUST CALM DOWN ONE MOMENT!
JUST KIDDING.
I AM CALM. IS THAT A PROBLEM?

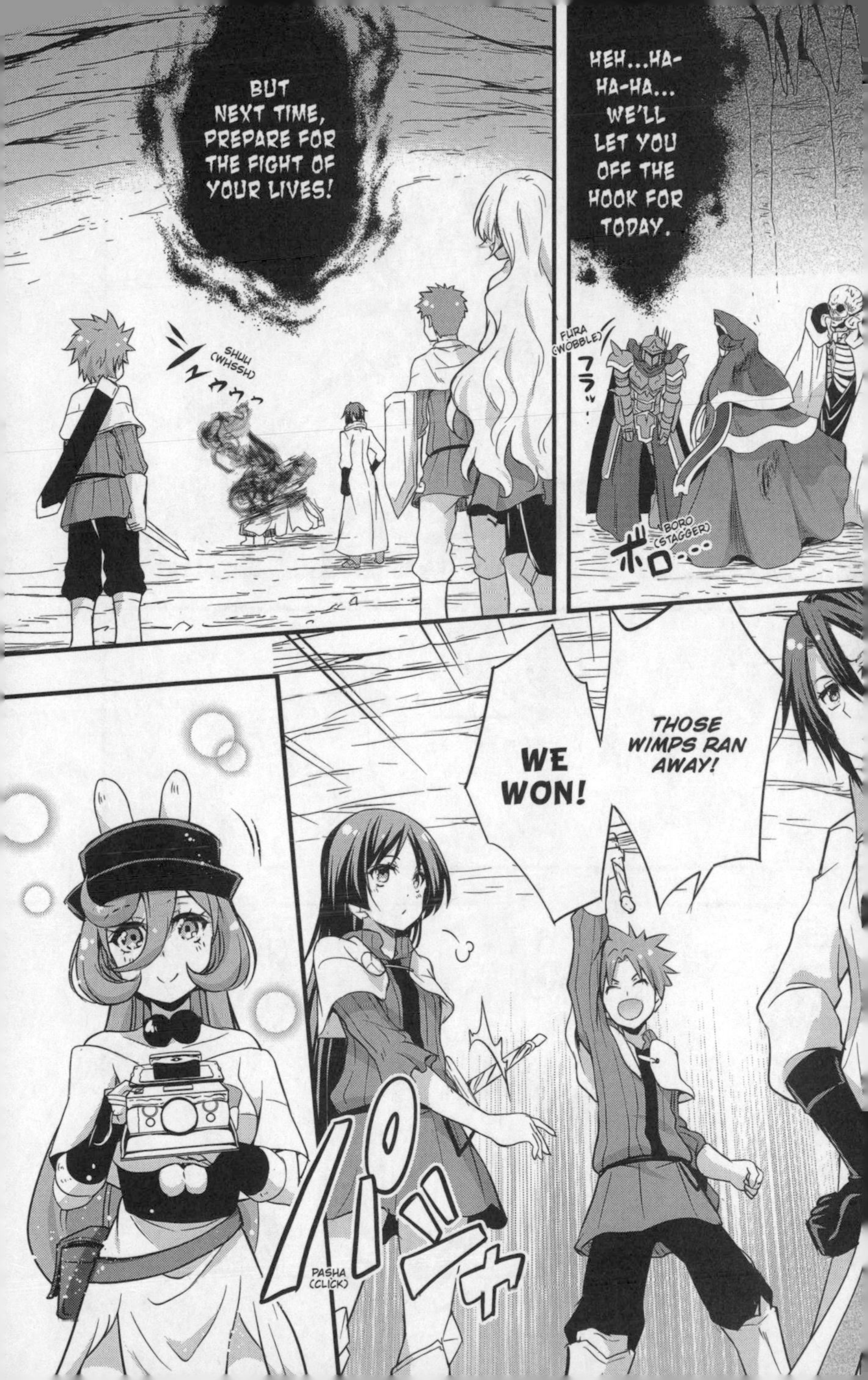
HEH...HA-HA-HA... WE'LL LET YOU OFF THE HOOK FOR TODAY.
FURA (WOBBLE)
BORO (STAGGER)
BUT NEXT TIME, PREPARE FOR THE FIGHT OF YOUR LIVES!
SHUU (WHSSH)
THOSE WIMPS RAN AWAY!
WE WON!
PASHA (CLICK)

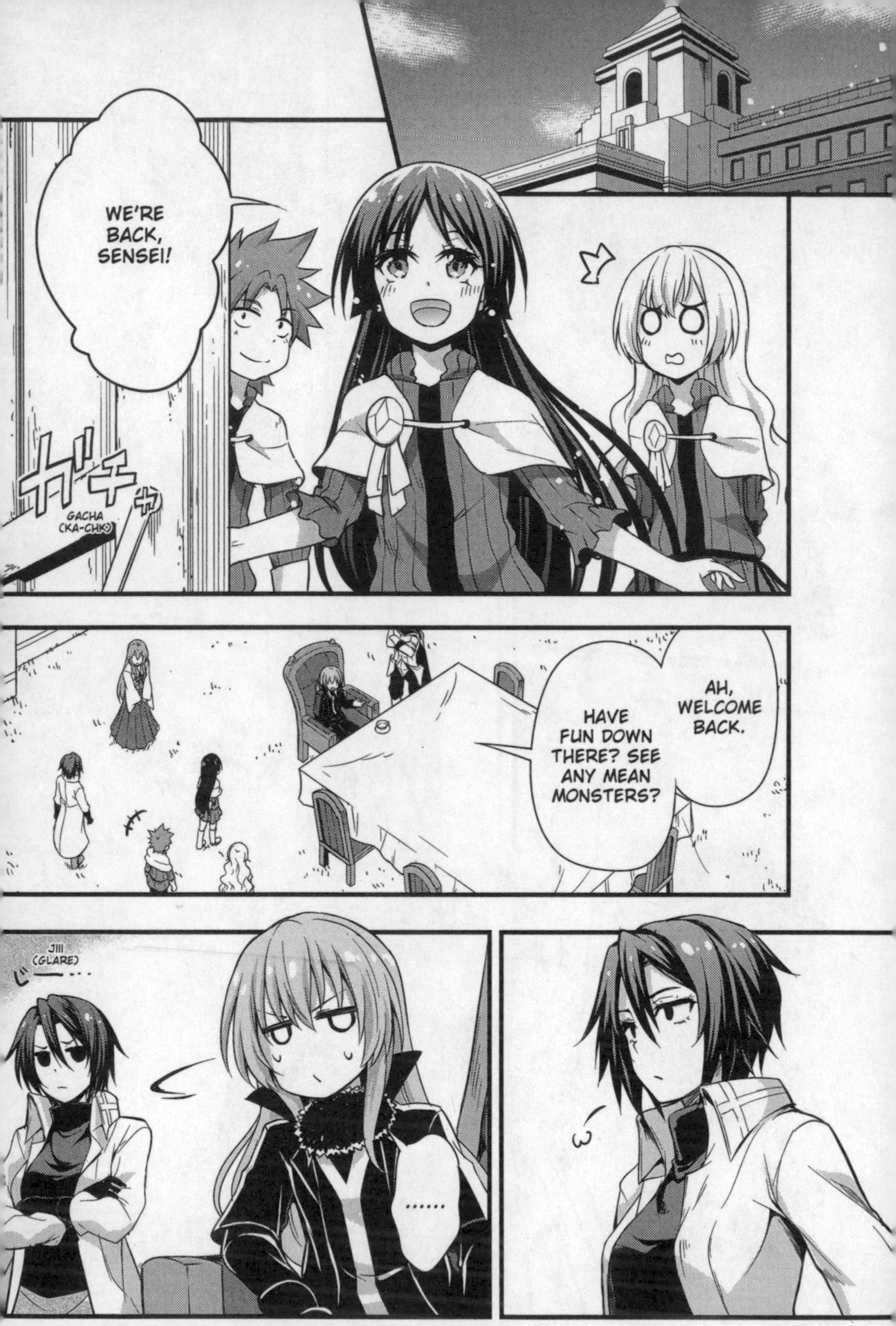
WE'RE BACK, SENSEI!
GACHA (KA-CHK)
AH, WELCOME BACK.
HAVE FUN DOWN THERE? SEE ANY MEAN MONSTERS?
JIII (GLARE)
......

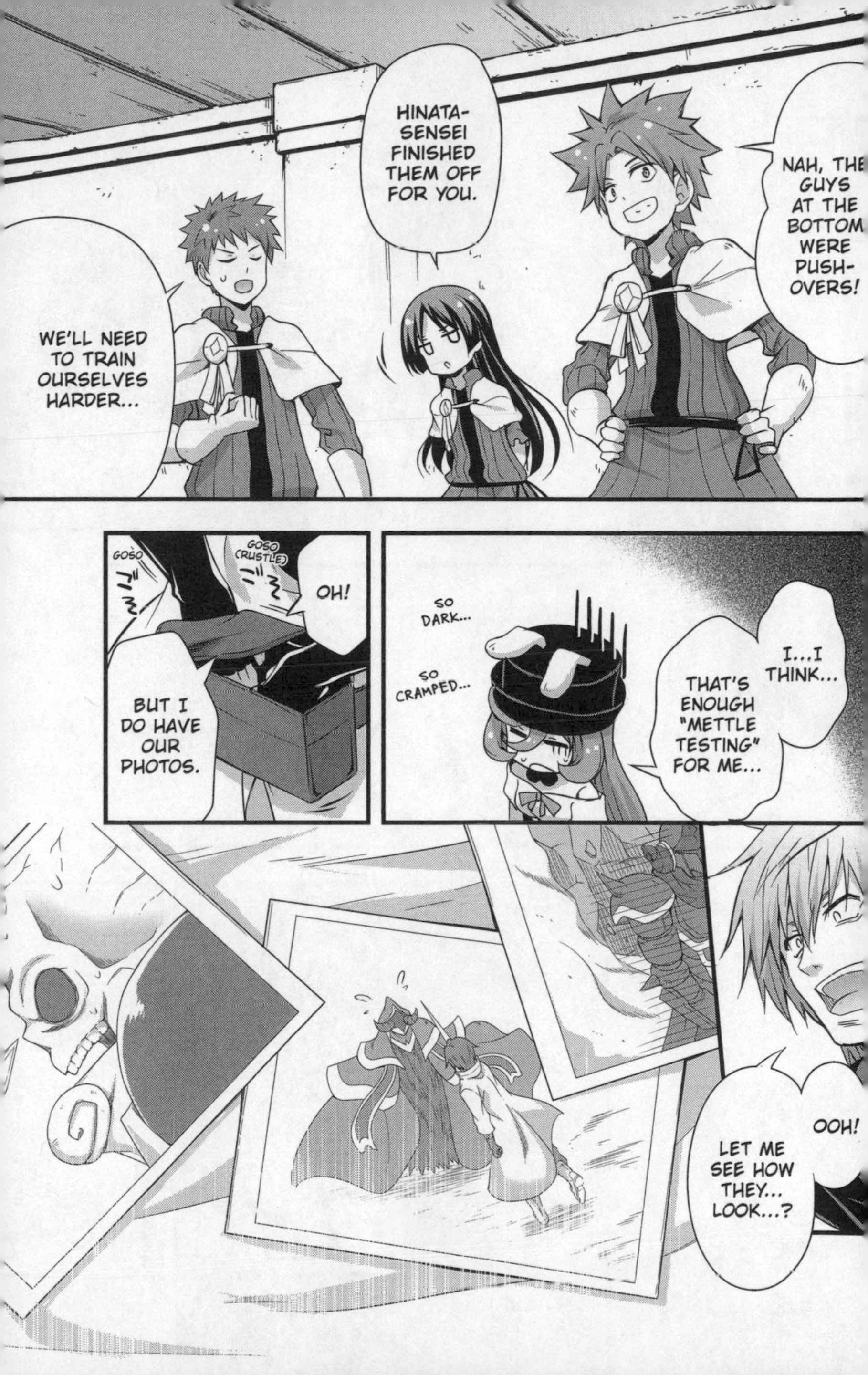
NAH, THE GUYS AT THE BOTTOM WERE PUSH-OVERS!
HINATA-SENSEI FINISHED THEM OFF FOR YOU.
WE'LL NEED TO TRAIN OURSELVES HARDER...
I...I THINK...
THAT'S ENOUGH "METTLE TESTING" FOR ME...
SO DARK...
SO CRAMPED...
GOSO (CRUSTLE)
OH!
GOSO
BUT I DO HAVE OUR PHOTOS.
OOH!
LET ME SEE HOW THEY... LOOK...?

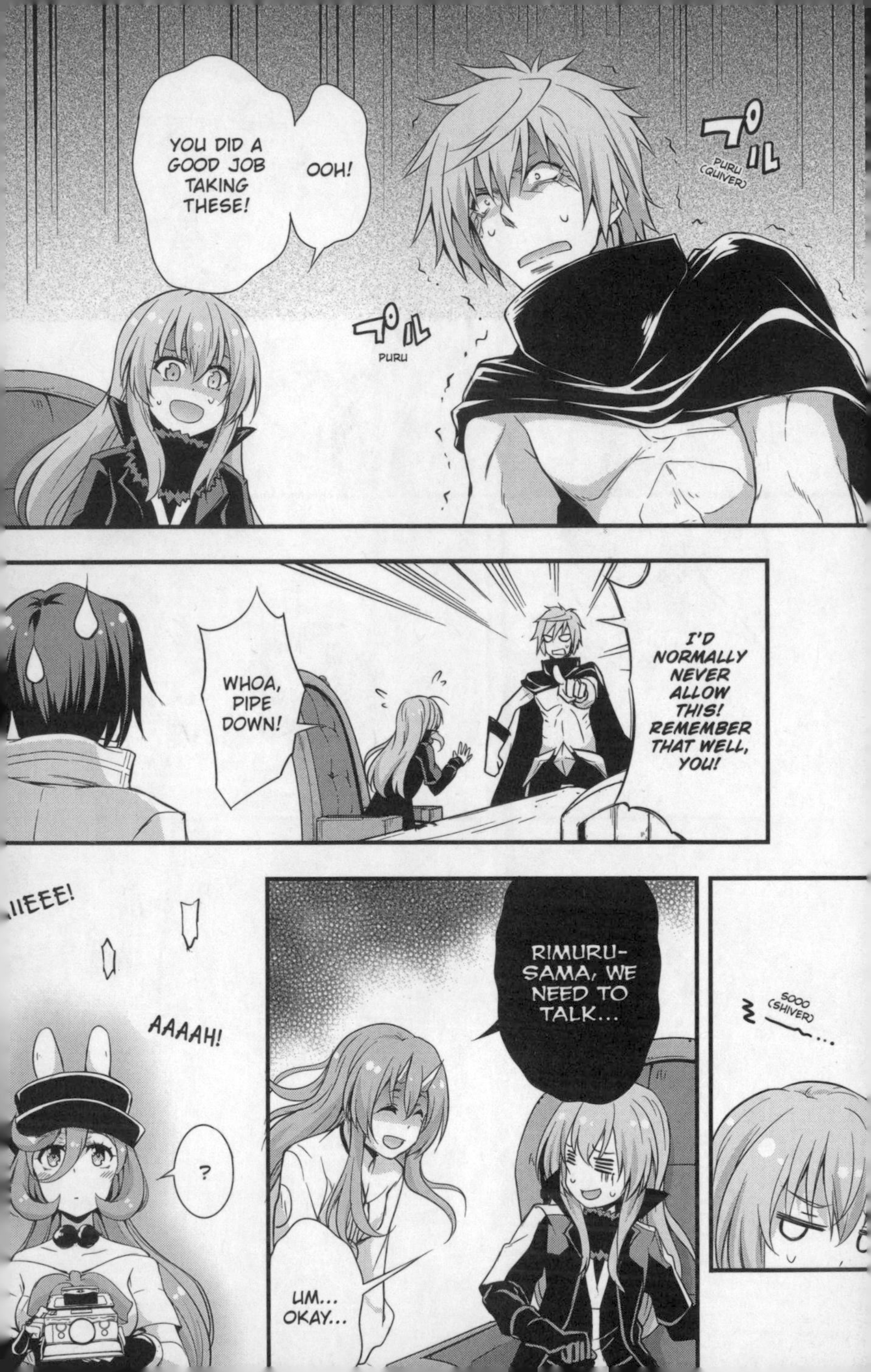
PURU (QUIVER)
OOH!
YOU DID A GOOD JOB TAKING THESE!
PURU
I'D NORMALLY NEVER ALLOW THIS! REMEMBER THAT WELL, YOU!
WHOA, PIPE DOWN!
SOOO (SHIVER)
...
RIMURU-SAMA, WE NEED TO TALK...
UM... OKAY...
IIEEE!
AAAAH!
?

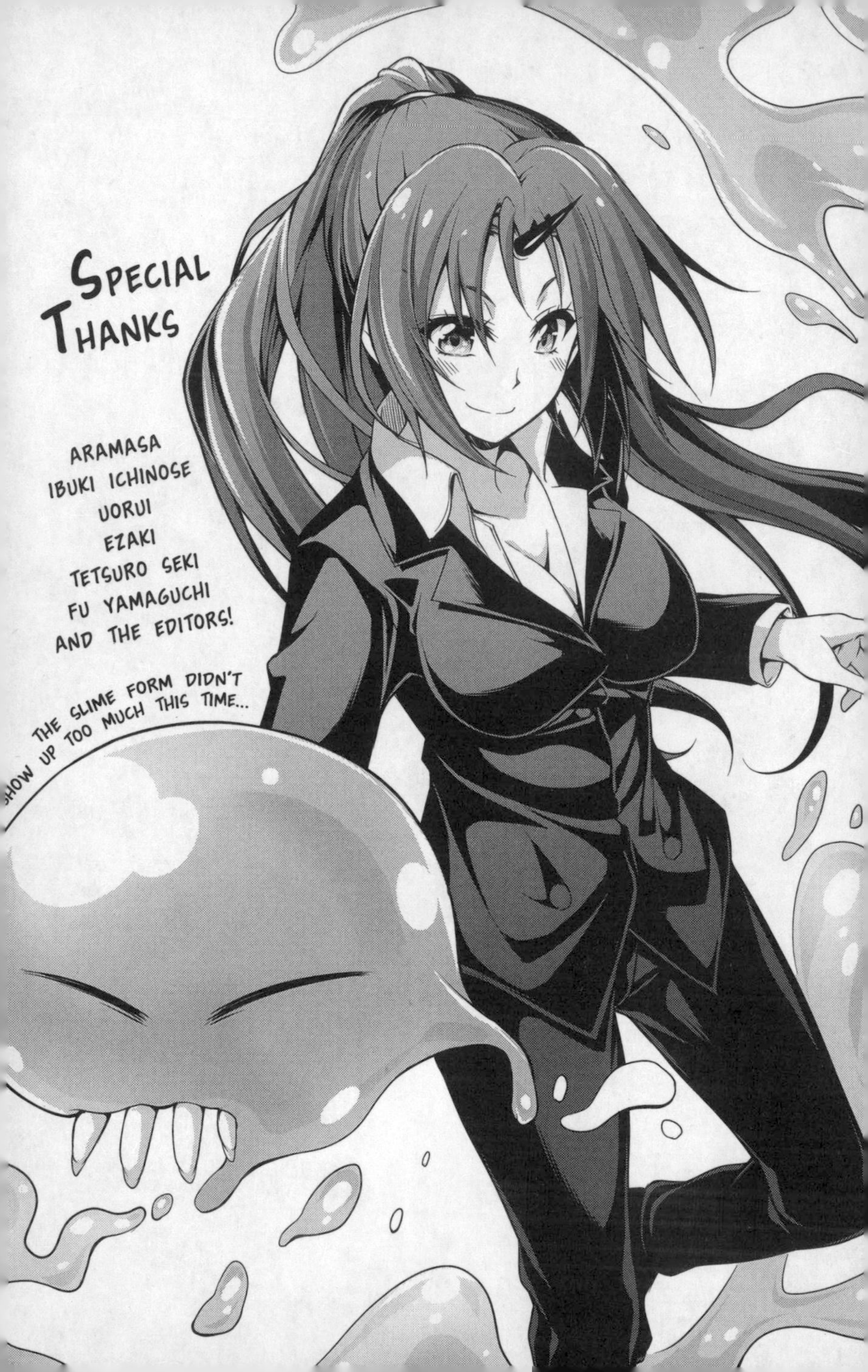
SPECIAL THANKS
ARAMASA
IBUKI ICHINOSE
UORUI
EZAKI
TETSURO SEKI
FU YAMAGUCHI
AND THE EDITORS!
THE SLIME FORM DIDN'T
SHOW UP TOO MUCH THIS TIME...

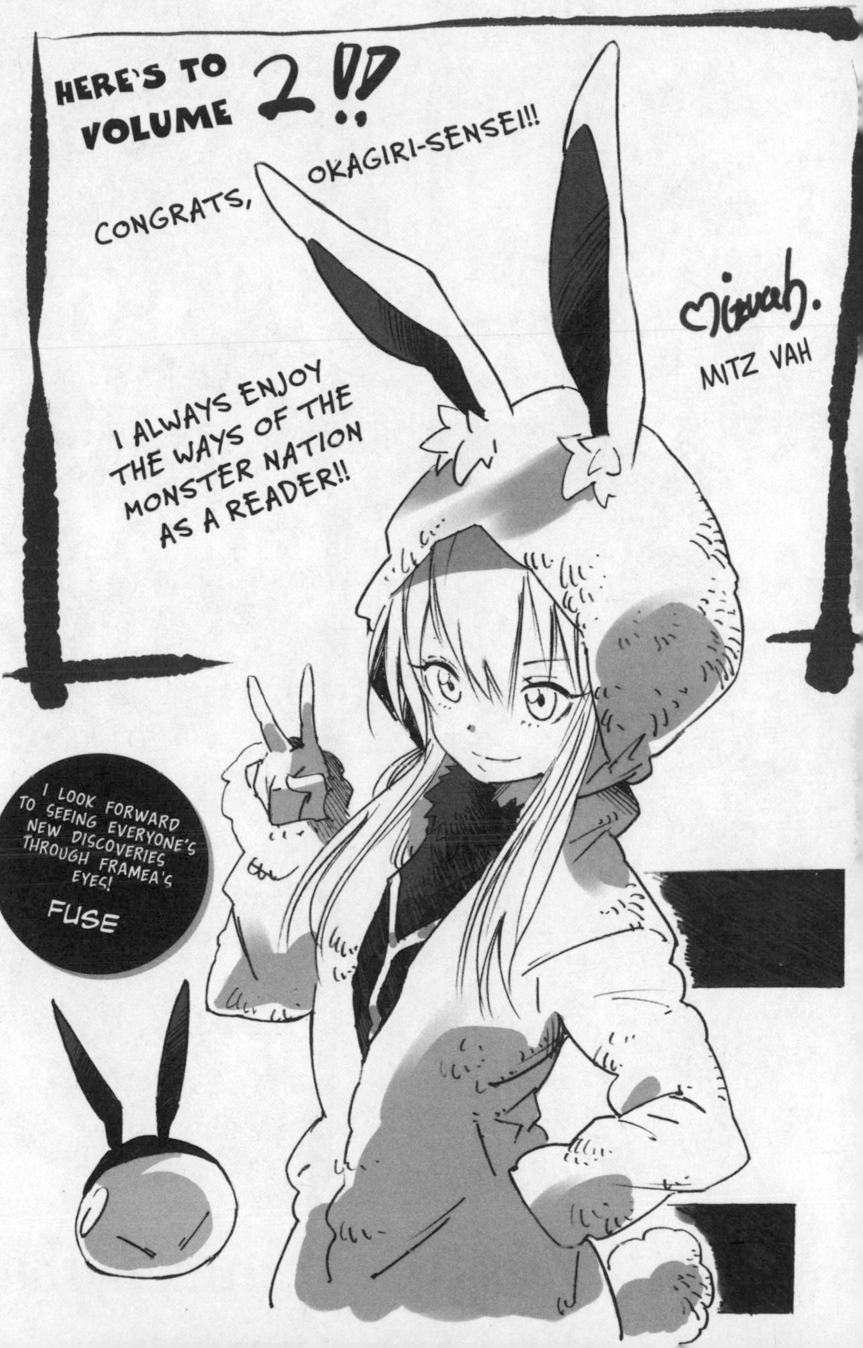
HERE'S TO VOLUME 2!!
CONGRATS, OKAGIRI-SENSEI!!!
I ALWAYS ENJOY THE WAYS OF THE MONSTER NATION AS A READER!!
MITZ VAH
I LOOK FORWARD TO SEEING EVERYONE'S NEW DISCOVERIES THROUGH FRAMEA'S EYES!
FUSE

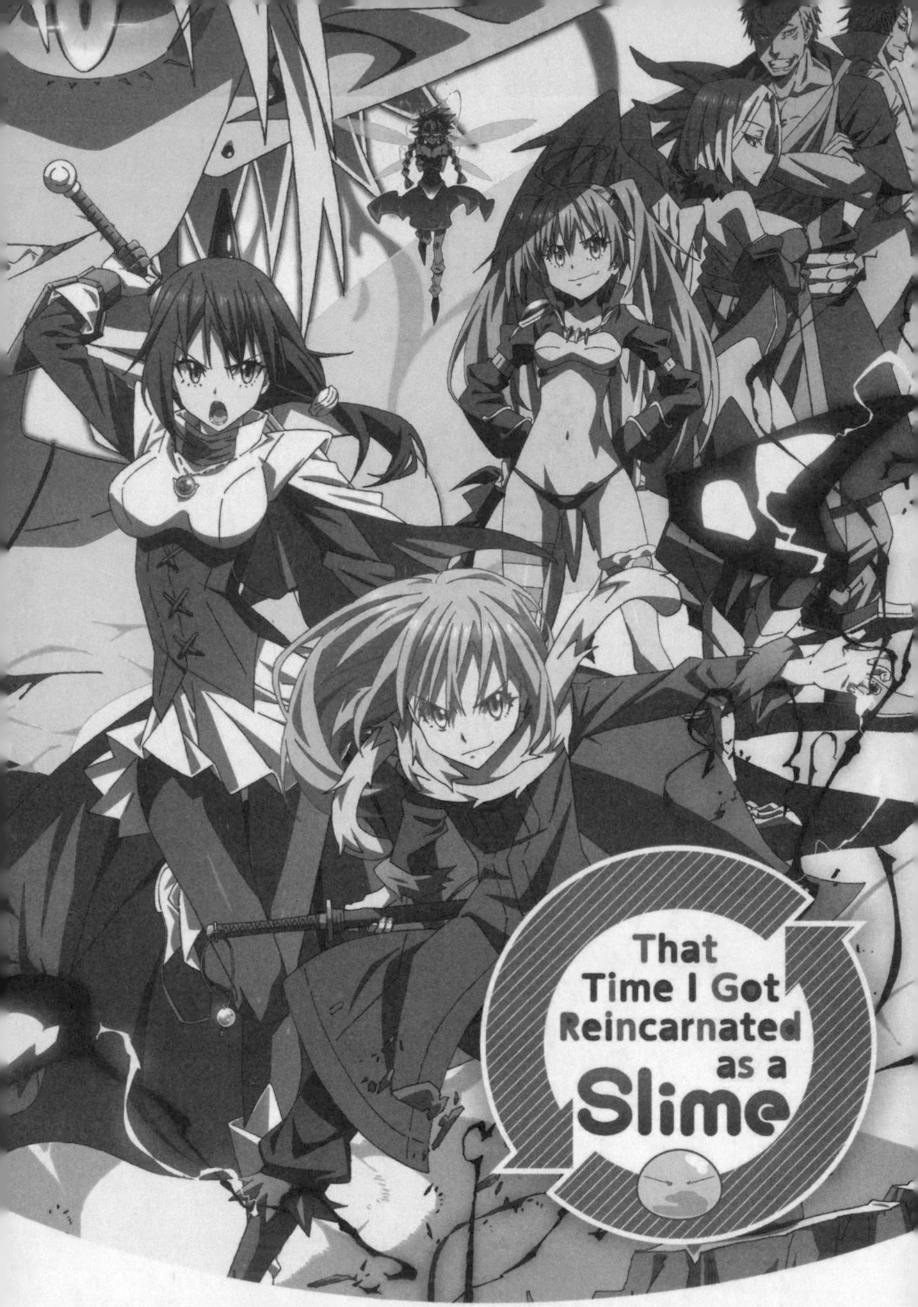
That Time I Got Reincarnated as a Slime

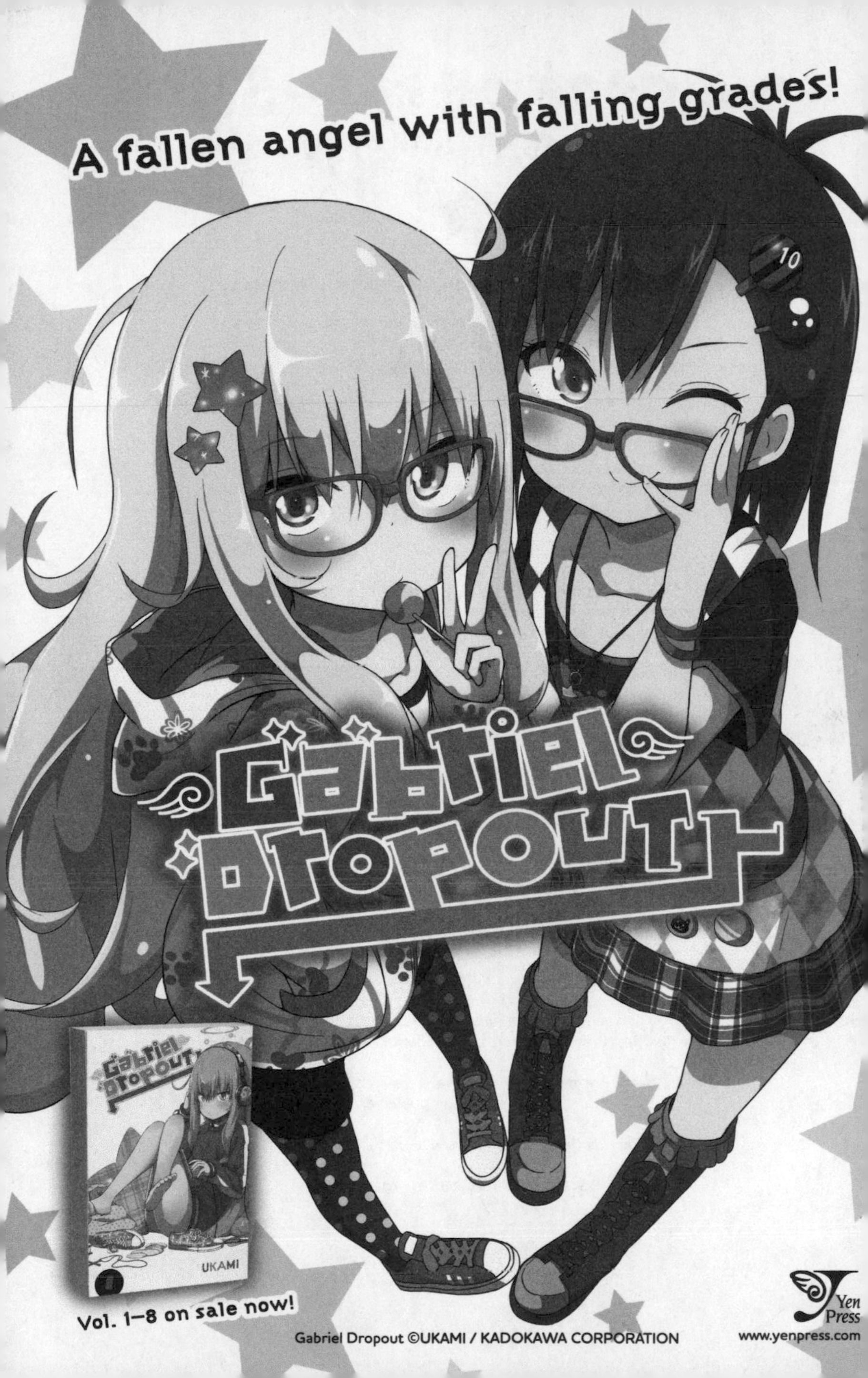

A fallen angel with falling grades!
Gabriel Dropout
Gabriel Dropout
UKAMI
Vol. 1–8 on sale now!
Gabriel Dropout ©UKAMI / KADOKAWA CORPORATION
Yen Press
www.yenpress.com

That Time I Got Reincarnated as a SLIME
The Ways of the Monster Nation

Translation: Kevin Gifford • Lettering: Barri Shrager

TENSEI SHITARA SURAIMU DATTA KEN ~MAMONO NO KUNI NO ARUKIKATA~ Vol. 2
©Fuse 2017
©Sho Okagiri, Mitz Vah 2017
First published in Japan in 2017 by MICRO MAGAZINE, INC.
English translation rights arranged with MICRO MAGAZINE, INC.
through Tuttle-Mori Agency, Inc., Tokyo.

Yen Press
150 West 30th Street, 19th Floor
New York, NY 10001

Visit us at yenpress.com
facebook.com/yenpress
twitter.com/yenpress
yenpress.tumblr.com
instagram.com/yenpress

First Yen Press Edition: October 2020

Yen Press is an imprint of Yen Press, LLC.
The Yen Press name and logo are trademarks of Yen Press, LLC.

The publisher is not responsible for websites (or their content) that are
not owned by the publisher.

Library of Congress Control Number: 2020936422

ISBNs: 978-1-9753-1353-1 (paperback)
978-1-9753-1354-8 (ebook)

10 9 8 7 6 5 4 3 2 1

BVG

Printed in the United States of America